Alexander and Dindimus.

Early English Text Society.
Extra Series. No. XXXI.
1878 (reprinted 1930).

Alexander and Dindimus:

OR,

THE LETTERS OF ALEXANDER

TO

Dindimus, King of the Brahmans,

WITH THE REPLIES OF DINDIMUS;

BEING A SECOND FRAGMENT

OF THE ALLITERATIVE ROMANCE OF

Alisaunder;

TRANSLATED FROM THE LATIN, ABOUT A.D. 1340-50;

RE-EDITED FROM THE UNIQUE MS. IN THE BODLEIAN LIBRARY, OXFORD.
BY THE
REV. WALTER W. SKEAT, M.A.,
LATE FELLOW OF CHRIST'S COLLEGE, CAMBRIDGE; AND M.A. OF EXETER COLLEGE, OXFORD.

———•◦•———

LONDON:
PUBLISHED FOR THE EARLY ENGLISH TEXT SOCIETY,
BY HUMPHREY MILFORD, OXFORD UNIVERSITY PRESS.
AMEN HOUSE, E.C. 4.
———
1878 (*reprinted* 1930).

OXFORD
UNIVERSITY PRESS

Great Clarendon Street, Oxford OX2 6DP
United Kingdom

Oxford University Press is a department of the University of Oxford.
It furthers the University's objective of excellence in research, scholarship,
and education by publishing worldwide. Oxford is a registered trade mark of
Oxford University Press in the UK and in certain other countries

© The Early English Text Society 1878

The moral rights of the authors have been asserted

Database right Oxford University Press (maker)

First Edition published in 1878
Reprinted 1930

All rights reserved. No part of this publication may be reproduced,
stored in a retrieval system, or transmitted, in any form or by any means,
without the prior permission in writing of Oxford University Press,
or as expressly permitted by law, or under terms agreed with the appropriate
reprographics rights organization. Enquiries concerning reproduction
outside the scope of the above should be sent to the Rights Department,
Oxford University Press, at the address above

You must not circulate this book in any other form
and you must impose this same condition on any acquirer

Published in the United States of America by Oxford University Press
198 Madison Avenue, New York, NY 10016, United States of America

British Library Cataloguing in Publication Data
Data available

Library of Congress Cataloging in Publication Data
Data available

Extra Series, 31

ISBN 978-0-85-991968-5

CONTENTS.

INTRODUCTION.   PAGE

§ 1. The three fragments of the Alexander-romances in alliterative verse. § 2. Description of the MS. of Fragment B. § 3. The French text of MS. Bodley 264. § 4. The apparent break in this text. § 5. Account of the meaning of this apparent break. § 6. Sources of the alliterative Alexander-romances. § 7. Fragment C. § 8. Fragments A and B by the same author. § 9. Resemblances between the language of the fragments A and B. § 10. The alliteration of the same. § 11. Mode of translation. § 12. Additional sources. § 13. Specimens from Julius Valerius and the Old High German. § 14. Abstract of the contents of fragment B. § 15. Remarks on the composition of it. § 16. On the name "Dindimus." § 17. The pictures in the Bodley MS. § 18. Conjectural date of Fragments A and B. § 19. Edition for the Roxburghe Club, by Mr. Stevenson. § 20. Variations from the MS. in that edition discussed. § 21. Mr. Stevenson's Glossary (reprinted). § 22 and § 23. On the Dialect of the Poem. § 24. Peculiarities of Alliteration in the Poem. § 25. List of French words in the poem i

ALEXANDER (FRAGMENT B) 1
NOTES TO "ALEXANDER B" 45
INDEX TO THE NOTES 59
GLOSSARIAL INDEX 61
INDEX OF NAMES 93

_{*} Fragment A (of the same poem) is printed at pp. 177—218 of the Romance of William of Palerne, &c., ed. by the Rev. Walter W. Skeat; E. E. T. S., Extra Series, 1867.

INTRODUCTION.

§ 1. In An Essay on Alliterative Poetry, written by myself, and prefixed to vol. iii of The Percy Folio MS., ed. Hales and Furnivall, I have explained that there are no less than *three* poems (all fragmentary) in alliterative verse on the subject of the Romance of Alexander the Great. These I denote by the letters A, B, and C; and they are as follows.[1]

A. A fragment preserved in MS. Greaves 60, in the Bodleian library, beginning—"Yee þat lengen in londe · Lordes and oþer." This was edited by me for the E. E. T. S. in 1867, being printed in the same volume with William of Palerne, pp. 177—218. It has never been printed elsewhere.

B. A fragment preserved in MS. Bodley 264, beginning—"Whan þis weith at his wil · weduring hadde." This was edited by Mr. Stevenson for the Roxburghe Club in 1849, and is now reprinted in the present volume.

C. A fragment preserved in MS. Ashmole 44, in the Bodleian library, of which a portion is also found in MS. Dublin D. 4. 12. It begins—"When folk ere festid & fed · fayñ wald þai here," and was also printed by Mr. Stevenson at the same time and in the same volume; without, however, collation with the Dublin MS., which is of later date than the Ashmole MS.

It will be understood that the remarks I have now to make relate to fragment B only, unless the contrary be expressed.

§ 2. There is but one copy of fragment B, and it is imperfect both at the beginning and the end. The portion preserved has been handed down to us in rather a curious way. The MS. in which it

---

[1] See also p. xxx of my Preface to William of Palerne, &c.

occurs (Bodley 264) is the well-known copy of the French Romans d'Alixandre, to which is appended a copy, in another hand, of Marco Polo's travels. It is remarkable for the number and beauty of the illuminations contained in it, which have been frequently admired. Nine similar illustrations (of a later date) refer to the present poem, and are described particularly in § 17.

§ 3. The text of this French romance is mainly the same as that printed in Li Romans d'Alixandre par Lambert li Tors et Alixandre de Bernay, edited by H. Michelant, and published by the Literary Society of Stuttgart in 1846. The French version of the story varies from the English one, and our three English fragments have, I believe, little to do with it. But the condition of fol. 67 of the French MS. is very remarkable. The page is divided, as usual, into two columns. Of these, the first ends with the line—"Li veillant lieue sus si li vuet affier;" followed by the rubric—"Comment les gens alixandre firunt noies pur le moure des femmes demorant en le lew." But the second column of the page, originally left blank, contains the following note in a later hand—"Here fayleþ a prossesse of þis rommance of alixander, þe wheche prossesse þat fayleth ȝe schulle fynde at þe ende of þis bok y-wrete in engelyche ryme; and whanne ȝe han radde it to þe ende, turneþ hedur aȝen, and turneþ ouyr þis lef, and bygynneþ at þis reson: Che fu el mois de may que li tans renouele; and so rede forþ þe rommance to þe ende whylis þe frenche lasteþ."[1] This note of course only occupies a few lines of the second column of the page, the rest being blank. The verso of fol. 67 is also blank. Fol. 68, col. 1, begins, as the above note states, with the line: "Che fu el mois de may que li tans renouele."

§ 4. But the really remarkable point is, that, notwithstanding the vacant three columns in the MS., there is *not* a "failing of a process;" there is nothing omitted whatever. At p. 333 of Michelant's edition above referred to, we read as follows:—

"li viellart salent sus, se li vont afier.
Ce fu è l'mois de Mai que li tans renovele."

---

[1] The first half of this note, down to "ryme," is printed in Warton's Hist. of Eng. Poetry, ii. 103, ed. 1840. The whole note appears, with four errors, in Weber's Metrical Romances, i. xxxi; and again, with the same four errors and six more, at p. iv of Mr. Stevenson's edition.

And this plainly shews that the story runs on without any break, as may yet more easily be seen by looking at the context. Moreover, since nothing is lost, the writer of the English note is clearly in error in saying that the English alliterative poem supplies the deficiency. It is not quite easy to account for the blank space, but there it is. We can hardly suppose it was left for the purpose of introducing an illumination, because the shape of the slender column is unsuited for this. It is more likely that the scribe of the French romance imagined there was a defect in the MS. from which he was copying, and that he left a space in case he should be able to supply it.

§ 5. The truth is, that the English fragment and the French romance belong to different versions of the story. And even if the English fragment could have been introduced, it is not introduced quite in the best place; neither does it fit properly either at the beginning or the end. If the English scribe had before him a long English poem, we should have been more obliged to him if he had preserved for us more of it; but, as it is, we are thankful that he has given us a part of it. It is not difficult, by a probable conjecture, to account for the present state of things. It would appear that the English scribe, for some reason or other, set some store by the portion of the story which includes the letters of Alexander to Dindimus, and of Dindimus to Alexander. Now he could not find these epistles in the French romance, not because a "process" had "failed," but because that particular version does not, in any case, include them. Turning to the point where he expected to find them, he observed, not a great way from the most fitting place (but still not quite at the fittest place), a blank page and a half. From this he concluded that the French scribe had *omitted* the epistles, and thought that the best way of supplying the supposed defect was by copying out a sufficient portion of the English version which he possessed. At the same time, he wished to preserve further a short account of the Gymnosophists, because of the similarity between these philosophers and those of which Dindimus was the king or master. Hence the result which we have in the present poem. It contains just the whole account of the Gymnosophists, and the whole account of the letters between Alexander and Dindimus, but purposely omits a portion of the narrative which comes *between* these, as pointed out in the footnote on p. 5. This is, however, not quite all. The scribe was determined not to lose the curious account of the trees which grew every day while daylight lasted, but disappeared every night; and, thinking this short account would seem out of place if merely added at the end of the Letters, boldly inserted it in the middle; at ll. 111—136. If this be not quite the right history of the matter, it is perhaps as nearly so as we can guess, and is quite sufficient for the purpose of understanding the present state of the text.

§ 6. I have said that the French romance follows, in the main, *one* form of the story, and the English romances *another*. The French romance is all printed, as explained above, and may now be dismissed, as we have nothing more to do with it. The three English fragments are all connected, and are founded mainly on the same Latin version. Repeating from p. xxxvii of my Introduction to William of Palerne and Alisaunder, I may remind the reader that the principal basis of these fragments is the Greek text known as the *Pseudo-Callisthenes*, whence three principal Latin versions are derived. These are (1) that by Julius Valerius; (2) the Itinerarium Alexandri (relating to Alexander's wars); and (3) that by the Archpresbyter Leo, which is also known as the "Historia de preliis." It is with the *third* of these that the three English fragments have most to do. This version begins with the words—"Sapientissimi egiptii scientes mensuram terre;" and an edition of it was printed in 1490, which has been my guide throughout, and from which I have given numerous citations. It is from this edition that the Latin text is quoted which appears at the foot of pages 1—42.

§ 7. All three English fragments are founded mainly on this Latin version, but the manner of translation is not the same in all. Fragment C may be taken first, as it is much the easiest to understand. This is a close translation of the Latin, with a brief original prologue of 22 lines only. It is of great length, extending to 5680 lines,[1] and is only slightly imperfect at the end.[2] As a result, it

---

[1] Only 5678 lines in Mr. Stevenson's edition, which omits two lines.

[2] That is, at first sight. But there is a gap after l. 722, where some leaves of the MS. have been lost.

contains *both* of the passages which exist also in fragments A and B. Fragment A corresponds to ll. 23—722 of C; and fragment B to ll. 4020—4067 and 4188—4715 of C. It is clear from this and from the manner of translation that C is independent of A and B, in the sense that it was made by a different translator.

§ 8. The next question is, whether there were two translators or three. As fragments A and B do not cover the same ground, but are taken, the former from a portion of the story near the beginning and the latter from a portion near the end, there is a chance that they may belong to the very same translation, and may have come from the same hand. In my Essay on Alliterative Poetry, I have observed that "the language of fragment B approaches that of fragment A, though I hardly think they belong to the same poem." In my Preface to William of Palerne, I have observed that "fragments A, B, and C, seem to be distinct from each other, and by different authors, the last bearing traces of a *northern*, the former two of a *western* dialect." That is to say that, though I had observed a similarity, both of language and dialect, between fragments A and B, I had not, at that time, made myself so closely acquainted with them as to feel sure that they could be definitely pronounced to be from the same hand. This hesitation gave rise to a paper by Dr. Moritz Trautmann, entitled "Ueber Verfasser und Entstehungszeit einiger Alliterirender Gedichte des Altenglischen,"[1] in which a great number of resemblances between these fragments are insisted upon, and there can now be little doubt about the matter. The result is satisfactory, as it introduces a simplification, reducing the number of independent versions from three to two. It may henceforth be understood that *fragments A and B are by the same author*, and that they are taken, presumably, from one and the same poem, which must, when complete, have been of very great length. It is, possibly, partly owing to this circumstance that only two fragments of it have come down to us.

§ 9. The following are a few of the more striking resemblances between fragments A and B, as pointed out by Dr. Trautmann.

[1] I have to thank Dr. Trautmann for his courtesy in sending me a copy of his paper.

FRAGMENT A.

þat all þe gomes were agrise · of his grim sight 986
with skathe wer þei skoumfyt · skape þei ne myght 86
þat þei gradden hur griþ · his grace to haue 151

how þe ludus of the land · alosed for gode 331
alosed in lond 139, 577
with all þe weies in þe won 164; if any wight in þis wonne 622
lengen in bliss 44
yee þat lengen in londe 1
teeneful tach 282

that moste was adouted 33, 400
or hee fare wolde 740; pass ere hee woolde 1080
hee shall grow full grim 858
his term was tint 30
þe dragoun dreew him awaie 998; hee drouned as a dragon · dredeful of noyes 985
and lordship of Larisse · laught too his will 131, 161
so hee stynted þat stounde 1079
too mark þe teene 497; as mich maugre and more · hee marked hem after 932
for no grace hur grete God · graunte ne might 539
Olympias þe onorable queene 576, 738 as hym leefe thought 60

FRAGMENT B.

þei were a-grisen of his grym 50

for skaþe of þe scorpion*us* · askape þei ne miȝhte 159
whan ȝe greden ȝour grace · to graunte ȝour wille 606; whan ȝe hem greden of griþ 764
þo þat ludu*s* in oure land · alosed arn wise 1112
alosed in lande 665
and for ȝe, weihu*ws*, of þat won wende ne mowe 1092
lengeþ in blisse 628
ȝif we lengede in ȝoure land 872
tenful tach 566; schamfule tacchus 463
þat most was adouted 1130
or he passe wolde 1135

þat is grimmest igrowe 252
ȝour daies to tine 589
dredful dragonus · drawen hem þiddire 156

mihte lordschipe lache 264

þat i mai stinte no stounde 97
he haþ marked ȝou men · mischef on erþe 1120

þei [your gods] graunte no grace 709

Olimpias · þe onorable quene 825, 1083 as him dere þoute 1133

§ 10. But though these coincidences are striking and of considerable force, the argument from them is less conclusive than the argument derived from the peculiarities of alliteration. This point is well and carefully worked out by Dr. Trautmann, and we may, I think, accept his conclusion, against which there is no antecedent probability. I ought to add here that another result of his more careful investigation is to shew that these two Alexander-fragments are *not* by the author of William of Palerne, as was supposed by Sir F. Madden, and as, at one time, believed by myself. Dr. Trautmann also expresses an opinion that the date of these fragments is later than I should put it; but here I am not convinced.

§ 11. It appears to me that there is another argument which is also of weight. I have said that fragment C is a *close* translation from one Latin text, but the others are not so. In both of them, however, the same treatment of the Latin versions is observed. The text of the "Alexander de preliis" is taken as a general guide, on which account it is here printed *at the foot of every page of the English text*, with a summary of the latter chapters on p. 43. It is, however, supplemented from other sources, and the author seems to have aimed at telling the story in his own way, plainly with the intention of making it more interesting and attractive.[1] Even where he follows the text "de preliis," he by no means translates closely, but gives rather the general sense of the passage, with poetical interpolations ad libitum. Take, for example, a couple of lines from the Latin text printed at the foot of p. 6; and observe the result.

Latin text. "Deinde amoto exercitu venit ad fluuium bragmanorum magnum, vocatum ga[n]gei; et castra metata sunt ibi."

Fragment C, ll. 4188, 4189; *close translation.*

"þen rade he in aray · remowis his ostis,
To þe grete flode of gangem · & graythid þer his tents."

Fragment B, ll. 137—142; *free translation.*

"As sone þe king sai · þat it so ferde,
He dide him forþ to flod · þat phison is called,
þat writen is in holi wriht · & wrought so to name.
From perlese paradis · passeþ þe stronde;[2]
In cost þere þe king was · men called it gena,
As was þe langage of þe lond · wiþ ludus of inde."

It is evident that our author has here had further access to some other text, whence he acquired the notion of identity between the rivers Phison and Ganges. The following passage from Palladius de Bragmanibus (of which more hereafter) shews the source of his knowledge. In speaking of Alexander's approach to the Ganges, the remark is made:—"Fluvius vero Ganges iste est qui nobis vocatur Phison, ferturque in S. Literis fluviorum quatuor Paradiso exeuntium unus;" ed. Bisse, p. 2.

§ 12. This point being perceived, we next proceed to consider the *supplemental* sources of information possessed by our author. I have

---

[1] For numerous examples of this in fragment A, see the Notes in my edition of it.

[2] I. e. stream; *not* strand.

already pointed out that, for fragment A, he used a compilation by Radulphus of St. Alban's extant in MS. no. 219 in the library of Corpus Christi College, Cambridge, and also the history of Orosius. I now point out that, for fragment C, he made use of certain Latin texts, of which three were printed by E. Bisse in 1665. These tracts, all of which bear more or less upon the matter in hand, are as follows.

(1) Palladius de Gentibus Indiæ et Bragmanibus; begins— "Ἡ πολλὴ φιλοπονία σου, καὶ φιλομαθία," with a Latin version—" Tua indefatigabili industria."

(2) S. Ambrosius de Moribus Brachmanorum; begins—" Desiderium mentis tuæ, Palladi," &c., being a letter to Palladius from St. Ambrose.

(3) Anonymus de Bragmanis; begins—" Sæpius ad aures meas fando pervenit."

The last gives the text of the letters between Alexander and Dindimus, of which there are five, viz. these.

(*a*) First letter of Alexander to Dindimus; see ll. 191—242 of our English poem.

(*b*) First answer of Dindimus to Alexander; see ll. 249—811.

(*c*) Second letter of Alexander; see ll. 822—966.

(*d*) Second answer of Dindimus; see ll. 973—1071.

(*e*) Third letter of Alexander; see ll. 1078—1127.

There is a MS. copy of these letters in the MS. C. C. C. no. 219, just mentioned above; and there are other MS. copies in the same library, viz. in MS. no. 370, at fol. 38, back, and in MS. no. 450, p. 279;[1] but these copies are imperfect. As Bisse's printed edition is a convenient one for reference, I take the opportunity of recording here the contents of a sentence which, owing to the imperfect state of the MS. used by him, he was unable to give properly. The gap occurs in col. 2, of p. 102, as indicated by dots, and may be filled up by help of the following. "Nonnunquam etiam suauitate odoris uel gustu dulcedinis aut contactus blanda mollicie refouemur. Quorum omnium suggerunt nobis elementa materiarum, que eciam uite nostre creduntur esse principia. Quorum permixtione contraria

[1] Described in Nasmith's Catalogue, p. 414, as "Epistola Originaniorum (*sic*) ad Alexandrum magnum;" certainly an odd rendering of the "Bragmanorum" of the MS.

humani generis structura conditur," &c.[1] By help of these tracts, I have been able to find, as far as can be found, the original of almost every sentence of our poem, and I have pointed out the principal results of this research in the Notes.

§ 13. For further information, see Zacher, *Pseudo-Callisthenes*, Halle, 1867; the editions of Julius Valerius by Angelo Mai (Milan, 1817), and Karl Müller (Paris, 1846); the Old High-German version edited by H. Weismann (Frankfort-on-the-Main, 1850), the second volume of which, in particular, contains much information; the introduction to Kyng Alisaunder in Weber's Metrical Romances; the remarks on the Alexander Romances in Col. Yule's edition of Marco Polo, p. cxxxvii; Vincent of Beauvais, Spec. Hist. iv. 66—71, &c. I give two passages, by way of example, for comparison with the English poem. The former, from Julius Valerius, answers to ll. 1—22. The latter, from the Old High-German Romance, written by Lamprecht in the twelfth century, and edited by Weismann, corresponds to ll. 111—136.

From Julius Valerius, De Rebus Gestis Alexandri, ed. Mai; Milan, 1817, lib. iii. cc. xvi—xxii.

"xvi. Quare domitis hostibus avectaque praeda, ad Oxydracontas, quae gens exim colit, iter suum dirigit. Non illam quidem gentem hosticam incursatur (neque enim illis studia sunt armorum) sed quod celebre esset, Indos, quos gymnosophistas appellant, hisce in partibus versari, opum quidem omnium et cuiusque pretii neglegentes, solis vero diversoriis sapientissimi, quae humi manu exhauriunt aditibus perangusta, enimvero subter capacibus spaciata, quod id genus aedium neque pretii scilicet indigens, et ad flagrantiam solis aestivam aptius habeatur. Ii igitur cum conperissent Alexandrum ad sese contendere, primates suos, quos scilicet a sapientiae modo censent, obviare adventanti iubent cum litteris huiuscemodi."

From the Old High-German Romance, beginning at l. 4946.

"Do sluge wir unze gezelt	Then we pitched our tent
uf an ein breit felt.	Upon a broad field
groz wunder ih da sah :	A great wonder I saw there ;
des morgenes, do uns quam der tach	In the morning, when day came to us,
do sah ih wassen boume—	I then saw trees grow—
des nam ih rehte goume—	Of it I took good heed—
di wohssen harte scone	Which grew very finely
uzer erde unz an di none ;	Out of the earth until noon ;

---

[1] MS. C. C. C. 370 fol. 47 back ; cf. MS. C. C. C. 219, fol. 70.

dar under blumen unde gras,	Thereunder (were) flowers and grass.
do die none liden was,	When noon was past,
do sunken di boume nider	Then sank the trees down
tiefe under der erde wider.	Deep under the earth again.
uf den boumen wohs gut fruht ;	On the trees grew good fruit ;
da begine ih groz unzuht ;	Then I did a great evil.
ih gebot minen knechten	I ordered my servants
daz si mir des obezes brechten.	To break off for me some of the fruit.
groz not in dar vone bequam.	A great peril came of it.
svilich irre daz obiz nam,	Whoever rashly took the fruit,
der wart so zebluwen	He was so severely beaten
daz ime daz moste ruwen	That it must repent him
daz er ie geboren wart.	That ever he was born.
si worden ouh an der vart	They were also upon the way
mit geislen sere zeslagen.	With whips severely struck.
sine wisten, uber wen doh clagen,	They knew not whom to accuse,
wande si ne gesahen niemanne ;	Since they saw no one.
doh horten si eine stimme,	But they heard a voice
di gebot unde sagete,	Which commanded and said,
daz nieman ne scadete	That no one was to harm
dem obize noh den boumen ;	The fruit nor the trees ;
daz si des namen goume	That they should take heed of it,
neweder wafen noh man.	Both as to weapon and man.
wurdiz ubir daz getan,	If aught were done against this,
dar umbe solde liden not	The man would suffer pain for it
unde den bitteren tot	And bitter death
oder scaden vil groz,	Or very great harm,
der des obezis nie ne genoz.	And still would not taste the fruit.
Ouh sahe wir dar	We also saw there
cleine fugele, daz ist war,	Little birds—it is true—
di waren samfte gemuot	Which were of gentle mood,
unde ne forhten niwit den tot.	And feared death no whit.
groze not er liden solde,	He was to suffer great pain
sver in scaden wolde,	Whoever should harm them ;
den brante daz himelfiur,	Heaven's fire should burn him ;
dem wart daz leben vil sur."	Life should be very bitter for him.

ABSTRACT OF THE CONTENTS OF FRAGMENT B.

§ 14. The general contents of fragment B may be briefly described. After Alexander had slain Porus, king of India, he came to the country of the Oxydracæ, the people of which go naked, and are called Gymnosophists. Their king sends a letter to Alexander, representing that he has nothing to gain by subduing them. Alexander offers them peace, and promises to grant them a boon; upon which they ask him, by way of taunt, to give them everlasting life. He replies that he cannot do that, but must still fulfil his destiny. Next he sees the wonderful trees which only grew during sunlight, and at sundown disappear. These trees were guarded by birds that spat deadly fire. He next comes to the Ganges, a river impassable except in July and August. He sees men on the other side of the river, and sends a message by boat to their king, who is called Dindimus. The rest of the poem concerns the five letters which pass between him and Alexander.

First letter; Alexander to Dindimus (pp. 8—10). Tell me some of your customs; it is good to impart knowledge; for a torch whence another is lighted loses none of its own brightness thereby.

Second letter; from Dindimus (pp. 10—30). I comply with your request. We live a simple life; we neither plough, fish, nor hunt. We live frugally, and die at a fixed age. We use no fire, avoid lusts, eat fruit, drink milk or water, speak truth, and never covet nor make war. Our wives neither paint their faces, nor use gay apparel. We dwell in caves; we dislike mirth. We admire the suns, stars, and sea, feed on the scent of flowers, and love the woods. But ye are evil; ye sacrifice your children, and make war. Your gods likewise are evil; Jupiter was lecherous; ye have as many false gods as the body of man has members. Each one presides over some member; thus Mercury is god of the tongue, Bacchus of the throat, and so of the rest. Your idols lead you into sins, for which ye shall suffer hereafter endless torment. Ye are like Cerberus or Hydra, and are born to sorrow.

Third letter; from Alexander (pp. 31—36). Why do you blame us? Your account of yourselves is a miserable one, neither to be envied nor imitated. Ye are as beasts, but we as men. We intersperse hard work with well-earned pleasure. Ye lose many joys, and dishonour the Creator. Your deeds are but folly.

Fourth letter; from Dindimus. We are but pilgrims upon earth. Your boastful deeds only make you proud. The gold which you prize cannot satisfy thirst, and we are wiser in treading it under foot. Ye know not how much ye err, and it is a kindness to tell you. The man who lives as if there were no death deserves to be struck down by lightning, as was Salmoneus.

Fifth letter; from Alexander. Ye are so set in an island, that no strangers can come to you; ye are like wretched prisoners. God has decreed for you misery in this life, and pain hereafter. Your deeds are a woe to you.

After the letters are ended, Alexander erects a pillar of marble to mark the furthest spot which he had succeeded in reaching. His men then begin their homeward journey; and the fragment ends.

§ 15. It thus appears that the poem is principally concerned with the correspondence that passed between Alexander and the king of the Brahmans. This correspondence has really nothing to do with the story of Alexander's adventures, but is a mere excrescence. It is easy to see that it originated with an ecclesiastic, and was introduced with a moral purpose. There are two leading ideas in it, both of them theological. The former is, the common and favourite contrast between the Active Life and the Contemplative Life, which so often meets us in mediæval literature; and the latter, the contrast between the Christian life and that of the heathen worshippers of idols. The arguments are so managed that the bias of one counteracts that of the other. We are led, on the one hand, to favour the Active Life as being more useful than the Contemplative; but, lest the scale should preponderate in its favour, it is linked with Heathenism as opposed to Christianity. The life of Dindimus, in as far as it is assimilated to that of a Christian, is preferable to that of Alexander. The life of Alexander, in its Active aspect, enlists our sympathies rather than that of Dindimus. The author of this ingenious arrangement strove rather for oratorical effect than sought to inculcate a lesson. To regard the various arguments in this light is to regard them rightly. It is merely a question of seeing what can be said on both sides. There is nothing else to be learnt from the story of it.

ON THE NAME "DINDIMUS."

§ 16. Though the poem deals with India, and attempts an account of the life of the Brahmans, there is little that is eastern about it. Bisse has pointed out the references to the Gymnosophists that occur in Strabo, lib. 15; in Plutarch's Life of Alexander; in Arrian, De Expedit. Alexandri, lib. 7; in Clement of Alexandria, Stromata, lib. 3; in Porphyrius, De Abstinentia, lib. 4; in Philostratus, Vita Apollonii lib. 3, capp. 4 and 5; and in other authors. The chief point of interest is in the name Dindimus,[1] given to the supposed king of the Brahmans. It should rather be *Dandamis*, answering to *Dandamis* in the Latin, and Δανδάμις in the Greek texts. It is not really a proper name, but a sort of title. It is the Sanskrit *dandin*, signifying 'bearing a staff,' or, as a sb., 'mace-bearer.' It occurs in the sense of 'warder' or 'door-keeper' in the Tale of Nala, iv. 25. It is an adj. formed from the sb. *danda*, a staff, mace, sceptre of justice; and this again is from the root *dand*, to chastise. It thus has the sense of 'sceptre bearer' or 'dispenser of justice.' Even in Sanskrit it is used as an epithet of Yama, and also as a proper name. The compound *tri-dandin*, lit. 'three-staves-bearing,' was applied in particular to an ascetic, as being one who has command over the three seats of action, viz. mind, speech, and body; see Benfey's Dict., p. 385. Hence the particular application of the epithet to a chief of ascetics is very appropriate. However, the simple form *dandin* was likewise used to signify an ascetic; and Prof. Cowell kindly refers me to a passage shewing that it was, in fact, a name for a man in the fourth (and highest) stage of Brahmanical life—the religious devotee. "His nails, hair, and beard being clipped, bearing with him a dish, a *staff*, and a waterpot, his whole mind being fixed on God, let him wander about continually, without giving pain to any living thing."—Manu, vi. 32.

ACCOUNT OF THE PICTURES.

§ 17. I here attempt an account of the illuminations or coloured pictures which occur in the MS. There are nine of these, viz. at ll. 137, 249, 355, 568, 681, 822, 973, 1078, and 1139, as indicated in the text itself. The subjects of them are as follows.

I. King Alexander stands just before his tent. At his feet flows a stream, in which swims a large eel, to represent the 'hound-fish' (l. 164), and just on the further bank stand two dragons (156). A man is rowing across the stream in a boat (168); two others, both naked, stand a little back from the stream, one of them bearing an offering of fruits (165).

[1] Printed *Duidimus*, in five places, in Warton's Hist. of Eng. Poetry, ed. 1840, p. 104; this misspelling is not corrected in the edition of 1871.

II. A tent. Alexander receiving a letter from a man who kneels before him (248).

III. Two naked men, of whom one is Dindimus, who bears a crown, and sits at the mouth of a cave, writing. The other, half hid in the cave, is the messenger to whom he is to entrust his letter.

IV. King Alexander before his tent. Before him stand four naked men, of whom the foremost, bearing a crown, is Dindimus.

V. In the middle of the picture is an idol, seated on a pillar or pedestal. The idol is in a constrained posture, pointing, apparently, towards its stomach. It probably represents Cupid (686). On the right of the idol stands Alexander. On the left of it stands Dindimus, naked but crowned, who is administering a reproof.

VI. Dindimus, naked but crowned, is receiving a letter presented to him by Alexander's messenger.

VII. Alexander is seated before his tent. He receives a letter from a naked messenger.

VIII. Alexander's page is kneeling down and offering a letter to Dindimus, behind whom are four men, one of whom is issuing from the mouth of the cave. In this picture Dindimus and his men are apparently naked, but are curiously tattooed or marked all over with something that almost gives them the appearance of wearing coats of mail.

IX. Alexander is setting up a large white pillar (1135).

CONJECTURAL DATE OF THE POEM.

§ 18. The chief value of the poem is in the language of it. It is a good specimen of Alliterative English, and contains, in common with all other such poems, a number of curious and characteristic words. My original impression was that it might be referred to about the year 1340; Dr. Trautmann argues that the date should rather be about 1370. It is hardly possible to decide the matter either way; and, if it may be argued on the one hand, that there are reasons for putting it earlier than William of Palerne (written about 1350), it may be said, on the other, that alliterative poems, by their retention of archaic forms, have an appearance of antiquity which is rather deceptive.[1] It is not of much consequence either way; and it is

[1] The French romance, in MS. Bodley 264, was written out in 1338, and

quite sufficient to know the date approximately. The dialect, which is more particularly discussed in § 22, is apparently that of the West of England. On account of the usefulness of references to good specimens of Middle English, I have attempted, in the Glossarial Index, to make a list of *all* the words in the poem, but omitting multiplication of references in the case of every word. See the note prefixed to the Glossarial Index on p. 61.

EDITION FOR THE ROXBURGHE CLUB.

§ 19. The poem has been printed before, as I have said, by Mr Stevenson, for the Roxburghe Club, in 1849; but the number of copies printed was limited, and the book is scarce; for which reason it is now reprinted for the Early English Text Society. Mr. Stevenson's text is not free from faults; it would seem to have been printed from an imperfect transcript without collation of the proofs with the MS. itself. The MS. itself has also several faults.[1] In the following list of the variations from the MS. in Mr. Stevenson's edition, the *former* of the two forms gives the word as it stands in the MS.; the latter the word as it stands in his edition; the numbers referring to the lines. It does not include the editor's numerous substitutions of *v* for *u*, of *th* for *þ*, and of capital letters for small ones. 1. *MS.* weduring; Stevenson *prints* wedering. 2. rommede—roumede. 4. wondurful—wonderful. 31. miȝht—might. 32. wele—wel. 39. werrede—wercede. 44. sikurede—sikured. 51. hiddem—hidden hem (*evidently an editorial correction; but no notice is given*). 55. Aftur—After. 65. speche—speeche. 74. my silf—myselfe. 81. skile—skill. 82. kinguus—kingus. 88. wrecheli—wrethelie. 100. seruauntus—servantus. 106. Whan—When. 107. enchesoun—enchesonn; oþur—other; kinguus—kingus. 108, &c. ouur—over. 109. oþure—othur. 124. &—In. grouuede—grounede. 127. &—in. 136. spilden—spildin. 142. ludus—ludis. 143. mascedonius—Mascedomus; (*cf. l.* 1073). 145. mascedonius—Mastredomus (*sic*). 148. hem—him.

illuminated in 1344. The English copy was written out perhaps about a century later, but then it was evidently copied from an older original.

[1] The chief of these are pointed out in the margin of the present edition; see ll. 51, 69, &c. Some others are discussed in the Notes.

INTRODUCTION.

150. miche — muche. 151. ou*ur* — over; romme — rounne. 152. watir—water. 155. aftyr—aftter. 164. þer inne—there inne. 176. &—In. 177. þi—the. 179. couaitede—covaited. 180. ic*h*—Ic. 185. þanne whitli — Than whith; ou*ur* — over; wat*ur* — wat*e*r. 187. say—saye. 193. grac*i*ouce—gracious. 194. on*u*rable—onerable. 200. fram oþ*ur*—from other. 203. sesoun—sasoun. 207. tyinge (*error for* typinge)—tynige. 210. meruailouse—marvailouse. 213. ȝour—your. 215. ic*h*—Ic. 222. þinguus—thingus. 230. hit— it; oþ*ur*e — other. 236. vn-wasteþ — onwasteth. 245. write — writte. 248. man*ere*—manner. 250. lond—loud. 251. pr*i*ncis— princes. 281. time—tune. 294. forwes—forues. 307. mod*ur*— moder. 336. mihte — miht. 345. ou*ur*come*n* — overcomen. 347. nol—ne of; pr*o*cre—prince. 351. keuered—keverid. 364. wiþ oute—without. 366. pr*o*cred—proceed. 395. y punched—ypiniched. 396. ȝour — ȝoure. 405. þei — thai. 420. sauiour — Savioure. 431. coruen—comen. 438. oþ*ur*—othir. 440. owen—usen. 442. any — ony. 443. wed*ur*es — wederes. 460. luþ*ur*ly — lutherly. 467. storri*us* — stormus. 470. game — gaine. 478. þe skiu*us*— skurus. 480. &—An. 483. waw*us*—wavus. 496. sauo*ur*on— saveron. 514. man*er*—manir. 517. lowe—lothe. 521. alle—all. 533. ou*ur*—over. 534. mihtest—mihhest. 541. quedfulle—qued fulle. 542. souorain—soverain. 543. vnblisful—unblissful. 545. gret — grett. 547. prouede — proude. 549. miht — might. 554. lecho*ur*us — lechurous. 565. hole — hol. 568. aftur — after. 569. luþ*ur* — luther. 570. auaunt — avaunte. 573. Miche — Swiche. 574. bet*ur*e — betere. 575. ged*ur*en — gederen. 578. ket*ur*e — kecere. 580. oth*ur* — other.   mirthe — in irthe. 583. ou*ur*-comeþ — overcometh. 597. leue*n* — liven. 605. For þei — For thi. 609. vnd*ur*stonde — understonde. 612. noþ*ur* — nothir (*twice*). 629. & — in; luþ*ur* — luther. 632. sinne — synne. 633. oþ*ur* — othir. 638, 639. No — Ne. 659. iaudewin—jandewin; ioiful—joyful. 662. rink—renk; wraþþe— wraythe. 663. main—mani. 664. found*ur*—founderer. 674. ȝiue — give. 682. fur — full. 685. soþ — sothe. 692. ell*us* — elles. 698. weihu*us* — weihus. 700. oþ*ur* — othir. 702. minst*r*alus— minstrelus. 717. vn — on. 722. oþ*ur* — othir. 729. spraiu*us* —

sprainus. 740. fau*re* — favere. 742. mais*t*rie — maistire. 763.
kun not—kunnot. 764. graunte—graunt. 769. any—an y. 772.
wreche—wirche. 775. ar—are. 776. tu*r*ment—tourment. 777.
wreche — wrethe. 786. wirche*n* — worchen. 797. ȝour—ȝoure.
799. yydr*a*—Thydra. 810. dindim*us*—Dindunus. 816. anon riht
anied — anonriht amed. 825. onorable — honorable. 834. ne — no
(*which is better*). 836. seye—seth. 840. dedes—dede. 846. tulye
—tulthe. 855, 865, &c. oþur—othir. 856. For-þi—Forthei. 863,
866. hungu*r* — hunger. 866. ȝou — you. 875. comine — comme.
881. hungur — hungurus. 884, 887. lech*u*rie — lecherie. 894.
charite*uus* — chariteus. 921. ioie — joie. 928. dimme — dunne.
929. siht—riht. 930. alse—alle. 936. Whan—When. 947. siht
— riht. & sau*ur* — saver. 958. þo — the. 986. kin*us* nie—
kinusme[n]. 1012. grete—Grece. 1017. burn*us*—turnus. dede*us*
—dedus. 1030. houngur—hounger. 1036. hit—it. 1037. cofly—
coflye. 1067. wit*h*—what. 1074. seye—sethe. 1075. bragmanye
brouht — Bragman ye brouht. 1082. grac*i*ose—graciouse. 1091.
you — thou. 1097. ȝour — ȝoure. 1100. & skile — in skile.
1118. iuge, ioie, iugged—juge, joye, jugged. 1121. þouh—Though.
1131. romme—roume. 1137. ic*h*—Ic. 1138. graie—grie.

§ 20. In several of these instances the MS. may, no doubt, be read either way. In particular, the scribe often makes but little difference between *y* and þ, or between *c* and *t*, and sometimes none at all between *u* and *n*, or between *m* and *in* or *ni*. Yet in most cases there can be no doubt about the matter, and I think the reader will in general be able to tell for himself why the readings in the present edition are preferable to those in the former. Thus, in l. 88, we must read *wrecheli*, i. e. wretchedly, miserably, not *wretheli*, i. e. wrathfully. In l. 124, *grouuede*=*growede*, i. e. grew; but *grounede* cannot well be explained. In l. 250, *lond* = land; but *loud* makes no sense. In l. 281, we must of course read *time*, not *tune*. In l. 467, the sense is 'to read stories,' not 'to read storms.' In l. 478, the sun and stars are visible *on þe skiuus*, in the skies; but not *on þe skurus*, which is explained to mean 'in the tempests.' In l. 578, *keture*, not an uncommon word, must be preferred to *kecere*, which does not exist. In l. 659, *iaudewin* can be explained, but *jandewin* cannot. In l. 729, *spraiuus*, sprays, is better than *sprainus*, giving no meaning. In l. 816, *anied* means 'annoyed;' the sense of *amed* we are not told, whilst the alliteration is then lost. In l. 846, the M. E. word for 'to till' is, of course, *to tulye*, not *to tulthe*. In l. 875, *comine peple* means 'common people,' but *comme peple* makes no sense. In l. 928, days are *dimme*, i. e. dim, rather than *dunne* or brown. In l. 1074, *seye* means seen, i. e. read over; *sethe* does not exist as a past participle, but means 'to boil.' In some cases the alliteration is a guide to the right reading, giving us, in l. 573, *Miche* for *Swiche;* in l. 929 and 947, *siht* for *riht;* and in l. 1017, *burnus* for *turnus*. In all four of these places, the MS. is quite right. Perhaps the most curious variation is in l. 347, where the MS. reading *nol no gome procre* (= will procure no man) appears as *ne of no gome prince*. And in l. 769 the reading of the former edition *an y* is explained in the glossary to mean 'an egg;' that is to say, "when the gods are loath to hear your prayers, the fact that they will not hear you hatches[1] an egg for you." The reading in the MS. is *any*, i. e. annoyance, vexation; and the right sense is "breeds annoyance for you."

§ 21. A glossary is appended to Mr. Stevenson's edition, but it is not a very full one. The number of words explained in it is 63; and, for the reader's convenience, I here reprint it, with the references, as given.

Aldurfadur, an ancestor, 1050. *Atlede*, attempted to go, 15. *Auht*, increased, 936. *Bakke*, a bat, 723. *Bliken*, to make fair, 411. *Boller*, a drunkard, 675. *Bourd*, a jest, 469. *Brigg*, strife, 393. *Cof*, quickly, 42; *Cofli, Cofliche*, quickly, 48, 64, 1076. *Dreche*, to drench, 1032. *Dreie* [*drie* in the text], to suffer, 857. *Englayme*, to cloy, 676. *Ferk*, to go, 300. *Fon*, foes, 339, 341. *Fulsum*, satisfied, 497. *Galfull*, lustful, 389. *Gaynes us*, it avails us, 181, 1028. *Giour*, a guide, 703. *Grith*, protection, 764. *He*, she, 654, 698. *Here*, to honour, 1046. *Hery*, to praise, 358. *Hihten*, to honour, adorn, 406, 408, 418. *Hue*, she, 656.

---

[1] The glossary to the former edition explains *norcheth* by *paineth not*. This is hardly fair; and, even then, the sense comes out just the opposite of what it should do. Besides, *norscheþ* occurs again, in l. 309.

Jandewin (?), 659. *Karre*, to turn, 886 [*read* 986]. *Laike*, to play, 465. *Licham*, the body, 492 [*read* 592]. *Lileth* (?), 474. *Lin*, to remain, 441, 448. *Lisse*, to please, 476. *Lite*, to mock (?), 732 [*read* 932]. *Lose*, praise, 221. *Lud*, a man, 205, 645. *Ludene*, human, 773. *Menskliche*, honorably, 1073. *Minegeth*, mentions, 573, 614. *Muniȝe*, to teach, 514. *Namecouthe*, celebrated, 823, 979. *Norcheth*, paineth not, 769. *Quedfulle*, full of wickedness, 541. *Reke*, extended, 594. *Sake*, contention, 388. *Schalk*, a man, 432. *Sichus*, sighs, 1115. *Side*, long, wide, 481. *Skurus*, tempests, 478. *Snelle*, keen, 437. *Solow*, a ploughshare, 295. *Sote*, sweet, 128, 496. *Spousebreche*, adultery, 885. *Tacchus*, manners, 463. *Taried*, harmed, 132. *Tendeth*, inflameth, 684. *Tenful*, sorrowful, 793. *Traie*, difficult, 710. *Whon*, a quantity, 353. *Wikke*, wicked, 537. *Wilnede*, desired, 150. *Won*, abundance, 499, 557, 575, 678, 891, 957. *Wond*, to depart from, 886, 957, 990. *Y*, an egg, 769.

In the references here given three corrections must be made; *karre* occurs in l. 986; *licham* in l. 592; and *lite* in l. 932; as noted above. And the explanations may, I think, be improved in at least 13 instances. *Dreche* = to afflict. *Jandewin* should rather be *jaudewin;* see my Glossary. *Laik* in l. 465 is a sb., not a verb. For *lileth* (the MS. reading) read *liketh*. *Lisse* is a sb., signifying joy. *Lite* means 'little;' *ille can lite* = knows little ill; or, more strictly, knows evil (but a) little. *Ludene* is not an adj., but the genitive plural. *Norcheth* = nourishes. *Sake* is simply *sake*. *Skurus* is an error for *skiuus* = *skius*, skies. *Traie* is a sb., meaning 'a vexation.' *Wond* is rather 'to shun, avoid.' *Y* is due to an error; the word is *any*. The explanation of *reke* is, besides, hardly satisfactory; if 'extended' be meant, the form should rather have been *rauht* or *rauȝt*.

ON THE DIALECT OF THE POEM.

§ 22. One difficulty in the way of studying the dialect of an old poem is that, when it presents mixed forms, we cannot well tell whether some of its peculiarities may not have been due merely to the scribe. We want to know which forms are original, and which have crept into the poem in course of transcription. Singularly enough, we have in the present instance a short sentence by the *scribe himself*, which tells us, at any rate, something. I allude to the note mentioned in § 3, which gives us the following hints. The scribe writes *fayleþ, lasteþ*, in the 3rd person singular of the present tense; *turneþ, bygynneþ*, but also *rede*, in the 2nd person plural of the imperative mood; *y-wrete* and *radde* appear as past participles of strong verbs; and we have also the phrases ȝe *schulle* and ȝe *han*. These indications are not to be disregarded; but point to a southern dialect, or to a midland dialect strongly marked by southern forms. It seems fair to infer that the numerous western forms found in the poem, such as the suffix *-us* for the present singular or for the imperative plural, are *not* due to the scribe, but to the original which he had before him; which makes some observations upon the forms in the poem all the more necessary and useful, as well as trustworthy. The bias of the scribe towards southern forms being ascertained, we can see our way more clearly than we could have done otherwise.

§ 23. For convenience, I consider the various peculiarities of the text in much the same order as I have done those found in William of Palerne; the present remarks may therefore be compared with those in my Preface to that poem, p. xxxviii. For *references* to the words cited below, see the Glossarial Index.

The plurals of nouns generally end in *-us*, as *wynterus, somerus, holus, answerus, ludus, costomus*, &c.; but this ending is also curiously varied to *-uus*, as in *skiuus, kinguus, weihuus, foliuus;* or else to *-eus*, as in *seggeus, dedeus;* or even to *-ous*, as in *þouhtous* (767), *godous* (772). In some cases, we find plurals in *-ys*, as in *heuys* (hues), *cauys* (caves), *stormys;* rarely in *-es*, as in *lettres, weies, dedes;* very rarely in *-is*, as in *holis* (57). Other plurals worth notice are *oxen* (296), *hous* (434), *fon* (foes), *tren* (trees, 853), *erene* = *eren* (ears), *eldrene, eldren* (elders), *breþeren, soulen* (souls). The pl. of 'fish' appears as *fihs, fihcs, fihch*, and *fihches*. The genitive singular also commonly ends in *-us*, as in *godus* (315), *catelus* (370), *licamus* (555). The genitive plural is found ending in *-ene*, as in *haþelene, briddene, bestene, ludene;* cf. *wommenus* (1016).

As regards adjectives, we find plurals in *-e*, as *meke, pore;* and *e* is commonly added to past participles in the plural, as in *clene-minded, corsede, bannede;* though it is also wrongly added to past

DIALECT OF THE POEM. xxvii

participles of weak verbs in the singular, a mark of the lateness of the transcription or of ignorance of spelling. We find the comparatives *bliþure, schenure, beture, keture, comelokur;* as also *lasse, werse;* and the superlatives *kiddeste, egrest, grymmest, grettest* (see 975, 976). The endings *-ly, -li,* and *-liche* are used both for adverbs and adjectives without distinction; thus we have *cofliche, cofli,* and *cofly.*

As to pronouns, for *I* the forms are *i, y,* and *ich* (1137); for *thou,* we have *þou;* pl. *ȝe* in the nominative, *ȝou, ȝow,* in the dative and accusative; see l. 540. The third personal pronoun is *he,* gen. *his, is,* dat. and acc. *him;* though in one instance (l. 703) the acc. is written *hin,* more likely by an error of the scribe than by a preservation of the *n* in the A.S. *hine.* The feminine of the third person is *hue* (as in Alexander A.), but *sche* occurs once, in l. 309; acc. *hure.* The neuter is commonly *hit.* The plural nom. is *þey* or *þei;* gen. *hure, hur;* dat. and acc. *hem.* We find *euerych a* = every (86). *Huo,* used for *who,* occurs interrogatively (941); *huo-so* or *ho-so* occurs for *who-so* (1001, 1060).

In the case of verbs, the infinitive ends in *-en,* as *reden, maken, forleten;* in *-e,* as *bereue, tine;* in *-ien,* as *tilien;* in *-ie,* as *þolie,* or *-ye,* as *tulye;* very rarely in *-yn,* as *helyn* (320). In the present tense, 2nd pers. sing., we find *-est,* as in *berest, bringest, lettest, sentest(e), wilnest;* cf. the contracted form *wost* (516). In the 3rd pers. sing., we most often find *-us,* as *farus, kairus, lepus, wendus, romwus;* but also *-es,* as *fondes;* and even *-eþ,* as *seseþ, askeþ,* with which compare the contracted forms *biclipth* and *et* (= *eteth,* 862). The plural ends in *-en* or *-e;* rarely in *-in,* as *wetin* (99), *worchin,* 361; once in *-on,* as *sauouron* (496), probably by an error of the scribe for *sauouren;* see numerous examples in ll. 712—733.

The imperative plural (2nd person) ends in *-us,* as in *giuus* (972); in *-es,* as in *ȝernes* (67); but also in *-eþ* (190), which is possibly due to the scribe. Of past tenses, we may note the use *sai* and *sie,* in the sense of *saw,* in the singular; and *saien* and *sihen,* in the same sense, in the plural; *sew* (sing.) in the sense of *sowed seed;* and *wreten* (pl.) in the sense of *wrote.* The 2nd person singular of strong verbs ends in *-e,* as *þou bade* (511). Examples of weak verbs are, in the singular, *helde, wente, brente, wiste,* with the fuller forms *askede,* *biggede, buskede;* and, in the plural, *tendide, spatten, spilden*. Of past participles, those of strong verbs end properly in *-en*, as *holden* (16), *coren* (chosen), *doluen, i-boren;* but the final *n* often drops off, as in *holde* (13), *graue, i-ʒoulde, schape, i-founde, smite* (smitten). Examples of past participles of weak verbs are *listned, i-eged, y-sustained, ydemed,* ending in *-ed; wastid,* ending in *-id;* also *i-kid, tend, iput, iset, kild, maad,* contracted forms. In two cases we actually find the ending *-eþ;* viz. in *yhanteþ,* 988, *vnwasteþ,* 236; these are probably errors. The prefix *i-* or *y-* is by no means uncommon, especially in weak verbs, as *i-kid, i-said, iput, i-set, i-eged, y-kid, y-maad, y-sustained, y-demed;* it is even found in strong verbs, as *i-ʒoulde, i-boren, ifounde.* Cf. *iset* (454) with *set* (481). The present participles end in *-inge,* as *rydinge, likinge, wastinge.* Substantives of verbal origin also end in *-inge,* as *wachinge, housinge, lesinge, swaginge, handlinge, heringe, queminge;* see ll. 948—952. We once find *-in* for *-inge,* as in *offrin,* l. 718. It is, perhaps, worthy of remark, that in the plural of the present tense of the verb signifying *to be,* we find both *arn* and *ben.* Both forms are due to the author, as is proved by the alliteration. In ll. 333, 423, 904, we find *ben,* as the alliteration requires; whilst in ll. 338, 345, 506, 1007, we find *arn,* also as required. A similar peculiarity occurs in Piers the Plowman. In ll. 446, 634, we have examples of the verb *worþen,* to become. Some peculiarities of spelling may be noted. For *fish,* we have the curious forms, *fihcs, fihs, fihch, fihches.* For *strength,* we find *strenke;* for *strengthen, strenkþen;* for *drinking, drinkinke;* for *nought, noukt.* In the word *world,* the *l* is frequently dropped, giving *word* or *worde;* but we also find the curious form *wordle,* as in some MSS. of Piers the Plowman. This form is still found in Somersetshire, as in the phrase *běeyaen aul dhu daiz een dhu wuurdl* (beyond all the days in the world), to quote from the representation of Somersetshire speech in glossic spelling, given by Mr. Elworthy in his Grammar of the Dialect of West Somerset, p. 103. We may also note the loss of *d* after *l,* as in *gol* for *gold;* as well as the use of *scl* for *sl,* as in *sclepe, sclowþe, sclain,* all in l. 344. Also the use of *sch* for *ch,* as in *schast* for *chast* (894), suggesting that *ch* had occasionally the sound of *sh.* The aspirate is sometimes misused, as in *holde* for *old*, l. 327; *hauter* for *altar*, l. 728. The number of curious words in the poem is considerable, not the least remarkable being the word *done* in l. 999, on which see the note. We also see that *to punch* is short for *punish*.

It hence appears that the dialect is much the same as that of William of Palerne, the chief difference being that there are no present participles in *-ande* as well as in *-inge*; but there are not many examples to judge from. I think the dialect is plainly West Midland, but not so far north as Lancashire; rather in the direction of Shropshire or Gloucestershire, as in William of Palerne.

ON THE ALLITERATION OF THE POEM.

§ 24. I note here a few peculiarities of alliteration.[1] Perhaps the most remarkable is the run upon *vowels*, which is also a marked feature of the Alexander A-fragment; see ll. 22, 27, 230, 240, 268, 290, 415, 461, 498, 500, &c. of that text. So here, we find an alliteration of *different* vowels in ll. 3, 15, 24, 157, 251, 338, 343, 345, 440, 442, 468, 506, 526, 568, 718, 720, 754, 812, 851, 936, 975, &c. We also find alliteration of the *same* vowel in many instances. Ex: *a, a, a;* 55, 63, 170, 198, 244, 377, 701, 822, 1007; *e, e, e;* 86, 201, 262, 360, 539, 744, 757, 862, 981, 1008; *o, o, o;* 327, 533, 711, 743. To these add l. 588, in which there are but *two* vowels, both *e;* also 153, in which we have *o, e* (in *eight* = viij.), *a;* also 518, in which *a* rimes with the diphthongs *au* and *eu*. The most remarkable instance is in ll. 1007, 1008, in which two *consecutive* lines have the vowel-rime. The letter *h* is also *sometimes* associated with vowels, as in these instances; 155, 219 (where *haþel* is for *aþel*), 277 (where *haþel* is again for *aþel*), 320 (*haþelene* for *aþelene*), 348 (*haþel* for *aþel*), 669, 728, 799, 842, 856 (*haþel* for *aþel*), 1137. This is the more remarkable, because *h* is also found as an alliterative letter, as in l. 16, 51, &c.

[1] I may further refer the reader to a careful dissertation entitled Die Alliterierende Englische Langzeile im xiv. Jahrhundert, by F. Rosenthal; Halle, 1877. This contains an analysis of the alliterations in the three texts of Piers Plowman, a work of great labour. Most of the remarks here made were written before I received a copy of this dissertation, which was kindly forwarded to me by the author.

C of course answers to *k;* as in 13, 26, 29, 38, 42, 48, &c. Also *ph* to *f;* as in 457, 1070. Also soft *c* to *s;* as in the word *Ceres*, 724; cf. *syte*, written for *cyte*, i. e. city, in l. 9; see the note. Also soft *g* to *i* ($=j$); 656. Scarce rimes are those with *i* ($=j$); 462, 553, 659, 697, 1118: with *qu;* 541, 608, 950, 1047: and with *v;* 671, 693.[1] Examples of double rime-letters are numerous; examples are *bl*, 411, 523, 543, 624; *br*, 134, 287, 393, 430, 503, 521, 586, &c.; *ch*, 107, 110, 417, 727, 894,[2] 941, 1080; *cl*, 489, 625, 636, 899, &c.; *dr*, 156, 529, 1032; *gl*, 676, 790; *gr*, 7, 87, 124, 133, 252, 254, 447, 502, &c.; *pl*, 296, 495, 847, 853; *pr*, 5, 161, 225, 280, 366, 509, 547, &c.; *sch*, 294, 330, 401, 412, 416, 421, 432, &c., especially the consecutive lines 959 and 960; *scl* = *sl*, 344; *sk*, 159, 871, 1020; *sm*, 1063; *sp*, 136, 172, 367, 699; *st*, 97, 114, 429, 487, 609, 686; *sw*, 310, 493, 719, 855, 921; *tr*, 513, 829; *wr*, 139, 660, 777, 814, 1136. There are even examples of triple rime-letters, as *spr*, 123, 729; and *str*, 756; but we must not include amongst these *sch* and *scl*, already mentioned, since these are merely ways of writing *sh* and *sl* respectively. But it was not thought at all *necessary* that, if a double consonant began one rime-word, the same sound should occur throughout the line. We have *br* riming with *b*, 175, 683, 714, 723; *fr* with *f*, 352; *gl* with *g*, 391; *gr* with *g*, 193, 274, 525, 824, 1025; *sp* with *spr*, 623; *st* with *str*, 530; and numerous other examples. The strangest example is an apparent rime of *br* with *pr*, 1075; but the word *prest* may be wrong.

We sometimes find *four* rime-letters in the line; as in 499, 544, 546; these lines are not very common, and the fourth letter is not needed.

Occasionally there is a failure of one of the sub-letters, as in l. 11,[3] 22 (where it is easy to supply *tid*); 81, where *k* seems to answer (by poetical licence) to *sk;* 290; 302 (where *refe* should be *bruten*, see note); 558; 782 (where *ȝou lif* should perhaps be *ȝou silf*); 793 (unless the *t* in *Tricerberus* is counted in); 815. One or other of

---

[1] No example of the rime of *v* with *f*, as in Piers Plowman and Richard the Redeles.

[2] The writing of *schast* for *chast* is a mere freak of the scribe.

[3] A bad line; the *g* in *gcnosophistiens* is soft, and does not well rime with *gomes*.

ALLITERATION OF THE POEM. xxxi

the sub-letters is often out of place, as in ll. 12, 47, 67, 106, &c.; but a certain amount of variation of this character is rather a beauty than a blemish, as it prevents the metre from being too painfully regular. Yet this licence is sometimes carried too far; in ll. 12, 47, 130, and some others, the accent has to be rather forced to bring out the rime. The worst is when the chief-letter fails, as in ll. 6, 1046; in the latter case, there is something wrong. Other unmusical lines are those where the chief-letter is ill placed, as in ll. 54, 163, 904, where the word *bi* is too weak to bear the whole weight of the verse. Similarly, l. 363 is bad. In l. 73, we may excuse the strong emphasis upon *not*, by supposing that Alexander meant to express his refusal unmistakeably. We may note ll. 31, 50, 394, 971, as examples in which the chief-letter comes nearer than usual to the end of the line.

As usual, prefixes are commonly neglected in the alliteration; thus, in l. 19, the accent is on the syllable beginning with *s* in *forsaide*, the prefix *for* being neglected. Other examples are: the rime with *m* in *amongus*, 28; *h* in *bi-holden*, 46; and with the italicised letters in the following, viz. a*b*oute, 54; bi-*r*eue, 82; a*g*ayn, 83; i*s*aid, 100; a-*p*ere, 104; en*ch*esoun, 107; a*s*tored, 114; for*d*on, 118; a*sk*ape, 159; a*sp*ien, 172; a*l*oweþ, 212; vn*h*armed, 227; vn*w*asteþ, 236; en*d*itinge, 243; a*l*osed, 250; rihte*w*isnesse, 258 (an odd instance); a*l*owe, 259; in*p*ossible, 268; vn*l*ich, 271; bi*l*eue, 272; &c., &c.

This neglect of the prefix is, of course, right; as it brings the *accented* syllable into play. But we sometimes find a very objectionable variation, viz. cases in which, contrary to the whole spirit of alliterative poetry, the rime-letter begins an *un*accented syllable. Examples of this occur, not only in the present poem, but (as I have before observed) in other alliterative poems also. As this point probably presents a difficulty to such as do not clearly apprehend the fact, I cite some instances.

   And *s*aide, *s*eg, to us *s*ilf · *s*ofisen þis cauus; 61.
   That us *d*erye no deþ · *d*esíre we nouþe; 71.
   Bigat *o*n *o*límpias · þe *o*nurable quene; 194.
   That we *d*iscórden of *d*ede · in many *d*one þinguus; 222.
   Alle þe *d*edes þat ȝe *d*on · *d*iscórden til oure; 273.

Ne oþir *d*ainteys *d*ere · *d*esíre we none ; 306.
To him þat *sch*op us to *sch*ap · *sch*al fáre to blisse ; 330.
And *d*elíten in no *d*ede · þat *d*oþ men to sinne ; 505.
*M*ichel holde ȝe of *m*iht · *M*inérua þe falce ; 653 ; cf. 722.
*D*iuísede here on his *d*ay · a *d*osain of wondrus ; 670.
That han no *r*ewárd to *r*iht · but *r*edlese wirchen ; 907.
þis *s*onde þat y *s*aid haue · *s*ire álixandre riche ; 967.

A crucial test is furnished by ll. 74, 75.

Of *m*é þat *m*iȝhteles am · *m*y-sílf so to kepe ;
I am *s*íkur of my-*s*ílf · to *s*úffre min ende.

Here, in the same word, viz. *my-silf*, without any change of accent, we have a change in the alliterative letter.[1]

No doubt our pronunciation has changed greatly since the fourteenth century, but accent is a much more persistent thing. No one will be so hardy as to maintain that such accentuations as *désire, ólimpias, déliten, minerva, diuisede, réward* could ever have been possible; and, for this reason, I refuse to believe in *sófisen*, or *díscorden* either. And I am prepared to maintain, as always, that even the chief-letter in the alliterative poetry of our forefathers sometimes fell on wholly unaccented and unimportant syllables, such as *schal* in l. 330, and *sire* in l. 967. So much the worse for the poetry, no doubt; but we must not shut our eyes to plain facts by pretending that poets could not err. Besides, it is easy to see *why* these unimportant syllables sometimes received the rime-letter. What the poet really wanted was *a help to the memory*, and this was attained quite as easily (now and then) by help of an unimportant syllable as by close attention to rule. The use of the word *schal* in l. 330 (as of *sire* in l. 967) was to give the reciter a start for his second half-line. The cue was quite sufficient for this purpose, and thus the line, though slip-shod, was allowed to pass. This is the simple explanation of the whole matter.

§ 25. I add a list (perhaps imperfect) of the principal words of *French* or *Latin* origin in the poem; omitting proper names. The list is as follows; the references to the lines where they occur will be found in the Glossarial Index.[2] Acorde, age, air, alowe, auterus

---

[1] We cannot shift the accent in a word like *mysilf*, as Chaucer does in the case of French words like *honour* and *fortune*. The case is quite different.

[2] The order of such words as are still in use is the alphabetical order of them in *modern* English; the *obsolete* words follow these, letter by letter.

(*altars*), amende, anied (*annoyed*), apere, armus, araie, asent, asingned, auowen. Obsolete: adouted, alosed, aseled, askape, aspien, astored, auaunt. Bal, best (*beast*), bochours (*butchers*). Obs.: bourde. Carien, cache, catel, cauys (*caves*), sese (*cease*), sertaine, sertefied, chalis, chaunce (*chance*), changede, chase, chaste, chere, chef (*chief*), chois, syte (*city*), claimen, clergie, closeþ, cost (*coast*), colour, comaundede, comine (*common*), conquerour, conscience, contre (*country*), cours, cortais (*courteous*), couaite, couaitous, cocodrillus (*crocodiles*), corone (*crown*), crye, costom. Obs.. sertus (*certes*), chariteuus, cheue, couaitise. Dainte, damned, degre, deliten, desire, dispit, destene, distroie, diuisede, discorden, dismembre, dite (*ditty*), diuerse, doctour, dolfinus, doute, dosain (*dozen*), dragonus, duk, dure. Obs.: defoule, dul (*dool*). Egre, ese, emperour, endite, endure, enemis, enforceþ, engendreþ, enquere, ensample, enuie (*envy*), erren, errours, echue (*eschew*), exkused. Obs.: enchesoun, englaymed, enoine (*anoint*). Fablus, face, failede, falce, faute (*fault*), fauure (*favour*), figure, fin (*fine*), flourus (*flowers*), folie, fol (*fool*), fourme (*form*), frut. Obs.: fenked, folliche; *and cf.* faiþ. Gay, gentil, gin (*a trap*), glose, glotenye, glotounius, grace, graciouce, graunt, *sb.*, graunte, *vb.*, grauntinge, gref (*grief*), greue (*grieve*), gruche, gile, gise. Obs.: gien, giour, gouernance. Hardy, haste, hastiliche, haunte, eritage, ypotamus, onurable, ost, huge. Idolus, inpossible, innocent, yle (*isle*). Iangle, iargoun, ioie (*with* ioiful, ioiles), iuge, *sb.*, iuggen, iuggement. Obs.: iaudewin. Langage, large, lecherie, lechour, lechourus, lettres. Obs.: los. Mentaine (*maintain*), manere, marbyl *or* marbre, meruailous, maistrus, maistrie (*mastery*), matere, maugre, megre, men (*mean*), mesure (*measure*), medle, medisine, membrys, mercy, message, minstralus, mischef, meven (*move*). Obs.: maumentrie. Nacion, nisete (*nicety*), noble, noblete, norscheþ. Obs.: noy, nien (*or* nye). Oxian (*ocean*), ordre. (*Add* offren, offringus, *from a Latin root.*) Pacen, paine, *sb.*, painede, paradis, part, *sb.*, parte, *vb.*, passe, pay, *sb.*, paieþ, pes (*peace*), perles (*peerless*), penance, peple, peril, perichen, philozofrus, pilegrimus, piler, pinchen (?), place, plain, plaunte, plente, point, pore, pouerte, poudur, power, praisen, praien, praiere, pres, praie (*prey*), prince, prented, presoun, preuey, procre (*procure*), profre, profit, profiteþ, proud (?), prove,

ALEXANDER. c

pulle (?), punched, purchas, purpre. *Obs.:* prest, prestly, prow, pris *or* prys. (*Add* preche, *of Latin origin.*) Quainte. *Obs.:* quaintise. Resoun, regne, remewid, renoun, reproue, reward, riche, richesse, rommede (*roamed*), robbed, romauncus, rout, reule. Sacrifice, saue, sauiour, sauur, *sb.*, sauouren, scole, sience, scorpionus, sel (*seal*), sesoun, seruantis, serue, simple, sengle, soile, solas, solempne, soueraine, space, spirit, spouce, stable, stat, stomak, storie, straiten, stidie (*study*), sodainly, sofisen, suffre (*soffre*), somme (*sum*), sur (*sure*), sustaine (sostaine). *Obs.:* swaginge. Taried, tariginge, tast, tastinge, tempren, tempest, templus, temted, tende, tendere, tentus, titelid, torche, turment, touche, touchinge, tribit (*tribute*), trye, turnen. *Obs.:* tache, tende. Vse (*use*), *sb. and vb. Obs.:* vndigne. Varied, verrai, vertue, vois. Werre (*war*), werrede (*warred*), wasten.

An inspection of these words may teach us some useful lessons. It is remarkable to what extent, in some cases, the language from which an English word is derived is indicated merely by its initial letter. Imperfect as is this list, and unsafe as it may be to generalise from so short a list of words as those which are included in the present glossary, I yet believe that the proportion of French to Anglo-Saxon words in Middle English is, approximately, capable of being ascertained from the above list. Thus the different words in the Glossarial Index beginning with the letter A are, roughly speaking, about 72; whilst the French words in the above list beginning with the same letter are 20. This gives a percentage of 27, neglecting fractions. Following out a similar calculation for the other letters, we obtain, merely as a rough guide, the following results.

Percentage of French words for each letter.

A	...	27	G	...	25	M	...	18	S	...	15
B	...	3	H	...	8	N	...	16	T	...	20
C	...	46[1]	I	...	28	O	...	12	U	...	7
D	...	29	J	...	100	P	...	80	V	...	100
E	...	43	K	...	0	Q	...	12	W	...	2
F	...	16	L	...	6	R	...	22			

Without insisting much on the accuracy of these figures, we may still see clearly that the letters under which we may most expect to

---

[1] Uncertain to some extent, because some words are written with initial *s*. Similarly, the percentage of the S-words is not quite clear.

find French words in fourteenth-century English are, J, V, P, C, and E; after which, probably, come D, I, A, and G. On the other hand, we may least expect to find French words under K, W, B, L, U, and H; after which, probably, come Q, O, F, N, and M. If we further take into account initial *combinations*, we may observe that SCH, SW, TH, WR, and WH are surely indicative of English origin, whilst CH is indicative of a French one.

I have little doubt that, in modern English, the percentage of French and Latin words under each letter has, in some cases, undergone a considerable change. To take an example, this is particularly the case with the letter A. Whilst the number of *English* words beginning with A remains much the same as it was, we have received a large number of additions to the *French* and *Latin* ones; the result being that the latter are now in a considerable majority. This change is due, in particular, to the very great influence of the Latin *ad* as a prefix. An investigation of this particular question is not without a certain interest, and it is of some use to the young to be told that K, W, TH, and SH, regarded as beginning a word, are essentially English, whilst J, V, P, and CH are essentially un-English. And the remark, as regards K, W, and TH, is almost equally true, in whatever part of the words those letters[1] be found. It is a good plan, with beginners, to learn the alphabet; which is not quite so easy a matter as it is commonly said to be.

[1] TH is really a *letter*, not a digraph. Add, that GH is a purely English combination, introduced into the word *delight* by a sheer blunder.

ERRATA AND ADDENDA.

P. viii. l. 14. *For* Li veillant *read* Li veillart.
P. 10, l. 240. *Dele* stop at end of line.
P. 17, l. 439. The sense of *lome* is not quite certain here. See the note and Glossary.
P. 27, l. 708. Insert a comma after *godus*.
P. 28, l. 738. 'y of reed' is the reading of the MS., as printed. Read *y-offred;* see note to the line.
P. 29, l. 774. After *schulle* insert [*wreche*]; see note to the line.
P. 30, l. 805. Insert two commas, and read:—& al is, burnus, aboute, &c.
P. 31, l. 834. The word *ne* is so in the MS.; it should rather be *no;* see note to the line.
P. 34, l. 920. The 'tene*n*' of the MS. should rather be 'tene'; see note to the line.
P. 35, l. 930. *For* oþur-wise *read* oþur wise; two words.
P. 37, l. 979. Insert a comma before *namkouþe*.
P. 39, l. 1042. The reading *helpe* of the MS. is certainly an error for ȝ*elpe;* see note to the line.

Alexander.

How alixandre partyd þennys. [Fol. 209]

Whan þis weith at his wil · weduring' hadde,
Ful raþe rommede he · rydinge þedirre.
To oridrace wiþ his ost · alixandre wendus,   *Alexander comes to the Oxydracæ.*
þere wilde contre was wist' · & wondurful peple,   4
þat weren proued ful proude · & prys of' hem helde.
Of' bodi wente þei bar · wiþ-oute any wede,   *This people go naked,*
& hadde graue on þe ground · many grete cauys,
þere here wonnynge was · wyntyrus & somerus.   8
No syte nor no sur stede · soþli þei ne hadde,
But' holus holwe in þe ground · to hiden hem inne.
þe proude genosophistiens · were þe gomus called ;   *and live in caves. They are called the Gymnosophists.*
Now is þat name to mene · þe nakid wise.   12
Wan þe kiddeste of' þe cauus · þat' was king' holde
Hurde tiþinge telle · & toknynge wiste,
þat alixandre wiþ his ost' · atlede þidire,
To be holden of' hem · hure hieȝest' prynce,   16

Historia Alexandri magni regis macedonie de preliis;
ed. 1490 ; leaf *g* iii. back.

Quomodo alexander inuenit Exidraces qui dicuntur Gimnosophiste.

[E]T inde amoto exercitu venit exidraces. Exidraces siquidem homines sunt in quorum mentibus nulla superbia dominatur ; vocantur itaque gimnosophiste. Non pugnant nec altricantur, et nudi ambulant ; ciuitates non habent, sed in tuguriis et in speluncis montium commorantur. Cumque audisset rex huius gentis aduentum alexandri misit sibi epistolam ita continentem.

Their king sends a letter to Alexander,	þanne weies ofᵗ worschipe • wittie & quainte	
	Wiþ his lettres he letᵗ • to þe lud sende.	
	þanne southte þei sone • þe forsaide prynce,	
	& to þe schamlese schalk • schewden hur lettres;	20
which he reads.	þanne raþe letᵗ þe rink • reden þe sonde,	
	þatᵗ newe tiþinge [tid] • itᵗ tolde in þis wise.	
"The Gymnosophists greet Alexander.	"þe gentil genosophistiens • þatᵗ goode were of witte,	
	To þe emperour alixandre • here answerus wreten,	24
	þatᵗ is worschipe ofᵗ word • worþi to haue,	
	& is conquerour kid • in contres manie.—	
	Vs is sertefied, segᵗ • as we soþ heren,	
If you come to fight with us, you will get nothing by it.	þat þou hastᵗ mentᵗ wiþ þi men • amongus vs fare.	28
	But ʒifᵗ þou, kingᵗ, to us come • wiþ caire to fiʒhte,	
	Ofᵗ us getist þou no good • gome, we þe warne.	
	For whatᵗ richesse, rink • vs miʒhtᵗ þou bi-reue	
	Whan no wordliche wele • is wiþ us founde?	32
	We ben sengle ofᵗ us silfᵗ • & semen ful bare,	
	Nouht welde we now • butᵗ naked we wende;	
We have nothing to lose.	& þat we happili her • hauen ofᵗ kynde	
	May no man butᵗ god • maken us tine.	36
	þei þou fonde wiþ þi folk • to fiʒhte wiþ us alle,	
	We schulle us kepe on-cauʒt • oure cauus wiþ-inne;	
	Neuere werrede we • wiþ wiʒth up-on erþe,	
We shall hide in our caves."	For we ben hid in oure holis • or we harm lacche."	40
	þus saide soþli þe sonde • þatᵗ þei sente hadde;	
	& al so cofᵗ as þe kingᵗ • kende þe sawe,	
Alexander lets them know that he will come in peace.	Newe lettres he letᵗ • þe ludus bi-take,	
	& wiþ his sawus ofᵗ soþ • he sikurede hem alle,	44
	þatᵗ he wolde fare wiþ his folk • in a faire wise

"[C]Orruptibiles gimnosophiste homini Alexandro scribimus. Audiuimus quod super nos venis pugnaturus, de quo miramur non modicum, quia nihil a nobis poteris extorquere. Nam cum nihil habemus vnde corpora nostra sustentantur, quid a nobis eripies? Quod si nobiscum pugnare volueris, simplicitatem nostram nullatenus dimittemus."

Qualiter alexander scripsit gimnosophiste.

[P]Erlecta igitur, alexander epistolam misit illis dicendo quod ad

To bi-holden here hom · & non harm wirke.
So haþ þe kingˑ to hem sente · & siþen wiþ his peple
Kairus cofli til hem · to kenne ofˑ hure fare.   48
Butˑ whan þei sien þe segˑ · wiþ so manie ryde,   *But they are afraid,*
þei were a-grisen ofˑ his grym · & wende gref þolie.   *and hide themselves.*
Faste heiede þei to holis · & hidden hem[1] þere,   [1 MS. hiddem, *an error for* hidden hem]
& in þe cauus hem kepte · fro þe kingˑ sterne.   52
þanne weren from hem wentˑ · wifis & children,   *Their wives and children remain visible.*
Wiþ oþur bestus aboute · þatˑ hem bi ferde.
Aftur ferde alixandre · & askede hem sone,   *Alexander asks why they too do not hide in caves?*
By ludus ofˑ þe langage · how þei leue miȝhte?   56
And ȝifˑ þei ne hadde none holis · on þe holw erþe,
As hadde þe weies þatˑ were · here wordliche makus?
þanne þei caire wiþ þe kingˑ · hur cauus to schewe,
& kennen þe conquerour · hur costomus alle,   60
& saide "segˑ, to us silfˑ · sofisen þis cauus,   *They say that they dwell in the caves too.*
Ofˑ oþur hous þan her arne · haue we no nede."
Whan alle þei til alixandre · hadde answere i-ȝoulde,
þe king cortais i-kid · cofliche saide,   64
"For i haue founde ȝou folk · faiþful of speche   *Alexander promises to grant them any boon whatever.*
Me to lere ofˑ ȝour lifˑ · with-oute les tale,
Ȝernes now ofˑ my ȝiftˑ · þatˑ ȝou leue were,
& whatˑ itˑ be þatˑ ȝe bidde · ȝour bonus i graunte."   68
þanne saide þei, "wordlich weiȝ · we wische of þi[2] ȝifte   [2 MS. 'þel'] *They ask for everlasting life.*
Ai-lastinge lif · to lacchen up-on erþe;
þatˑ us derye no deþ · desire we nouþe,
For oþur wordliche won · atˑ wille we haue."   72
"Nai, sertus," saide þe noble · "þat may notˑ be graunted   *He replies that he himself is but mortal.*
Ofˑ me, þatˑ miȝhteles am · my silfˑ so to kepe.

---

eos cum pace alacriter venit et ingressus est ad eos. Alexander
autem intuens illos nudos ambulare et habitare in abditis tuguriis et
speluncis, filios vero et vxores separatos cum animalibus ambulantes,
interrogauit eos dicens; "Non sunt sepulcra vobis?" At illi ostenderunt
tuguria et speluncas in quibus habitabant, et dixerunt:—"Hic
per dies singulos requiescimus." Deinde dixit Alexander, "Quid
vultis petere, dabo vobis." Illi autem dixerunt, "Da nobis immortalitem,
quia nihil aliud peroptamus." Quibus alexander Respondit,

I am sikur of⟨t⟩ my silf⟨t⟩ · to suffre min ende ;
I ne haue no lordschipe of⟨t⟩ lif · to lengþe my daies." 76

They ask, "why then do you want to conquer the world?"

"Seg⟨t⟩," saide þei again · "syn þou so knowist⟨t⟩,
þat⟨t⟩ þe is demed þe deþ · to dure nouht⟨t⟩ longe,
Whi farest⟨t⟩ þou so fihtinge · folk to distroie,
& for to winne þe word · wendest⟨t⟩ so romme ? 80
How miȝht⟨t⟩ þou kepe þe of⟨t⟩ sckaþe · with skile & with troupe
Aȝeins ryht⟨t⟩ to bi-reue · rengnus of⟨t⟩ kinguus ?"
þanne agayn saide þe gome · wiþ a good chere,

He says he is king by the grace of God,

"þorou þe grace of god · i gete þat⟨t⟩ .i. haue. 84
þei han demed me, or deþ · þorou dintus of⟨t⟩ miȝhte,

[¹ MS. 'saide']

Of⟨t⟩ erþe to be emperour · in euerych a side.¹
Sin i haue grace of⟨t⟩ þat⟨t⟩ grauntt⟨t⟩ · grimmest⟨t⟩ to worþe,
I wrouthe wrecheli now · & wraþede drihten, 88

and must fulfil his destiny.

Ȝif⟨t⟩ i for dul of⟨t⟩ any deþ · my destene fledde,
þat⟨t⟩ is markid to me · & to no mo kinguus.
Men seþ wel þat⟨t⟩ þe see · seseþ & stinteþ,

[Fol. 209, back]

But⟨t⟩ whan þe wind on þe watur · þe wawus arereþ. 92
So wolde .i. reste me raþe · & ride ferþe,
Neuere to gete more good · no no gome derie,
Bute as þe heie heuene goodus · wiþ herteli þouhtus
So a-wecchen my wit⟨t⟩ · & my wil chaungen, 96

He cannot rest still anywhere.

þat⟨t⟩ .i. mai stinte no stounde · stille in o place,
þat⟨t⟩ i ne am temted ful tid · to turne me þennus.

[² MS. 'worschen']

& sin we wetin hur wil · to worchen² on erþe,
We mowe be soþliche isaid · hur seruauntus hende. 100

Were all men wise alike,

Ȝif⟨t⟩ god sente euery gome · þat⟨t⟩ goþ up-on molde
Wordliche wisdam · & wittus iliche,
Betur miȝhte no burn · be þan an oþur ;

"Mortalis cum sim, immortalitatem nequeo exhibere." At [*ed.* Ait] illi dixerunt, "Miser, si mortalis es, quare huc et illuc discurris tot et tanta facinora committendo ? Hec omnia nisi a summa prudentia gubernantur"—Alexander itaque respondit eis et dixit, "Nescitis quod mare nullatenus conturbatur, nisi cum a ventis validissimis **commouetur**. Uellem siquidem in pace consistere, sed habeo in me

A-pere miȝhte þe pore · to parte wiþ þe riche.   104
þanne ferde þe worlde as a feld · þat ful were ofˢ bestes, *all would be equal, like beasts.*
Whan eueri lud liche wel · lyuede up-on erþe.
For þatˢ enchesoun god ches · oþur chefˢ kinguus, *But some must be kings,*
þatˢ scholde maistrus be maad · ouur mene peple; 108 *and Alexander their chief.*
And me is markid to be · mostˢ ofˢ alle oþure,
For-þi y chase to cheue · as chaunce is me demed."—
Whan þis sawe was said · þe semliche prynce
Fro þe fore-saide folk · fondes to ride   112
þanne he farus to a feld · ful fair & ful large,
þatˢ stod on an hie stede · a-stored wiþ frutus. *Alexander sees some trees,*
þere sai he semliche tres · wiþ þe sonne woxe, *which bear fruit while the sun*
þatˢ frutˢ baren hem a-boue · on bowus ful þikke. 116 *shines,*
& al so sone as þe sonne · sesede to schine,
þatˢ don[1] was þe day · fordon ofˢ þe cloudus, [1 MS. 'þat siȝt don']
þe tres seseden ofˢ siȝhtˢ · & sonken to gronde,
þatˢ frekus miȝhtˢ no friþ · no no frutˢ kenne.   120
As raþe as þe sonne ros · & reed gan schine,
þatˢ his lem on þe loftˢ · liȝhtˢ ȝafˢ aboute, *but disappear when it is dark.*

---

spiritum, qui meo sensui tam fortiter dominatur, quod nullo modo hoc facere me permittit." Et hec dicens dimisit eos illesos.

[*A portion of the story is here omitted in the English poem; it relates to the finding of the pillars of Hercules and a nation of Amazons; to elephants in the woods of India; to a nation of bearded women; and a nation of men and women walking about unclothed. Then comes a description of intolerable cold and severe snowstorms, so terrible that five hundred soldiers died; there was also a great fall of rain, after which it seemed as if burning torches fell from heaven. Alexander offers sacrifices, and the storms cease. The story then goes on with the arrival of Alexander at the river Ganges; see l. 137 of our English version. The substance of ll. 111—136 occurs further on in the Latin, being evidently taken from the chapter I here transcribe, which begins on leaf h 6, back.*]

Quomodo alexander inuenit arbores que nascebantur cum sole.

[I]Nde amoto exercitu deuenit ad alium campum in quo arbores consistebant mire magnitudinis, que cum sole oriebantur et cum sole occidebant. A prima siquidem hora diei egrediebantur de sub terra et vsque ad horam sextam cressebant (*sic*) altissime. A sexta vero hora vsque ad occasum solis intantum descendebant, vt nullatenus super

þe tres spradden hure spraies · & spronngen on hiȝþe,
& grete grouuede frut⁺ · on þe grene braunchus.   124

He sends for some of the fruit.
[¹ MS. 'siee']
þan comaundede þe king⁺ · cofli to feche
Of⁺ þat⁺ freliche frut⁺ · þat⁺ þe frekus sie.¹

[² A word omitted; see l. 135.]
þanne [buskede]² a bold knihť · & to a bow stirte,
þe sote-sauerede frut⁺ · sone to pulle.   128

[³ MS. 'as'; see l. 117.]
The man who attempts to pluck it is slain.
But⁺ al³ so raþe as þe rink · gan þe ris touche,
Doun fel he wiþ dul · ded in þe place ;
& siþen sent⁺ was a vois · sone fro heuene,
þat⁺ non trinde þe tres · last⁺ þei taried were !   132

In each tree sat a bird,
For eueri grene growe tre · þat⁺ on þe ground spronge
Hadde bremliche a brid · þe braunchus alofte,
þat⁺ whan þer buskede a burn · a bow for to touche,

that spat sparks of deadly fire.
þei spatten sparclus of⁺ fir · & spilden him raþe.   136

How alixandre remewid to a flod þat is called phison.

[*A picture*. I.]

Alexander comes to the Pison,
AS sone þe king⁺ sai · þat⁺ it⁺ so ferde,
He dide him forþ to flod · þat phison is called,
þat⁺ writen is in holi wriht⁺ · & wrouht⁺ so to name.

a river of Paradise, also called the Ganges.
From perlese paradis · passeþ þe stronde ;   140
In cost⁺ þere þe king⁺ was · men callede hit⁺ gena,
As was þe langage of⁺ þe lond · wiþ ludus of⁺ inde.

---

terram viderentur. Et quottidie fructus amenissimos conducebant.
Has cum vidisset, Alexander precepit cuidam militi vt sibi de ipsis
frondibus portaret. Ille vero, dum domini sui mandatum vellet im-
plere, mox percussit eum spiritus malignus, et, presentibus omnibus,
expirauit. Et audierunt vocem in aere dicentem, "Quicunque istis
arboribus propinquus accesserit, morte velocissima morietur." Erant
autem in ipso campo aues mitissime super volantes, et cum aliquis
tangere vellet eas, continuo exibat ex eis ignis et eum crudeliter
incendebat.

[*After this, we again turn back to leaf g 5, back.*]

**Quomodo alexander venit ad fluuium bragmanorum, vbi habita-
bant yppotami, cocodrili, et serpentes.**

[D]Einde amoto exercitu venit ad fluuium bragmanorum magnum,

þere made þe mascedonius kingᵗ · his men for to stinte,
And bi þe banke ofᵗ þe strem · he biggede his tentus.
þanne þe mascedonius men · in þe men tyme   145
Bi-ȝonde phisonus flod · saien folk rome.   *He sees some men beyond the river,*
For-þi bad þe bolde kingᵗ · þatᵗ burnus of inde
Scholde talken hem til · & tidliche enquere   148
þe name ofᵗ hure nacion · nedli to knowe;
For miche wilnede þe weiȝhtᵗ · to witen ofᵗ here fare.
Ride miȝhte nouhtᵗ þe rink · ouur þe romme stronde   *but cannot reach them for the serpents there.*
For þe wormus þatᵗ were · bi þe watir founde.   152
For, outᵗ-taken .viij. wokus · ofᵗ al þe twelf monþe—
þatᵗ is soþli to saie · þe sesoun ofᵗ iuli,   *Except in July and August,*
And heruestᵗ þatᵗ hastly · aftyr him folweþ—
Dredful dragonus · drawen hem þiddire,   156   *there are dragons,*
Addrus & ypotamus · & oþure ille wormus,   *hippopotamuses,*
& careful cocodrillus · þatᵗ þe kingᵗ lette.   *and crocodiles there.*
For skaþe ofᵗ þe scorpionus · askape þei ne miȝhte;
So riue romede þei · þe riuer bi-side.   160
As prestᵗ as þe pris kingᵗ · sai his pres stinte,
þatᵗ he fer wiþ his folk[1] · fare ne miȝhte,   [¹ MS. 'flok']
For þe bestus ofᵗ bale · þatᵗ bi þe watur ferde,
& harm ofᵗ þe hound-fich · þatᵗ houede þer-inne,   164
Of' þe seggus þatᵗ he sai · bi-ȝonde þe side stronde   *Alexander calls to one of the strangers to come over in a boat.*
Ho dide calle ffor to come · to carpen him tille.
Whan þei hurden [h]is houp · hastiliche aftur
A lud to a litil bootᵗ · lepus in haste,   168
And raþe to þe riche kingᵗ · romwus alone,   [Fol. 210]
And aftur of alixandre · askeþ his wille.

---

vocatum gagei (*sic*); et castra metata sunt ibi. Et respicientes vltra flumen viderunt tres homines, quos iussit alexander indica lingua inquiri qui essent. At illi dixerunt, "Bragmani sumus." Desiderabat autem alexander cum eis loqui, sed ipsam latitudinem fluminis nemo poterat preterire; eo quod erant ibi yppotami multi et scorpiones agrestes et cocodrilli, qui per ipsum fluuium omni tempore discurrebant, excepto mense iulii et augusti. Cumque vidisset alexander quod nullo modo poterat ipsum fluuium transire, tristabatur valde. Statimque iussit vt nauiculam de viminibus fabricarent, et vestirent

ALEXANDER'S FIRST LETTER.

	A wel-langaged lud · let' þe king' sone
	Aspien ful spedliche · bi speche of' þe lande, 172
He asks who they are.	In what' kyþ were þei kid · & what' hit' called were,
	& ho were lord of hur land · & ledere of' alle.
They say they are Brahmans, and their king is Dindimus.	"We were in bragmanie bred" · saide þe burn þanne,
	"& dindim*us* þe dere king' · our demere is holde."
	"Sert*us*," saide alixandre · "þi sawe me quem*us*, 177
	Me haþ longe to ȝour land · liked to wende ;
	Wiþ ȝou to carpe in þis kiþ · couaitede y ȝorne ;
	For miche lud*us* of' ȝour lif' · listned ic*h* haue." 180
Alexander gives the stranger a letter, for Dindimus.	þanne let þe lordliche king' · lettres endite,
	& þere-on sett*us* his sel · & siþen hem tak*us*
	To þe burn on his bot' · & bad him in haste
	To þe king' of' hur kiþ · carien his sonde. 184
	þanne whitli þe weiht' · ou*ur* þe wat*ur* ster*us*,
	And þe lettr*us* to his lord · led*us* ful sone.
	As sone as his king' say · þat' sonde him yprofred,
	He hit' lacchus of' þe lud · & lok*us* þer-inne ; 188
Contents of the letter.	& ȝif' ȝe lud*us* haue list' · þe lettr*us* to knowe,
	Tendeþ how þis tale · is titeled þer-inne.
"Alexander,	"þe kidde king' alixandre · þat couþ is in erþe,
	þat' name haþ of' noblete · & neuere ma*n* dradde, 192
son of Ammon,	þat' grete god amon · in graciouce tim*us*
	Bi-gat' on olimpias · þe on*ur*able quene,
greets king Dindimus.	Dindim*us* þe dere king' · doþ for to grete,
	þat lord of bragman*us* lond · & ledere is holde, 196
	& in þis same wise saiþ · & sendeþ him gon,
	& til alle þat' arn · aft*ur* him þare.—
We have often heard of you.	We han, lud*us*, of' ȝour lif' · listned ful ofte, 199
You never plough,	þat' michil ben ȝour maner*us* · fra*m* oþur men varied.
[¹ MS. cren]	For ȝe non erþe ne eren[1] · þat' erne ȝou miȝhte
[² MS. 'flok']	Fode for to fare wiþ · as oþ*ur* folk[2] vsen.

---

eam de coriis animalium vt per ipsum fluuium transirent. Factum
est, et intrauit in eam vnus miles, cui dedit alexander literas, vt portaret eas didimo regi Bragmanorum, continentes ita :—

   [R]Ex regum et dominus dominantium Alexander filius dei

On se saile ȝe nouht' · in sesoun of¹ ȝere,
For to fihche on þe fom · or finde any praie.   204   nor fish.
But¹ litil leue we þat¹ · lud, i þe warne,
For-þi bi-seche y þe, seg¹ · ȝif¹ it soþ were,   Is this true?
Send me typinge¹ tid · & tel me þe soþe,   207   [¹ MS. 'tyinge'; see l. 240.]
þat¹ y may witen of¹ ȝour werk · & of¹ ȝour wonus alle.
For ȝif¹ men saiþ bi ȝow soþ · þe sawe þat¹ y hirde,   If so, I never heard of a more wonderful people.
Of¹ more meruailouse men · miȝhte i nouht' kenne.
Ȝif¹ y wisdam or wit¹ · in ȝour werk finde,
þat¹ god aloweþ ȝour lif¹ · & likeþ ȝour dedes,   212
Y schal ȝour costomus, king¹ · couaite to holde,
& fonde for bi² miȝht' · ȝour fare to sinke.³   [² Sic; 'mi'?] [³ Sic; 'sewe'?]
For fram þe ȝouþe of¹ my ȝer · ȝerned ich haue
Of¹ wide werkus to wite · & wisdam lere ;   216
We weren tauht' in oure time · & tendide lorus,   We were taught that no people are so holy that they can blame us.
Of¹ oure doctourus dere · demed for wise,
þat¹ non haþel vndur heuene · so holi is founde,
þat¹ mihte a-legge any lak · our lif¹ to reproue.   220
But¹ for y, ludus, of¹ ȝoure lif¹ · swich a los hurde,
þat¹ we discorden of¹ dede · in many done þinguus,   But you differ from us greatly.
And þat¹ ȝour doctours dere · don ȝou to knowe
þe best¹ lorus of¹ lif¹ · & lawus of¹ wise,   224
And we ȝou praien, sire prince · prestly me sende   Tell me your customs.
Alle þe lorus of ȝour lif¹ · in lettres a-seled ;
And y bi-hote ȝou her · vnharmed to leue.
For more may hit', in cas · ȝou menske þan greue ;   228
Whan may hit' greuen a man · þat¹ mich good knowiþ   It cannot harm

---

Amonis et regine Olimpie Didimo regi Bragmanorum gaudium.
Postquam ad tantam etatem peruenimus quod inter bonum et malum
potuimus discernere qualitercunque, desiderauimus repellere ignoran-
tiam et replere sapientia mentem nostram ; quia, vt nostrorum philo-
zophorum doctrina declarat, 'Eloquentia sine sapientia nocere valet
potius quam prodesse.'   Hinc est quod ad aures nostras relatione
plurium peruenit quod mores vestri a ceterorum nostrorum moribus
sunt diuisi ita, quod nec in terra nec in mari aliquod auxilium re-
quiratis ; Aliam doctrinam quam a nostris doctoribus didicimus ob-
seruantes. Quapropter attentius deprecamur quodque uniuersam doctrinam vestram et sapientiam nobis in vestris literis intimetis. Poteri-

any one to impart knowledge.	To carpe of¹ his konninge · & kenne hit¹ til oþure¶
	For þe wers is no weih · wis ȝif¹ he seme,
	þouȝ he finde oþur folk · folewen his dedus. 232
Take the case of a torch; its light is not lessened, though it lights others."	Of¹ a torche þat¹ is tend · tak an en-sample ;
	þat¹ þouȝ ludus of þe lem · lihtede an hundred,
	Hit¹ scholde nouht¹ lesen his liht¹ · no þe latur brenne,
[¹ MS. 'waxs']	While þe weke & þe waxe¹ · vn-wasteþ lasteþ. 236
[² MS. 'fiok']	& so it¹ farus bi folk² · þat¹ fain is to teche ;
	Hit¹ wasteþ no wisdam · weihes to lere.
	For-þi busiliche, burn · we bidde þe nouþe
	Wiþ-oute tariginge of¹ time · tiþinge sende. 240
	Of¹ þat¹ we ȝernen of¹ ȝou · ful ȝare to kenne,
	To witen of¹ þe wisdam · þat ȝe wiþ faren."
Dindimus reads the letter,	Whan dereworþe dindimus · þe enditinge hurde
	Of¹ alixandre askinge · as he write hadde, 244
	Oþir lettrus he let¹ · of¹ hur lif¹ write,
and sends an answer.	& agyn to þe gome · goodliche he sente.
	As cof¹ as hit¹ come was · þere þe king¹ dwelde,
	In þis manere dide þe man · þe massage arede. 248

How king dindimus sente lettrus to king alixandre.

[*A picture*. II.]

[Fol. 210, back]	"Þe dere king dindimus · þe doctour of¹ wise,
	þat¹ lord of¹ bragmanus lond · alosed is þare,
"King Dindimus to Alexander, greeting.	To emperour alixandre · egrest¹ of¹ princis,
	þat¹ is grimmest¹ igrowe · and grettest¹ of¹ kingus, 252
	Sendeþ lettres of¹ lowe · & to þe lud writes
	Miche gretiþinge of¹ grace · & grauntinge of¹ ioie.—

---

mus quoque ex vestris manibus comprehendere bonitatem. Nec vestra sapientia in aliquo minuetur. Talis enim est solicitudo sapientie, qualis natura accense facule comprobatur ; a qua cum plures facule ignem recipiant, nihilominus ipsa candet que facit alios coruscare.

Responsiua regis Bragmanorum missa Alexandro.

[D]Idimus Bragmanorum didascolus alexandro — Salutem ; per tuarum tenorem cognouimus literarum, quod animus tuus cupit vera

Bi þi message, man · þat¹ þou to me sentest¹,
Whan we sihen þi sonde · wiþ þi sel prented,   256
We kenden þi couaitise · & þat¹ þou, king¹, wilnest¹   We have discerned your desire.
þe rihte-wisnesse wite · þat¹ to a weih longus.
In þat¹ alowe i þe, lud · þat þe lef¹ were
þe beste lawe to lere · & lor*us* of witte;   260
For riht¹ wisdam is worþ · al þe world riche.
For non emperour on erþe · þat¹ eu*e*re was founde,   No emperor can dispense with wisdom.
þat¹ wantede wisdam · his wihes to gye,
Mihte lordschipe lache · of¹ oþ*ur* low peple;   264
Bute þe loweste þat liuede · his lord mihte worþe,
And wiþ him fare as a fol · þat¹ failede his witt*us*.
Neþeles, sire noble king¹ · y þe now warne,   Yet, I warn you,
To oure painede peple · in-possible hit¹ semeþ,   268
þat¹ ȝe oure maner*us* mihte · mekliche endure,   you cannot endure our customs.
Or in þe lif¹ þat¹ we liue · laste any while.
For oure lif¹ & oure lawe · vnlich is to ȝoure,
And al luþ*ur* bi-leue · we loþen in herte.   272
Al þe dedes þat¹ ȝe don · discorden til oure;
For we ne grete noht¹ þe god*us* · þat¹ ȝe gode holden.
Of¹ þat¹ þou senteste, sire king¹ · to say þe tru[t]he   As to your request,
Of¹ al þe lore of¹ our lif¹ · wiþ-oute long¹ dwelle,   276
Haþel, for þin hendschipe · haue vs exkused,   pray excuse us.
For we ne konne þe nouht¹ kenne · our costom*us* alle.
þouȝh .i., lud, of¹ our lif¹ · lettr*us* þe sende,   279
Prince, hit¹ profiteþ nouht¹ · to preche of¹ oure ded*us*;   It profits not to tell you.
Ȝe ne haue no tome no time · to tende my saw*us*,
For ȝe so busiliche ben wiþ¹ · aboute þe werre.   [¹ *Sic;* 'wis'?]
But¹ say þou nouht¹, sire king¹ · for sake of¹ enuie,

---

scientia et sapientia perfecta informari, que omni regno meliores existunt, et nequeunt precio computari; de quo discretionem tuam non modicum commendamus. Imperator enim qui sapientiam ignorat non imperat subiectis, Sed subiecti suo dominantur imperio. Scripsisti siquidem vt vitam moresque nostros indicaremus tibi per literas seriatim; quod impossibile reputamus. Et si tibi de vita nostra aliquid scriberemus, nullatenus tamen mens tua enucleare posset saporem, eo quod mentem tuam cause bellice obtenebrarunt. Sed ne

CUSTOMS OF THE BRAHMANS.

<small>Yet think not I grudge telling you.</small> Þat' me were loþ of' our lif' · ludus to teche ; 284
For as michel as y may · in minde bi-þenke,
Bi þis a-selede sonde · soþliche i telle.
<small>We are poor Brahmans.</small> We, bredde breþurne in god · bragmanus pore,
Leden clanliche our lif' · & libben as simple. 288
<small>[¹ MS. 'wolde']</small> We ne wilne in þis world · to welde¹ no more,
<small>We live a simple life, in all poverty.</small> Bute as we simpleliche our lif' · sostaine mowe.
We ben to penance iput' · & pouerte drien ; 291
We holde hit nedful to nime · þat' nouht may be wastid
Hit' is no leue in oure lawe · þat we land erie
<small>We plough not.</small> Wiþ no scharpede schar · to schape þe forwes ;
<small>[² MS. 'fled'] We sow not.</small> Ne sette solow on þe feld² · ne sowe none erþe,
In ony place of' þe plow · to plokke wiþ oxen ; 296
Ne in no side of' þe se · to saile wiþ nettus,
<small>We fish not.</small> Of' þe finnede fihes · our fode to lacche.
<small>We hunt not.</small> For to hauke ne hunte · haue we no leue,
Ne foure-fotede best' ··ferke to kille ; 300
Ne to faren in þe feld · & fonde wiþ slyhþe
For to refe þe brod · of' briddus of' heuene.
& whan we faren to fed · we finde no faute, 303
We han so michel at' þe mel · þat we no more wilne.
Oþir goodis to gete · giue we no tente,
<small>We desire no dainties. [³ MS. 'vus']</small> Ne oþir dainteys dere · desire we none,
Þan oure modur of' mete · may vs³ forþ bringe,
Þat' we kennen for kinde · & callen þe erþe. 308
<small>The earth sustains us.</small> Sche vs norscheþ at' nede · & i-now sendeþ,
Wiþ-oute swet' oþur swink · swich as we hauen.
Hit' ne is no leue in our land · þat ludus þer-inne

credas quod inuidia moueamur, quantum poterimus tibi de moribus nostris duximus indicandum. nos siquidem bragmani simplicem et puram vitam deducimus ; peccata non committimus, nec vltra volumus habere quam ratio nature requirit. Omnia patimur et omnia sustinemus. Id apud nos dicimus optimum, quod superfluum non probatur. Terras nostras non aramus, et ipsis semina non immittimus. Boues currui non iungimus. Retia in mari ad comprehendendum pisces non ponimus. Uenationes aliquas quadrupedum aut auium non facimus. Nihil etiam ad manducandum querimus nisi quod terra sine labore hominum producit. His etiam cibis non implemur,

Scholde more of' hure mete · þan mesure take; 312 We never eat too much,
For-þi[1] sounde we be seie · & sike in no time, [1 MS. 'For-þei']
Bute helþe haue we hir · til we henne passe. and are always in health.
To godus pay is our peple · in bettur point founde,
Him to louen as hur lord · & like him to serue, 316
þan fale oþir folk ben · þat' fillen hure wombe,
& nimen more þan i-now · whan no ned were.
We maken no medisine · no no man prayen We make no medicine,
Wiþ ony haþelene help · to helyn oure bodius. 320 nor need any.
We han a sertaine somme · a-singned of' ȝerus,
Whan we schulle lese þis lif · & laste no more; We die at a fixed age.
For we mowe tellen our time · whan þe time fallus.
For litil lengure a lud · liueþ þan an oþir; 324
But' bi cominnge[2] of' kynde · as heuene king' demus, [2 MS. *obscure;* 'co—ge,' *with* 8 downstrokes between o and g.']
We schal doute þe deþ · whan þe day fallus;
Bi an ordre of' oure kinde · whan we holde waxen,
Whan mihte lakken our limus · & lesen our hete, 328 We grow old, and then die, and go to heaven.
We schulle for-leten oure lif' · & leue þat' þe soule
To him þat' schop vs to schap · schal fare to blisse.
For no cold þat' vs comeþ · in oure kinde age,
We ne faren to no fir · our fingrus to warme; 332 We use no fire.
Of' bodi hole we ben · & no bale fele.
Ay we founden to fle · flechliche lustus; We flee lusts.
We maken þorou mekenesse · alle manir þingus
þat' mihte vs soile wiþ sinne · sese in a while. 336
I rede þe,[3] riche emperour · ful raþe þat þou founde [3 MS. 'þat þe,' *where* þat *is superfluous.*]
To ouyr-comen enemis · þat' arn þe[4] wiþ-inne; [4 MS. 'ȝe']

---

quia illicita est nobis. Nihil apud nos ventres producit. Ideo absque morbo sumus. Et dum viuimus semper fruimur corporum sanitate. Nullam facimus nobis medicinam. Nullum etiam adiutorium querimus pro nostrorum corporum sanitate. Et vno termino mortis vita nostra concluditur, quia plus altero vnus non viuit, sed secundum ordinem natiuitatis cuiuslibet mortis terminus superuenit. Ad ignem pro afflictione frigoris non sedemus. Nullum estum corpora nostra sentiunt; semper nudis corporibus ambulamus; corporis desideria non facimus. Omnia per patientiam supportamus. Omnes inimicos nostros interiores occidimus, vt exteriores nullatenus timeamus. Leuius enim capitur ciuitas quando ab interioribus et exteri-

[¹ MS. 'þei']	For haddestᵗ þou fenked þe fon · þat in þi¹ flech dwellen,
[Fol. 211]	None mihte þe now · nye wiþ-oute. 340
Thou fightest against outward foes,	Butᵗ þou fihtestᵗ wiþ þi fon · þat faren þe biside,
	& hem þat in þi¹ bodi ben · ay berestᵗ wiþ þe.
	Butᵗ ifᵗ we ony enimis · wiþ-inne vs aspie, 343
we slay the foes within us.	We nolle sclepe in no sclowþe · til we hem sclain haue ;
	þer-for we al ouurcomen · þatᵗ arn vs wiþ-inne,
	We ne haue fere ofᵗ no fon · þatᵗ faren wiþ-oute,
[² MS. 'do']	Ne we agayn hem to² go · nol no gome procre,
	Ne ofᵗ no haþel vndur heuene · any help seche ; 348
We fear no one, and desire to conquer none.	We ne doute none douhtie · ne no dede sterne,
	Ne we no wilne no win · ofᵗ watur no ofᵗ londe.
	Wiþ trene bowus we ben · on þe body keuered,
We eat fruit and drink milk.	& vs findeþ þe frut · fode atᵗ oure nede. 352
	Ofᵗ mylk haue we miche whon · amongus our peple,
	þatᵗ we no wante no wite · ofᵗ wordliche fode.

How dindimus enditid to alixandre ofᵗ here leuy[n]gᵗ.

[*A picture.* III.]

We drink of the river 'Thabeus.'	WHan we ludus in þis land · liste to drinke,
	We turnen tid to flod · thabeus is called. 356
	þere-ofᵗ we taken a tastᵗ · whatᵗ time þatᵗ vs nedeþ,
	And herie þe heie god · with herte & with tounge.
	Whatᵗ so we worchen in þis worlde · or waken or slepe,
	Or in erþeliche ese · eten oþur drinke, 360
We do all for the sake of God.	For his sake þatᵗ itᵗ sente · soþli we worchin,
	To sustaine his seruantis · as him-silfᵗ likus.
	We hopen haue þe lifᵗ · þatᵗ come schal her-aftur,

---

oribus impugnatur. Tu autem, imperator, cum exterioribus pugnas, vt quidem nunc porcos demones nutrias et conserues. Securi semper viuimus ; in mari in terra, nullum adiutorium postulamus. Corpora nostra frondibus arborum, quarum fructibus vescimur, sunt operata. Aquam tebaliani fluminis semper bibimus et gustamus. Unum solum deum altissimum colimus, sibique assidue laudes predicamus. Uitam venturi seculi concupiscimus. Rem aliquam que vtilitati non

& derely wiþ-oute deþ · dure schal euere. 364
Tale tende we non · þat' turneþ to harme, *We never indulge in tale-bearing.*
But' hit' be preched for prow · & procred to goode.
We no spende no speche · but' whan we speke weele;
We ne sain but' soþ · & sesen by time. 368 *We always speak truth.*
We no recche of' no ricchesse · no renoun of' landus,
No catelus couaitise · comyþ at' oure herte; *We are not covetous.*
For þat is soþliche a sinne · þat' seggus haunteþ,
& to miche mischef' · many men bringeth. 372
Al we libben in loue · & loþen enuie, *We loathe envy.*
& hit paieþ our peple · in pouert' to libbe.
For we hit' rekenen for riche · & redileche finden,
þat' hit' foleweþ oure folk · til þei fare hennus. 376
Ay ar we in pes · and armus forsaken, *We forsake warfare.*
& to no wikkede werk · woned be we fare.
þer nis no lawe in oure land · ludus to chaste,
For we no dede no don · domus to þolie. 380
We holden hit' a vertu · at' hom in oure lande,
Among' þe men of' our march · mercy vnknowe; *We shew no mercy.*
For we ben meved to no man · mercy to gran[t]e.
We ne gilte noht god · no no gome here, 384 *We never do any sin for which we have to ask for mercy.*
Where-fore we mosten haue in minde · mercy to crye,
þat' god scholde of' oure gilt' · for-giuen vs þe sinne
Of' ony wikkede werk · þat' we wroute euyre.
Ne we for sake of' our sinne · no sacrifice maken 388 *We do not sacrifice to devils.* [¹ MS. 'galsule'; cf. l. 668.]
To oure galfule¹ god · wiþ gold nor wiþ siluer,
As ȝe dulfully don · to deuelus of' paine,

---

pertinet, nullatenus audire affectamus. Non multum loquimur, et cum ad loquelam prouocamur dicimus veritatem et ipsam continue predicamus. Diuitias non amamus. Inter nos nullus liuor nullaque inuidia dominatur. Nullus etiam inter nos altior vel fortior reperitur. Ex paupertate quam habemus diuites sumus, quam communiter omnes supportamus. Litem non facimus, nec arma corporalia occupamus. Pacem semper ex consuetudine retinemus. Iudicia non habemus, quia mala non facimus, vnde ad iudicium vocemur.

Una vestra lex est contraria nostre, quia misericordiam nullam facimus, eo quod nulla committimus quibus misericordiam consequi mereamur. Nullum laborem qui auaricie pertineat sustinemus,

	To make hem glad of 3oure gilt' · & glose 3ou here!	
We flee lusts.	Alle leccheries lust' · vs lopeth to founde,	392
	Or to bringe vs in brigge · for to breke spouce;	
	Or any mis-dede make · where-fore we miht aftur	
	Ben y-punched in paine · & parte [fram] blisse.	
We gainsay your guilt and your false gods.	& þus we gayn-saie 3oure gilt · & 3our godus false,	396
	As 3e wolde fare by 3oure fon · þat 3e fals knewe.	
	We ben rihtful of' red · & resoun alowen;	
[¹ MS. 'For-þei']	For-þi¹ ne se we no seg' · sodainly deie;	
	For we ne li3the noht' our lif' · wiþ no luthur dede,	400
	Where-fore we scholde with schame · be schorted of' daies.	
We dye no cloth.	We don deie no cloþ · of diuerse heuys,	
[² MS. 'worchipful']	No in no worschipful² wede · oure wiuus a-tiren,	403
	Where-fore a lud mihte like · to louen hem þe bettere,	
[³ MS. 'tolk']	Or þei fairere þan a-fore · [to] folk³ miht' seme;	
	So to hihten hem her · we holden hit' sinne,	
	To maken hem comelokur corn · þan hur kynde askyþ.	
Our wives never paint their faces,	Þere-fore þei haten to be hiht' · on hed or on face	408
	Wiþ ony wachinge of watur · or ony werk ellus,	
	Or fonde wiþ fals craft' · hure face to enoine,	
	For to bliken of' hur ble · þe bliþure of chere,	
nor try to look better than they are by nature.	Or hem schenure to schene · þan þei schape were	412
	Of him þat lente hem hur lif' · & hure limus made.	
	For þey þat' crauen by craft' · comelokur seme	
	þan þei ben kindeli coren · as heuene king' likus,	
	God scholde þat' him schop · schine by rihte	416
	For his children hem to chese · þat changede his schappus.	
[Fol. 211, back]	For be he burn oþur burde · þat hure bodi hihten	

---

membra nostra libidini non tradimus. Adulterium non committimus, nec aliquod vicium facimus vnde ad penitentiam retrahamur. De defectibus non querimus, quia quod rectum est omnes facimus et tractamus. Subitaneam mortem non facimus, quia per sordida facta aerem non sordidamus. Aer noster nullatenus est corruptus. Nullum colorem nostris vestimentis tradimus. Femine nostre non ornantur vt placeant, cum ipsis non causa libidinis sed causa procreande sobolis commiscemus. Ipse autem nullum ornamentum querunt nisi quod eis diuina prouidentia concessit. Et quis auderet diuinum opus mutare?

Oþir-wise þan it' was · in þis word schape,
þey gayn-sain hure sauiour · þat' hem so made, 420
& ben aschamed of' his schap · & schewen hem ellus.
þou douhty doutede king' · we don þe to knowe,
þat' oure bodies ne ben · in no baþ wahche. *We never use a bath.*
We han while we here ben · hete of' þe sonne, 424
& vs by-dewen aday · þe dewus of heuene.
We ben busy of' no swink · nor no burn maken *We never labour*
For to wirchen our wil · & wordliche serue.
Vs no likeþ of' no lud · lordschipe haue; 428
Non is sternere of' stat' · ne stouter þan oþir. *All are equal amongst us.*
Sin we ben breþeren of' brod · brouht' into þis worde,
Alle coruen of' a king · þat' kid is in blisse,
Whi scholde any schalk · þat god schop on erþe 432
Haue maistrie of' men · more þan an-oþir?
We ne han none hous bote holus · in þe holou cauus, *We have no houses but caves.*
Vndur hillus ful hie · to holden us inne; 435
þere comeþ no wawe of' þe wind · no watur of' þe rainus.
Hie boldus[1] to bulde · be we not' snelle; [1 MS. 'holdus'; see l. 848.]
To legge lym oþur ston · loþ is us alle;
Vs ne likeþ no lome · in oure land vse, *We use no tools.*
As oþir erþliche men · owen aboute. 440
We lin, whan us sclepe list' · lowe vndur erthe,
Al wiþ-oute any swink · of' ert[h]liche werkus;
Swich housinge we han · to holde out' þe wedures, *Our caves keep off the weather.*
& leden þerinne our lif' · þe lengþe of' our daies. 444
Whan god likeþ from lif' · lede vs to blisse,
We liggen doun in our den · þere we ded worþen.
þanne is vs g[r]ayþed no graue · in þe grounde doluen, *When we die,*

Si quis autem naturam mutare voluerit, criminale reputamus. Balnea non facimus vt corpora nostra sanemus. Solis ardore calemus et aeris rore perfundimur. Nullam cogitationem habemus nec hominibus nec animalibus dominabimur. Crudele dicimus hominem ad seruitium premere, quia diuina dispositio sic nos liberos liberauit et creauit. Lapides in calcem non resoluimus vt nobis domos et palacia fabricemus. Uascula de terra non facimus. In fossis sine solicitudine aliqua repausamus. Nos enim tales domos habemus in qui-

we lie where we lay.	But' þere we lin as we laie · whan we lif' hadde.	448
	Wiþ us schineþ euery schalk · in schippus for to saile,	
We do not go to sea.	For to winne on þe watur · wordliche fode.	
	For þei þat' sailen on þe see · as we soþ knowen,	
	In gret' peril ben iput' · & perichen ful ofte.	452
We do not cultivate learning.	We ben lered in oure land · lore of' no scole,	
	Ne to no sience i-set' · vs silue to wisse,	
	þat' mihte vs kenne in þis kiþ · to carpen as wise,	
	But' þat' comeþ us by kinde; · we konne noht ellus.	456
	We ne faren to no philozofrus · to fonden hure lorus;	
	For ay longeþ þat' lore · to lesinge & iangle.	
	Alle oure sawus ben simple · þat' we soþ tellen,	
We never lie.	& for to lie is us loþ · or luþurly wirche;	460
	But' swiche wordus of' wise · we wilnen to lere,	
	þere nis no iargoun no iangle · ne iuggeme[n]tis falce.	
	Vs ne schewiþ no schalk · schamfule tacchus,	
	Where-wiþ we mihte mis-do · or ony man gile.	464
We dislike play and mirth.	We ne louen in our land · no laik nor no mirthe;	
	But' whanne we meuen our mynde · mirþe to here,	
We only read romances.	We raiken to oure romauncus · & reden þe storrius,	
	þat' oure eldrene on erþe · or þis time wroute.	468
When the tale is a merry one,	& whan we tenden any tale · þat turneþ to bourde,	
	þat' were game for a gome · or good of to lauȝe,	
we are sad.	We sesen of' solas · & sorwen in herte;	471
	& maken mourninge of' mirthe · whan men scholde glade.	
	Of' oþur wondrus we witen · in þis word here,	
[¹ MS. 'lileþ']	þat' likeþ¹ us to loken on · on þe loft' heie;	
	We sen selkouþe þing · þat is ta sain, heuene,	

---

bus dum viuimus habitamus, et dum morimur in ipsis sepelimur. Ad negociandum maria non nauigamus. Artem huius loquendi non discimus, sed simplicitate qua fruimur que nos mentiri non sinit omnia enarramus. Philosophorum scolas non frequentamus, quorum doctrina discors est, nihilque certum aut stabile, sed super mendacia discurrunt. Ludos non amamus. Dum uero ludrica volumus exercere, nos nostra et nostrorum predecessorum facta perlegimus; et cum deberemus ridere, plangimus et turbamur. Alia vero videmus quibus corda nostra letantur. Uidemus siquidem celum stellis innumerabilibus choruscantem, solem rubicundum, cuius claritate totus mundus

þere as lem is of loft¹ · & lisse to gode ;   476
þe sonne set¹ in his cours · & þe seue sterres,   *We observe the sun and the seven stars,*
And alle þat segge*us* mowe sen · siþe*n* on þe skiu*us*,
þat¹ to hure schappere hem schewen · schining¹ rede,
& siþen liht¹ fro þe loft¹ · to þe land caste.   480
þe side se we mow sen · set¹ vp-on erþe,.   *the wide and purple sea,*
þat in kinde colour · a-cordeþ to purpre ;
But¹ whan þe watur wiþ þe wind · þe waw*us* vp casteþ,
& þouh hit¹ turne any time · to tempest¹ of¹ wind*us*,   484
Hit¹ ne a-wecheþ no wawe · nor no wat*ur* rereth,   *which has no waves.*
As hit¹ among*us* ȝou men · is many time founde
þat¹ stiue storm*us* of¹ þe wind · stiren vp þe waw*us*.
But¹ here, whan þe wind haþ · his hugeste blastus,   488
þe clere watur he bi-clipth · & closeþ hit¹ inne.
þer-inne soþli we sen · selcouþe kindus
Of¹ þe fletinge fihs · þat¹ in þe fom lepen.
þere maken dolfin*us* dine · & diuerce fihches,   492   *We see therein dolphins and other fish.*
þat¹ þere swimme*n* ful swiþe · & swange*n* aboute.
We han mirthe ful miche · in med*us* & feldus,
þere faire plac*us* & plain · han plente of¹ flourus,   *We can feed on the scent of flowers.*
þat¹ sote sauo*ur*on til us ; · & wiþ þe siht¹ clene   496
We ben as fulsom i-founde · as þouȝ we fed were.
Vs is likful and lef¹ · in land*us* to walke,
þere won walleþ of¹ watur · i*n* þe welle-springus.
Miche wilne we wende · in þe wod*us* thikke,   500   *We love the woods,*
For to rome vnd*ur* ris · þat¹ rif¹ is of¹ leu*us* ;
þere we mowe graspe*n* on þe grene · & gret¹ ioie here
Of brem briddene song¹ · [in] þe braunchus a-lofte.   *and the songs of birds.*
þis is oure costom of¹ kinde · þat¹ we kyþe*n* alle,   504
& deliten in no dede · þat¹ doþ men to sinne.
Sire emp*er*our alixandre · þis arn oure lawes,   *These are our customs.*

---

splendet et calet. Mare purpureum semper videmus ; Et quando tempestate moueter non dissipat vicinam terram, sicut accidit in partibus vestris. Illud vt sororem amplectimur et congirat (*sic*), et ibi varia genera piscium contemplamur. Delectamur etiam videre florigeros campos ex quibus in nostros nares suauissimus odor intrat. Delectamur etiam in optimis locis siluarum et fontium in quibus iocundissimas

	Boþe oure reule & our riht' · þat we þe rede holde.
	ʒif' þou our lif' wole alowe · & oure lawe vse, 508
[¹ MS. 'þei']	Hit' schal þe profite, prince · whan þi¹ pres faileþ.
[Fol. 212] [² Sic. Read 'of' (?)]	Hit' is noht' long' in² us, lud · þei hit' loþ seme,
	For y haue sent' þe my sonde · as þou þei-self' bade.
Be not angry.	But' be þou nouht', bolde king' · balful no tened, 512
	þat' þou miht' trystli trye · þe treweste lawe.
	For we schulle minnge þe, man · swiche maner lorus,
	þat' þou miht lihtliche, lud · þe beste lawe kenne.
	Whan þou hit' wisliche wost' · wilne hit' in herte, 516
Mend thy life.	& lowe þi lordschipe · & þi lif' mende.
	Asie & aufrik · & europ þe grete
	þou hast' lowed to þe, lud · in a litil while.
Thou preventest the sun from shining by thine armies.	þe lem of' þe sonne-liht · þou lettest' to schine, 520
	So brem bringest' þou þi men · alle in bryht' armus;
	& þe guldene ger · þat' þi gomus vsen
	Wiþ þe blasinge ble · blenden þe sonne.
	þou hast' robbed wiþ þi rout' · ij. riche strondus, 524
Thou hast robbed two streams of gold.	þere þe grauel of' þe ground · was of gold ore.
	þat' on was called erenus · & þat oþur large
	þe peple callede paccolus · þat þou pore madest';
	So fale folewen þe folk · to fonde þi heste, 528
Thine armies drink up the Nile.	þat with hure drinkinke drawht' · whan þei drie þirsten,
	ʒe maken stinte of' his strem · a stronde ful huge,
	þat nilus þe noble flod · namned is wide. 531
	So miche holdest' þou þe, man · of' miht' & of' strenke,
	þat' þou miht' ouur oxian · wiþ þin ost' saile.
	So wis wenst' þou þe be · þat þou by wit' mihtest'

---

auium audimus cantilenas. Istas siquidem naturas et consuetudines obtinemus, quas si tenere volueris, tibi vident asperum et amarum. Si autem eas obtinere nolueris et imitari, nobis aliam imponere non valebis, quia secundum tenorem tue epistole actus nostros et doctrinam tibi per presentem mittimus. Uolumus autem tibi de tua natura paululum enarrare, quia vita tua nobis dura esse videtur. Tu asyam Affricam et Europam paruo tempore te dicis concludere. Tu lumen solis facis deficere dum cursus sui terminos armatorum rabie postulas. Tu pactoli et herimi fluuios splendentes auro arentes et absque colore et pauperes reddidisti. Tu bibendo nilum fluuium minuisti; tu mon-

WICKEDNESS OF THE GREEK GODS.

þorou þi maistrie miche · maken to sclepe — *Thou makest Cerberus to sleep.*
Tricerberus þe helle-hound · þat holden is kene 536
Boþe wakrongᵗ & wikke · & wardain ofᵗ paine.
ȝe no fonde no fastᵗ · but fillen ȝoure wombis, — *Ye never fast.*
Eten euere whan ȝe list · & in ese libben.
Vn-kinde kiþe ȝe ȝou · to kille ȝour children, 540 *Ye sacrifice your children.*
To queme quedfulle godus · þat quenchen ȝour blisse ;
& to ȝoure souorain ofᵗ sinne · sacrifice maken
Wiþ þatᵗ vnblisful blod · þatᵗ þei bled hauen.
Miche maugre ȝe maken · amongᵗ many kingus, 544 *Ye make war ever.*
& gretᵗ werre in þis world · to waste þe peple.
Many men vp-on molde · ful mek & ful simple
þorou þe, prouede prince · ful proude ben woxe.
ȝe wene winne nohtᵗ i-now · on þis worde one, 548 *Ye cannot have enough.*
But ȝifᵗ ȝe heuene miht haue · & holden hitᵗ alse.
Michel gilte ȝe, gome · bi ȝour godus falce, — *Your gods used to work all evil.*
As þei were woned in þis word · to wirchen in hure liue.
For ensample, bi my sawe · soþ mow ȝe fonge 552
Of iubiter þe ioilese · iugged to paine.
He was alosed in his lif · lechourus ofᵗ kinde, — *Jupiter was lecherous.*
þatᵗ in his licamus lustᵗ · as a lie brente.
He hadde, while he here was · to hordom i-eged 556
Gret won in þis word · ofᵗ wommen aliue.
For-þi¹ ȝe holde him a god · þatᵗ in helle lengus, — [¹ MS. 'Forþei']
& þatᵗ sorwful sinne · for his sake vsen.
Y prove hitᵗ by proserpine · þatᵗ ȝe praisen alle, 560 *Proserpine was equally wicked.*
& holden godesse god · to gien ȝou here ;
Hure was lecherie lufᵗ · þe while hue liuede alse,

---

strasti vt horribile mare nauigaretur; tu tartareum custodem, id est canem cerberum supra posse precio confirmasti; tu in sacrificio tuo filios occidis tuos; tu inter homines humiles semper discordiam seminas. Suades hominibus vt nequaquam spacia terrarum sufficiant, sed celorum querere habitacula preparata. Per dies tuos multa committis vt illi faciunt, et fecerunt. Nam testimonium potest accipi a ioue deo tuo et proserpina dea tua quos colis. Iupiter enim multas adulteratus est feminas; Prosperina vero multos fecit sui adulterii perticipes (*sic*). Miserrime ergo colis deos tuos et aduersos et adulteros.

              & many lud by hure lay · hur lust to ful-fille.

[¹ MS. 'hure'] Many men vp-on molde · made hue¹ by slithe   564
              To haunte hure in hordom · hur hole lif-time.
Ye imitate her. Of' hure tenful tach · ȝe taken ensample,
              & ay wilnen hire wone · in werkus to fonde !

How he sparep not' alixandre, to telle him of' his gouernance.

[*A picture*. IV.]

Ye are all unjust. Alle ȝe vsen vnrith · and aftur þat wirchen ;   568
              Ȝe ben lupur of' ȝour lif' · & lawus ȝe chaunge.
              Of' more make ȝe auaunt' · þan ȝe mow forþen ;
Ye esteem flatter- Wis holde ȝe no whi · but' ȝif' he wel conne
ers.
              Faire tempren his tounge · his tale to schew.   572
              Miche matere of' wit' · minegeþ ȝour tounge ;
              But' beture holde y a burn · þat' bereþ him al stille .
              Ȝe geduren ȝou gret' won · of' gol & of' siluer,
Ye like to have & miche likus ȝou lache · lordliche holdeus,   576
many servants.
              & siþen many seruantis · ȝou-silue to abowe,
              To be keture y-kid · þan any kouþ peple.
              & ȝit' y liue þat' ȝe liue · þorou lasse fode
              þan oþur seggus þat' semen · simple [in] mirthe.   580
              Of richesse & of renoun · romme be ȝe kidde,
              & ben baldere y-wist' · þan any burn elles ;
We surpass you But' oure kinde konninge · ȝou ouur-comeþ nouþe
in all things.
              In alle dedus þat' ȝe don · in ȝoure daies time.   584
              We witen, weies, ful wel · þat' ȝe were alle

Nec permittis homines in sua viuere libertate, sed illos in seruitutem redigis et retorques. Recta iudicia minime iudicas. Leges indicis commutari. Bona dicis, et ipsa nullatenus imitaris nec operaris. Neminem reputas sapientem nisi loquendi habebat facundiam. Omnem sensum in lingua tua habes, et tota sapientia in ore tuo consistit. Aurum diligis, domos maximas construis, et habere peroptas copiam seruitorum. Intantum manducas et bibis, quod stomachus nimia perturbatione concussus in varias egritudines commutatur, et sic ante tempus mortis periculum sustentas. Omnia vis tenere, deinde omnia tenent te vt seruum. Sola Bragmanorum scientia vniuerse sapientie

Bremliche y-brouht' forþ · & bred of' þat' modur
þat' is stable to stonde · & stonus engendreþ, *Ye are but earth-born.*
And þe erþe is called · þat' euery man helpeþ. 588 [Fol. 212, back]
Whan god demeþ ȝou deie · ȝour daies to tine,
Grauus of' gret' prys · ȝe grayþe ȝou tille— *Ye build fine tombs.*
& but' hit' fair be & fin · folie ȝe holden—
To legge in ȝour licam · þat' lodlich[1] is founde. 592 [1 MS. 'bodilech']
& so ȝour bodies ȝe buren · þat' bettur riht' hadde
In rouh erþe to be reke · to roten hure bonus.
And by þe dedeus that men don · to þe dede bodies,
Ludus keneþ huo hem louen · to hure liuus ende. 596
We, for loue of' þe lord · þat' we leuen inne, *We, for love of God,*
None bestus i-boren · balfulli kille, *kill no beasts,*
Ne no tidi a-tir · in templus a-raie,
No figure of' fin gold · fourme þer-inne; 600 *nor carve idols.*
Where-fore þe heie heuene god · heren us scholde,
Whan any burn to him bad · [h]is bone graunte.[2] [2 MS. 'graunde'; see l. 764.]
But ȝe,[3] folliche folk · ȝour fals godus alle [3 MS. 'so']
Wil-fully worschipen · wiþ wordliche godus, 604 *Ye worship your gods,*
For þei scholde hasteli ȝou here · & ȝou help kiþe,
Whan ȝe greden ȝour grace · to graunte ȝour wille,
Whan ȝe for sake of' ȝoure sinne · sacrifice maken, *and sacrifice to devils.*
& quellen any quik best' · to queme þe deuelus. 608
Ȝe ne vndurstonde nouht' þat stounde · þe storie of þis
    wordus,
þat' god hereþ no gome · but' for his goode dedus, *God hears not man because of sacrifices.*
& for no bestene blod · þat' any burn quelleþ,
Noþir of' kide, noþur of' calf · noþur of kild oxe. 612

---

tue dominatur. Quia si bene consideramus, illa mater te genuit que
lapides et arbores procreauit. Tu ornas sepulcra tua et in vasa gem-
mea puluerem tui corporis collocas et recondis. Quid peius esse potest quam ossa que terra recipere debet, non sinis ipsam terram de
corpore recipere alimentum? Nos autem in honore deorum pecudes
non occidimus, templa non construimus vbi statuas aureas vel argen-
teas erigamus. Tu solem legem habeas vt de omnibus bonis tuis im-
molationem facias vt exaudiant preces tuas. Nonne intelligis quod
deus non precio nec sanguine vitulorum nec arietis aut hirci, sed

GOD IS A SPIRIT.

But' he hereþ euery haþel · þat' hertely biddeþ,
& wiþ mekenesse of' minde · minegeþ his nede.

[¹ MS. 'word-liche'; see l. 621.]
God's Word is the Son of Man.

Godus worþliche¹ word · as we wel trowen,
Is sone soþliche of' man · þat in him-silf dwelleþ, 616
By which molde is y-maad · & man vp-on erþe,
& al þat weihes in þis word · scholde wiþ fare;
Al bestus þer-by · þat' lif bere mowe,

All are sustained by Him.

Ben soþliche i-sustained · as him-silf' likus; 620
þat' ilke worþliche word · we worschipen alle,
& hit lelliche louen · as our lif' likus.

God is a Spirit.

God is spedful in speche · & a spryt' clene,
Boþe blessed & blyþe · þat' blendeþ alle sorwe. 624
He clameþ nouht but' clennesse · & clepeþ to [h]is ioie
Clene-mindede men · þat' meke ben founde.

Ye are all fools,

Where-fore we holde ȝou folk · folus echone,
Þat' ȝe ne leuen in þat lord · þat' lengeþ in blisse, 628
& lede clanly ȝour lif' · & no luþur wirche,
As ȝe haþ of us herd · holly þe dedus.

and live in lust.

But ȝe in lechoures lust' · al ȝour lif spende,
And serue sory idolus · þat ȝou in sinne brynge. 632
Wiþ oþur folies fale · ȝe foulen ȝour soulen;

After death ye will suffer pain.
[² MS. 'aclulle we']
[³ MS. 'we']

& so ȝe duren in ȝour dede · til ȝe ded worþeþ.
þanne schulle ȝe² for ȝour sinne · soffre paine,
For ȝe³ unclene bi cleped · & cleuen in ȝour sinne.' 636
þere may ȝow borewen of' bale · no bost' nor no pride,
No no god þat' ȝe giuen · to ȝour godus falce,

No sacrifice of beasts will help you.

No no sory sacrifice · þat' ȝe so maken
Wiþ any bestene blod · þat' euire burn schadde. 640

---

propter bona opera et orationis eloquium moueatur? Ex eo audit deus
hominem propter verbum, quia ex verbo deo similes efficimur; deus
verbum est, et ex hoc verbo omnia viuunt permanent et consistunt;
nos hoc verbum semper amamus et hoc etiam veneramur. Qua propter
reputamus te nimium infelicem, quia credis naturam deorum vel cum
diis communicationem habere, cum ad deum fornicatione et idolorum
seruitute quottidie sordides; cum hec facis, hec amas, et post mortem
inde tormenta innumerabilia sustinebis. Nos vero contraria facimus
et amamus, vt post mortem diuina gloria potiamur. Tu non seruis

VARIOUS LIMBS DEDICATED TO THE GREEK GODS.

Ȝe ne herien nouht' herteli · þe heie god alone,
þat' heuene holdeþ & haþ · to his hole regne,
But' al so fale falce godus · ȝe fonden to queme   *Ye have as many*
As a burn bereþ now · in his body membrys.   644   *false gods as a man has limbs.*
For ȝe liknen a lud · to a litil wordle,
& this sawe ȝe sain · soþliche echone,
þat', al so many as a man · haþ membrys y-schape,
Him falleþ al so fale godus · faiþfuly herie;   648
& so ȝe sacrifice don · to selkouþe fendus!
For euery lime þat' a lud · longeþ to haue,   *Every limb is*
Ȝe kyþen carefule godus · & kallen hem nowþe,   *dedicated to some god.*
Aftur dedeus þat þei dede · diuerse names.   652
Michel holde ȝe of' miht' · minerua þe falce,
For hue[1] foundede first' · folies manye;   [1 MS. 'he'; see l. 656.]
& þis is, seggus, ȝour sawe · as ȝe sain alle.   *Minerva sprang*
Hue was engendred wiþ gin · of' iubiterus hede;   656   *out of Jupiter's head,*
For-þi[2] ȝe holden hure wis · & hollyche segge,   [2 MS. 'For-þei']
þat' hue þe hilþe of' þe heed · haþ for to kepe.   *and therefore guards the head.*
Þe iaudewin iubiter · ioiful ȝe holde;
For he was wraþful i-wrouht' · & wried in angur,   660   *Jupiter was wrathful,*
Gomus holden him god · þat' gieþ þe herte;   *and guards the seat of wrath,*
For þere ariseþ in a rink · þe rotus of' wraþþe.   *the heart.*
A god mihtful of' main · martis ȝe holden;
For he was fihtere fel · & foundur of' werre,   664
He is alosed in lande · lord of' þe breste;   *Mars is lord of the breast.*
For þere þe miht' of' a man · most' is i-sene.
For mercurie miche spak · to mentaine iangle,   *Mercury is god of*
Ȝe holden him galful & god · & god of' þe tounge.   668   *the tongue;*
For hercules þe endelese · þat' euere is in paine,   *Hercules, with his*
Diuisede here on his day · a dosain of' wondrus,   *dozen of wonders,*

---

vni deo, qui regnat in celo, sed plurimis diis. Tot deos colis quot in tuo corpore membra portas. Nam hominem dicis paruum mundum; et sicut corpus hominis habet multa membra, ita et in celo dicis multos deos existere. Iunonem [*lege* Iouem] credis esse deum cordis, eo quod iracundia nimia mouebatur. Martem vero deum pectoris esse dicis, eo quod princeps extitit preliorum. Mercurium deum lingue vocas, ex eo quod plurimum loquebatur; herculem deum credis bra-

	þat¹ ȝe a-uowen verraie · & vertu*us* holden,	
	þat¹ a man moste do · wiþ mihte of¹ his arm*us*,	672
	A god holde ȝe him · helplich of¹ grace,	
presides over the *arms*.	þat¹ haþ ȝour arm*us* to ȝeme · & may ȝou ȝiue strenke.	
Bacchus the drunkard,	For bacus þe bollere · þat¹ ȝe abowen alle,	
	Englaymed was in glotenye · & glad to be drounke,	676
over the *throat*.	Ȝe callen him kep*er*e of¹ þe þrote · & kinde god holden,	
[Fol. 213]	& wis witiere of¹ win · þat¹ alle won bryng*us*.	
Of Cupid, ye say	Cupid*us* þe corsede · þat is in care punched,	
	Ȝe worchen al worschipe · & in þis wise tellen—	680

How he telleþ alixandre of his maumentrie.

[*A picture.* V.]

that he loved lechery,	Þat¹, for he leccherie louede · in his lif¹-time,	
	And þat folie fur · foundede on erthe,	
	A bryht brenninge brond · he bereþ on his hondis,	
	And alle lech*ur*us lust¹ · of þe lem tendeþ.	684
	And so ȝe sain þat¹ he is · a soþ god iproued,	
and presides over the *stomach*.	þat¹ haþ þe stomak in stat¹ · stifly to kepe ;	
	For þere þe hete that¹ men han · is holden wiþ-inne,	
	þat¹ enforceþ þe flech · folie to wirche !	688
Ceres, over the *womb*.	Also, segg*us*, ȝe sain · þat¹ ceres þe falce	
	Is a goodesse god · & gieþ þe wombe ;	
	For hue tilede in hur time · on þe touh erþe,	
	& whete soþliche sew · or any segg*us* ell*us*.	692
Venus, over the *privy members*.	Ful verrai of¹ vertue · ven*us* ȝe holden ;	
	& for hue lady was alosed · of¹ leccherouse dede*us*,	
	Ȝe holden hure a goodesse god · þat haþ for to kepe	
[¹ MS. 'He proueþ']	þe preuey¹ membr*us* of¹ a man · þat¹ marke is of¹ king*us*.	
Juno can	Iuno þe ioilese · ȝe iuggen for noble ;	697

chiorum eo quod duodecim virtutes exercuit preliando. Bachum deum gutturis esse putas, eo quod ebrietatem primus inuenit; cupidinem esse deam (*sic*) dicis, eo quod fornicatrix extitit; tenere dicis facem ardentem cum qua libidinem exitat (*sic*) et ascendit [*lege* accendit], et ipsam deam iecoris existimas. Cererem deam ventris esse dicis ; et venerem, eo quod fuit mater luxurie, deam genitalium membrorum

VARIOUS SACRIFICES TO GREEK GODS.

  & wei-huus sain þat he witeþ · in his worde one,   *foretell things to come.*
A spild spiritᵗ of þe air · þatᵗ may speke wondrus,
& telle whatᵗ bi-tide schal · of tene oþur ofᵗ welþe. 700
ȝe leuen alle in appolin · & also ȝe tellen   *Apollo, who practised medicine and minstrelsy, is god of the hands.*
þatᵗ, for he medisine made · & minstralus craftus,
· ȝe holde hin giour ful good · & god ofᵗ þe handus.
So þer leueþtno lime · lasse no more, 704
þatᵗ in ȝour power is putᵗ · butᵗ parted to fendus.
ȝe ne leuen notᵗ on a lord · þat lengus in heuene,
þat al þe membrus of a man · made atᵗ his wille.
And þouȝ ȝe falce godus folk · founden to serue, 708 *Your false gods only grieve you.*
þei ne graunte no grace · butᵗ greuen ȝou ofte,
& taken ofᵗ ȝou tribitᵗ · þatᵗ traie is to paie,
Ofᵗ ȝoure offringus alle · ofte in þe ȝere.
To martis þe mithtelese · men ofren in time 712 *To Mars, ye offer a boar;*
A gretᵗ bor & a bold · as burnus han vsed.
To bacus þe balful · men bringen in temple   *To Bacchus, a kid;*
A kide, as is costum · of comine peple.
A fair pokok ofᵗ pris · men paien to iuno, 716 *To Juno, a peacock;*
& him wirchen þer-wiþ · worschipe vn erthe.
þe offrin ofᵗ appolin · as ȝe alle knowe,   *To Apollo, a white swan;*
Ys a swan swiþe whitᵗ · swich as ȝe bryngen.
ȝe schullen bi ordre ofᵗ vse¹ · offren to venus,² 720 [¹ MS. 'of on vs']
A ful derworþe douue · on his den take.   [² MS. 'vectus']
  To Venus, a dove;
Minerua men worschipen · in oþur maner alse,   *To Minerva, a bat;*
& bringen hure a nihtᵗ-brid · a bakke or an oule.
To ceres þe sorwful · ȝe sacrifice maken, 724 *To Ceres, corn;*
& carien bi costum · corn to hure temple.
ȝe mensken alle mercurie³ · wiþ mirthe & wiþ ioie, [³ MS. 'mercurie']
& him a chalis ful chois · wiþ good chere bringen.   *To Mercury, a cup.*

---

esse profers. Totum siquidem corpus hominis in deos diuidis, nullam
in te particulam reseruando. Nec credis quod vnus deus qui est in
celo corpus tuum creauerit. Deos colis alienos qui te in seruitutem
redigunt, Et ipsis offers tributa. Marti enim offers aprum, Bacho
hircum, Iunoni pauonem, Ioui thaurum, Appollini agnum, Ueneri
columbam, Minerue noctuam, Cereri farra, Mercurio mella, Altaria herculi ex frondibus arborum plurimum coronata. Templum

THE GREEK GODS ARE BUTCHERS.

Ye put boughs on Hercules' altar;
Þe hauter oft he[r]cules · alle ȝe hihten,   728
& hitt spreden wiþ spraiuus · oft springinge braunchus.

and flowers on Cupid's.
Cupies þe corsed · wiþ comeliche flourus
Ȝe herien ful hertely · & hihten [h]is temple.
Þus manye mihteles godus · & mo þan y telle,   732
For þe hope oft hur help · ȝe herien on erþe.

Ye cannot serve them all at once.
& ȝitt may þer no man · in any maner wise
Wiþ solepne sacrifice · serue hem att onus,
Butt eueri wile oft a wehy · his owene wone haue,   736
Be itt bole oþur bor · betur oþur werse.
Oft swiche bestus þatt ben · oft burnus y of reed,
Þei han mihtt vp-on molde · & oft no mo þingus.   739

Why do ye believe in false gods?
Whi fauure ȝe þanne falce godus · & folliche seggen
Þatt þei han power oft peple · þatt pacen on molde,
Whan þei ne han miht oft no mor · nor no maistrie on erþe,
Butt of hur owne offringe · & onliche oft bestes?

For your sins,
For ȝour errours on erthe · sire emperour riche,   744
& for þe dedus vn-dingne · þat ȝe don alle,

[¹ MS. 'worþei']
As ȝe ben worþi¹ oft wo · whan þe word failus,

ye shall be punished.
Ȝe schulle be punched & putt · in paine for euere!
Ȝour godus ful of gile ben · þatt ȝe so good holden, 748
On hem is help oft non harm · no hap oft no grace,

Your gods are butchers.
Butt bochours ben þei echon · ȝour body to dismembre,
& euerich pinchen his partt · þere paine is vnended.
As many mihtelese godus · as ȝe on molde seruen,   752

[Fol. 213, back]
As fale painus in fir · ȝou fallus to drie.

Your idols make you sin.
For ȝour ydil idolus · don ȝou ille wirche;
Summe to lechorus lustt · ȝour likinge turneþ,   755
Summe ȝou strenkþen to striue · & straiten ȝour minde,
& somme eggen in ese · to eten & to drinke.
Þei by-sette ȝou so · in sinne & in gile,

---

cupidinis rosis et floribus siue frondibus ornas. Totam potestatem tuam ponis in illis, et non est in corpore tuo membrum quod illis non attribuas. Reuera non deos quos vocas adiutores, sed carnifices sunt vocandi; quoniam membra tua diuersis tormentis affligunt. Oportet enim vt tot tormenta subeas quot deos seu deorum culturas agis. Unus deus instruit te fornicari, alter bibere, alter

þatͥ ȝe wirchen hur wil · & worchipen alle.   *Ye work their will.*
&, seggus, for ȝe so don · ȝe semen vn-wise, 760
Hem to seruen in sinne · þatͥ mowe no segͥ helpe.   *Ye serve them by sin.*
þei beþ vn-mihtful y-mad · men for to wisse,
And kun not saue hem-selfͥ · fro sorwful painus.
Whan ȝe hem greden ofͥ griþ · to graunte ȝour bone, 764
Wheþur hey hit heren or nouhtͥ · to harme hitͥ ȝou turneþ.
Whan ȝe hem praiere profre · ȝifͥ þey prestͥ heren,   *When ye pray, they harm you.*
þei casten in ȝoure consience · corsede þouhtous.
And, ludus, ȝifͥ hem loþ be · to listne ȝoure bonus, 768
Hitͥ ȝou norcheþ any · for thei ȝou nouhtͥ heren.
So wheþur þei graunte hitͥ or gruche · þei greuen ȝou ofte,   *Whether they hear you or not, ye suffer.*
For eueri time hitͥ ȝou turneþ · to tene & to harme.
þo ben ȝoure gostliche godous · þatͥ gon to do wreche 772
Aftur ludene lifͥ · for hure luþur werkus.
For þei schulle in þis word · wirche for sinne,
Whan þatͥ burnus ar bured · þatͥ balfully wrouthe
Tokne ofͥ þatͥ turmentͥ · tolde ȝoure eldren, 776   *Your elders spake of torment to come.*
How wreche scholde ben wrouht · for wrongful dedes,
& dul aftur þe deþ · ȝour doctourus saide,
þatͥ seggus scholde for sinne · suffre in þis worde;
& ȝe ben soþli þe same · ofͥ wham þei so tolde, 780
þatͥ scholde lenge aftur lif · in lastinge paine.   *Ye shall dwell in endless torment.*
For ȝifͥ ȝe seggus ȝou[r] lifͥ · soþli bi-þenke,
Wers wirchen no folk · þan ȝe weiȝes alle.
For sake ofͥ ȝoure sauyour · ȝe ne soffre no paine, 784
Butͥ liuen in ȝoure likinge · & luþurli wirchen;

---

litigare. Omnes tibi imperant, et omnibus obedis; quia mala facis et non vis a malo vllatenus respicere. Igitur talis diis seruis qui mala facere hortantur. Si exaudierint te dii tui, mala tibi euenient, quia de malo rogas eos. Si vero non exaudierint te, tuis desideriis obuiabunt. Ergo si te exaudierint vel non, semper tibi inferunt detrimentum. Tales sunt dee tue que furie nuncupantur, que et peccata hominum per furorem post mortem vindicant. Hec sunt tormenta tua que tibi doctores tui dixerunt, que te velut mortuum cruciant et tormentant. Quot si vis recte considerare, nil peius quis sustinere valet quam tu sustines; quecunque enim signa doctores tui apud inferos esse dixerunt, certissime cognoscuntur pene tue in in

	ȝe waken for wikkednesse · & wirchen but' ille.
Ye commit murder, adultery,	ȝe speden for to spille men · & spouce-breche fonden;
	ȝou is lechurie luf' · & liben wiþ stalþe, 788
and theft.	To robbe men of' hure riht' · ful redy ben alle.
	ȝe ben glotouniu̅s gle · glad for to haunte,
	& han no mesure on molde · of' mete ne of' drynke.
	ȝe ben to þe helle-hond · holliche i-like, 792
Ye are like Cerberus.	Tri-ce[r]berus þe tenful · of' wham i tolde haue;
	Foure hedus ben on him · þat' haþ but' on wombe.
	& so it' fareþ by ȝou folk · þat fillen ȝou-siluen;
	For alle þe godus þat' ȝe geten · of' gomus vp-on erþe 796
	Seruen for to sustaine · ȝour vnsely wombe.
There is an adder in hell called Hydra,	Also ȝoure docturus sain · in sawus ful olde,
	þat' an addre is in helle · þat yydra is called,
	To cache is couaitous · corsede soulus; 800
never glutted.	& fonde he fewe oþur fale · ful is he neuere.
Ye are like him.	Þanne mow ȝe ludus of lif · be likned him tille;
	For ȝe ben couaitouse kid · & kunne nouht' blinne,
	But' euere wenden to winne · wordliche godus, 804
	& al is burnus aboute · ȝour body for to fede.
[¹ MS. 'sain']	Alle þe foliuus, folk · þat' ȝe fain¹ wirchen,
	Ben purchas of' penaunce · whan ȝe parte hennus.
[² MS. 'panne'] Ye were born to sorrow."	To bale were ȝe þanne² bore · for bannede werkus, 808
	þat' schullen schamly be schent' · & schapen to paine.
	Þus dindimus þe dere king' · enditeþ his sonde,
	& god by-secheþ to saue · þe soueraine prinse."—
When Alexander heard this,	Whan emperour alixandre · wiþ erene hit' hirde, 812
	& tendede þe tiþinge · þat' y told haue,
he was wroth.	He was wroþ, for þe writ' · of' wrong' gan a-lose
	His godus þat' he held · to gyen þe peple.

---

ferno. Tu enim vigilans penas paris, vtpote [ed. vtpute] furta, fornicationes, et adulteria que committis. Dicunt enim quod in inferno semper sitiunt habitantes et minime possunt satiari. Et tu tantam habens cupidinem acquirendi vt nunquam possis diuitiis recreari, Deinde omnia que in inferno esse dixerunt in te sine dubio commorantur. Heu ibi misero, qui debes post mortem tuam innumerabilia tormenta substinere!— Relata epistola Alexandro, iratus

But' nouþeles anon riht · anied in his herte, 816 *Being annoyed, he sends a letter back.*
Sone sente he again · his sel & his lettrus.
Wiþ-oute tariynge tid · þis tiþingus come
To dindimus þe dere king' · þat' þe dite radde.
Now liþus, ȝe þat' listene wele · þe lettrus to þe ende, *Hear it!*
For þus redely þe rink · a-radde þe sonde. 821

How alixandre sente answere to dindimus by letter.

[*A picture.* VI.]

"Þe aþel king' alixandre · of' armus alosed, *"Alexander,*
  þat' noble is & name-kouþ · & neuere man dradde,
þat' grete god amon · in graciouse timus 824 *son of Ammon,*
By-gat on olimpias · þe onorable quene,
Ful derely to dindimus · enditeþ his sonde, *to Dindimus, greeting.*
& his sawe to the seg' · saiþ in þis wise.— 827
Ȝif' alle þe lorus þat' þou, lud · in lettrus me sentest *If all is true, ye are very good men.*
Ben trewe to be trowen on · & trysty to leue,
þanne be ye sykur[1] to be saf' · for sake of' ȝoure werkus. [1 MS. 'sylur']
For ȝe ben burnus of' lif' · best' vp-on erþe,
Ȝif' ȝe nouht' wirche but' wel · in þis word here; 832 [Fol. 214]
Hit' comeþ ȝou bi custum · so clanly to libbe.
Whi deme þanne þat' we don · ne dede vp-on erþe *Why deem ye that we sin?*
But' sinne þat' is sorwful · oure soule to spille?
Whi seye ȝe seggus also · þat' sinne ȝe holden 836
Any werkus to wirche · of' wordliche craftus?
Whi be ȝe, ludus, so lef' · to lakke þe werkus *Why blame the works of man?*

---

est valde propter deorum iniuriam, et continuo scripsit ei hoc modo.
  Responsio Alexandri ad regem Bragmanorum.
  [R]Ex regum et dominus dominantium Alexander filius dei Hamonis et regine olimpie dindimo salutem. Si omnia in vobis reperiuntur que nobis vestris literis intimasti, soli potestis homines nuncupari, qui, vt dicitis, nulla facinora perpetratis. Sed pro certo sciatis quod huiusmodi vitam non ex virtute sed ex consuetudine obtinetis, quia secundum consuetudinem aut dicitis vos deos esse aut inui-

MISERIES OF THE BRAHMANS.

     þat' man-kinde haþ y-mad · on molde to be vsed?
     ȝif' hit' be soþ þat' ȝe sain · hit' semeþ, by ȝoure dedes, 840
     þat' ȝe no giuen of' no gome · no none godus trowe,
Ye are envious. Or ȝe en[u]ye to hem han · & hatien hur sondus,
     For to libbe in ȝour land · as ludus aboute.
     Many wondurful wonus · wisli we knowen, 844
     þat' ȝe amongus ȝou men · in ȝour march vsen.
Ye say that ye plough not, ȝe telle vs þat ȝe tende nauht' · to tulye þe erþe,
     Ne place erie wiþ plow · no plaunte winus,
nor build. Ne bulde boldus an hih · for burnus to wonye, 848
     Ne non erthely note · nedfully wirchen.
     In þat' þou leredest' me, lud · þat ȝe no land erien,
Ye have no iron. ȝe ben exkused echon · for iren ȝou wantus,
     Where-wiþ mihte ȝe men · maken any boldus, 852
     Or tren plaunten in place · or any plow dryue.
Ye have no tools. Whan ȝe mow take no tol · to tilien on erþe,
     No swiche werkus to swinke · as oþur swainus vsen,
Ye must live hard. For-þi bi-houus ȝou, haþel · harde to libbe, 856
     & wo drie in þis word · for wante & for nede!
     So mowe ȝe, ludus, ȝour lif' · leden as bestus,
     In gret' mischef' of mete · as ȝe mote nede.
A hungry wolf must eat earth. ȝe witen wel, whan a wolf' · wanteþ [h]is fode, 860
     þat' he ne fundeþ no flech · to feden him vppe,
     Of' þe erþe he et' · for ellus he scholde
     Be wiþ hungur y-holde · & happily sterue. 863
     þanne mow ȝe weies to þe wolf' · ful wel ben y-likned;
Ye have to do the same. þat', for ȝe finde no fode · as oþur folk vsen,
     Swich hungur as ȝe han · by-houus ȝou þolie,

---

dia mouemini contra nos. Dixistis siquidem; Non aratis, non funditis semina, et non scinditis vites aut arbores plantatis. Edificia fabricare non vultis. Manifesta ratio est, quia ferramenta quibus laborare possetis penitus indigetis. Vnde laborare, nauigare, construere, et seminare uobis [*ed.* nobis] omni modo [*ed.* mode] denegatur. Ideo pascentes herbas oportet vos vt pecora vitam ducere aridam et agrestem, quia frumenta, nec carnes, nec pisces habere potestis. Nonne lupi hoc faciunt, qui cum nequeunt carnibus saturari de terre penuria saturabuntur? Quot si liceret vobis ingredi terram nostram,

&, be 30... of oþur loþ · libben in wante.
þere-fore no like no lud · of his luþur fare,   868
No hope for his harde lifᵗ · to haue no mede.
For almus-dede do 3e non · as 3e demen alle,   *Ye do no alms.*
Butᵗ skarsete & skaþe · vn-skilfully fonden.   871
3ifᵗ we lengede in 3oure land · ful loþ were oure bestus   *Our beasts would scorn your life!*
To ben so simple of vs silf · & suffre þat tene !
We scholde folewe oþur folk · & fonden echone
To a-corde ofᵗ oure costom · wiþ comine peple ;
Butᵗ 3e han daiute in dul · 3oure daies to spene,   876
& ben y-sustained so · wiþ sorwe in þis worde.
Butᵗ 3e ben litil to a-lowe · of 3oure luþur fare ;   *Ye are not to be praised.*
For nouhtᵗ butᵗ nisete · nedful 3ou makus !
3oure owne folie, folk · doþ 3ou ful ofte   880
In hungur & in hard lifᵗ · to holde 3oure peple.
Also 3e sain in 3our sonde · þatᵗ soþly 3oure wiuus   *Your wives use no gay apparel,*
Ne gon in no gay tyr · as gise is ofᵗ oþure,
& þat ludus in 3oure land · no lechurie haunten,   884   *and no man commits adultery.*
Butᵗ sparen alle spouse-breche · þe space ofᵗ hure liuus ;
& þou 3e wonde swich werk · me wondrus ful lite !
How mihtᵗ 3e lechurie loue · or likinge haue,   *How can he, with such fare?*
Whan luþur fare haþ alaid · 3our lustus echone,   888
þatᵗ 3e megre ben maad · wiþ mischefᵗ & hungur ?
For 3e so simple ben seie · & semen so pore,
3ou wantus wordliche won · 3our wiuus to hihte.
þere-fore as bestus 3e ben · & ofᵗ body chaste,   892   *Ye are chaste perforce.*

---

non reciperemus sapientiam de vestra penuria quam habetis, sed ipsa fames in suis finibus remaneret. Si vero in fines [*ed.* finines] vestros nostra tabernacula figeremus, paupertate sicut vos potiremur. Non enim est laudandus vir qui semper in angustia viuit, sed qui temperate diuitiis perfruitur. Quot si laudandi [*ed.* laudendi] essent viri in angustia positi, Ceci claudi et leprosi deberent super ceteros homines commendari. Dixistis etiam quod femine vestre non ornantur, et cuiusmodi ornamenta portabunt, quia non habent et nullatenus possunt habere. Item quod adulteria non committitis, sed semper in castitate manetis ; quomodo fornicabuntur qui non comedunt ? Libido enim non procedit nisi ex calore epatis et ciborum ; vos autem non comeditis nisi herbas sicut porci, et fa-

	Vn-mihty, for mischef · to medle wiþ burdus,	
	þatᵗ nis no chariteuus chois · so schastᵗ for to libbe;	
	Sin ȝe maugray ȝour mihtᵗ · mote hitᵗ wiþ-drawe!	
	Also ȝe sente vs to saie · in þe same time	896
	Ofᵗ oþur manerus mo · miche for to lakke;	
Ye never study;	þatᵗ ȝe no stidie in no stounde · ne no statᵗ wilne	
	Of clergie þatᵗ clene is · to claimen in scole;	
and neither expect nor shew mercy.	& þatᵗ ȝe mercy on molde · in no maner wilne,	900
	No mercy don to no man · a-mongus ȝou founde.	
	þanne hitᵗ semeþ by ȝoure sawe · ȝifᵗ ȝe soþ tellen,	
	þatᵗ kindely ȝoure consience · a-cordeþ to bestus.	
Ye are as beasts.	For as bestes ȝe ben · by no skile reuled,	904
	Ne hem ofᵗ kinde no comeþ · no konninge ofᵗ witte;	
	So be ȝe, ludus, by-lad · & lawe-les alse,	
	þatᵗ han no reward to riht · butᵗ red-lese wirchen.	
We are wise.	Butᵗ we faiþful folk · þatᵗ faren as wise,	908
	Ben y-demed to do · dedus of rihte.	
	For-þy vs kenneþ our kinde · to a-corde in trowþe,	
	In swiche lawus to liue · þatᵗ longen to gode;	
We sow and plant.	For to sowe & to sette · in þe sad erthe,	912
	& oþur wordliche werk · wisly to founde.	
	Sin man-kinde is y-maad · so michel & so riue,	
	Among so perles a peple · in-possible hitᵗ were—	915
	Butᵗ somme were reuled by ryhtᵗ · as resoun hitᵗ axeþ—	
Some men ought to work.	Hem-selfᵗ to sostaine · wiþ selkowþe þingus,	
	For to liue by þe land · as ludus ben schape	
	To haue welþe aftur wo · as þe word farus.	
After work comes pleasure. [¹ MS. 'swine']	For tenen sum-time tid · & sumtime mirthe;	920
	& aftur swaginge of swinc¹ · swiþe comeþ ioie.	

mem [ed. famen] non expellitis et ideo nullum potestis habere stimulum luxurie et coeundi. Studium non habetis discendi nec misericordiam queritis, et hec omnia cum bestiis communiter retinetis; quia sicut a natura non habent vt aliquod bonum faciant, ita nec in bono aliquo delectantur. Nobis autem ratiouabilibus qui liberum habemus arbitrium in ipsa natura multe blandicie sunt concesse. Impossibile enim est vt maxima mundi machina possit absque mobilitate consistere, vt post tristiciam non succedat leticia. Humana

But' so, weihuus, as ȝe witen · þat' weduringe chaungeþ, *Seasons change.*
Now broun & now briht' · & now breme stormys,
So is þe wit' & þe wil · of wordliche peple   924   [Fol. 214, back]
In selkouþe sesounus · seen[1] for to chaunge.   [¹ MS. 'fain']
Whan wedur waxeþ al bryht' · þat' wel is to like,   *In fair weather,*
Mirie ben men of' mod · in minde & in herte;   927   *men are merry;*
But whan þe daies dimme ben · hit' doþ hem to mourne,   *but in dim days,*
For siht' of' þe sesoun · þat' semus vnbliþe.   *sad.*
Ȝit' chaungeþ wit' of a weih · in oþur-wise alse,
þorou þe grete de-gre · þat groweþ in age.   *Man changes according to his*
For when he is innocent' · þat' ille can lite,   932   *age.*
þanne haþ he solas of' him-silf' · simple to worþe;
For betur likede him a bal · þan a borou riche;   *In youth,*
& he is hardy to non harm · but' hauntus his gamus.   *he plays with a ball.*
Whan he is eldure of' age · þat' auht' is his strenke,   936   *In riper years, he shews his*
þanne wol he prouen him proud · & prys of' him holde,   *valour.*
& wexe wilde of' his wil · & wikke to staunche.
Whan he is fare so forþ · fer in his age,   *In old age,*
þan[2] stoute is he, stedefast' · & stille of' his herte.   940   *he is quiet.*
         [² MS. 'þat']
Huo wole a cherched child · chese for hardy,   *Who would look for hardiness in*
Or a ȝoung' man meek · þat mirþe couaiteþ ?   *an infant?*
Huo wolde wene þat' a weih · woxen on elde
Were wist' for vnstedefast' · of' word or of' dede ?   944
Manie mirþus on molde · þat oþur men vsen,   *Ye omit many*
Ȝe leuen þorou ȝour luþur wit' · þat' longen to peple.   *joys,*
Summe in siht' þat' we sen · & sauur of' mouþe,   *of sight, savour,*
Summe in handlinge of' hond · & heringe of' ere,   948   *handling, hearing,*
Summe þat' longen to a lud · of' likinge smellus,   *and smelling.*
& queminge of' quaintise · þat' quencheþ our tene,

---

siquidem voluntas variabilis est que cum celi mutatione mutatur, quoniam scincerus dies scinceram mentem reddit hominis et gaudentem. Tenebrosa autem dies tristem reddit sensum hominis et obscurum. Et per diuersas etates similitur variatur. Infantia siquidem in simplicitate letatur, iuuentus presumptione, senectus stabilitate commode gratulatur. Multa delectabilia visui nostro occurrunt que uobis penitus denegantur. Alia per visum contemplamur, alia percipimus per auditum, alia attrahimus per odorem, alia sentimus per

	& in menskinge of¹ mouþ · mirþe we hauen,
	In tendere touchinge of¹ þing¹ · & tastinge of swete. 952
We enjoy fruit.	& sin we frekus ben so fre · þat¹ we frut¹ hauen,
	& al þat¹ growus in þe ground · of¹ graciouce þingus ;
We find fish.	We finde fihch in þe se · þat¹ vs fedeþ alle ;
	We lachen likinge y-now · of¹ þe lof¹ briddus ; 956
	& ȝif¹ ȝe wonde of¹ þat¹ won · to winne ȝour fode,
	Ȝe schulle be demed þat¹ ȝe don · dispit¹ to þo kindus.
Ye dishonour the Creator.	Þanne schewe ȝe to hur schappere · schame for his sondus,
	þat¹ so schinden his schap · þat¹ he ȝou scheweþ here.
	Or ȝe han hertely hate · to oure hole peple, 961
	For we ben beture of our lif¹ · & swich bote finden ;
	Sin swiche godus as we sen · ben sen[t] to us alle,
[¹ MS. 'do']	& nouht¹ so to¹ ȝou now · nedful burnus. 964
Your deeds are folly."	Alle þe dedus þat ȝe don · y deme þat it¹ turnus
	More to folie þan to faiþ · of¹ any ful witte."
	Þis sonde þat¹ y said haue · sire alixandre riche
	Let¹ bringe wiþ his brode sel · to bragmanus prince, 968
	& raþe whan hit¹ rad was · ful redy wiþ oþur
Dindimus replies.	To þis adoutede duk · dindimus sente.
	Whan hit¹ was sent¹ to þe seg · he dide hit¹ sone red ;
Hear his reply !	Now how hit¹ goodly by-gan · men, giuus tente ! 972

How dindimus sendyd an answere to alix-
andre by letter.

[*A picture.* VII.]

| "Dindimus | "**D**indimus þe dere king¹ · the docktour of¹ wise, |
| | þat¹ lord of¹ bragmanus land · & ledere is holde, |

tactum, et per gustum alia saporamus.   De terra etiam omnes fructus attrahimus, de mari pisces, de aere volucres, et auium deliciis gratulamur.   Si autem ab his uolueritis [*ed.* nolueritis] abstinere, aut superbia vos tenebit aut inuidia contra nos torquebimini, eo quod nobis et non vobis ista sunt donata.   Ego autem secundum oppinionem meam iudico quod mores vestri ad stulticiam magis quam ad sapientiam retrahuntur.—Recepta epistola dindimus legit, et statim alexandro secundo more scripsit hoc modo.

[D]Idimus bragmanorum didascolus Alexandro salutem.   Non

To emperour alixandre · egrest' of' princes, — to Alexander, greeting.
þat' is grymmest y-growe · & grettest'[1] of' kingus, 976 [1 MS. 'greftest']
Ioie graiþus wiþ grace · & gretinge of' mouþe,
As to þe kiddeste y-core · þat' corone weldus!
We do þe namkouþe king' · to kenne & to here, 979
þat' in þis wastinge word · we ne wone nouht' euere; — We do not always live in this world.
For erþe is nouht' our eritage · þat' euere schal laste,
Ne we ne ben nouht' ibor · to abide þer-inne.
But' we ben pore pilgrimus · put' in þis worde, — We are pilgrims on earth.
For we by destene of' dome · schulle deþ þolie; 984
þanne schulle we hie to þe hous · þat' hie is in blysse,
& karre to oure kinus nie · to kenne of' oure fare.
We ben of'-set' wiþ no sinne · for vnsely godus, — We do no sin.
Ne we sitte in no sete · þere sinne is y-hanteþ. 988
But for oure kinde consience · þat' kenneþ vs to goode,
We wonde wikkede werk · & wende fro skaþe.
We ne sain noukt', king', be þou sur · for sake of' our pride, — It is not pride or envy that makes us such as we are.
þat' we bolde godus ben · burnus to gie, 992
Ne enuye to hem han · ne hate in þis worde.
For we ne giue vs to no gilt' · þat' scholde god wraþe,
Ne nouht nien him her · by niht' no by day.
God, þat' alle gomus schop · & alle gode þingus, 996 — God made men of many kinds.
Made here vp-on molde · many manere choisus;
For maad mihte hit' nouht' be · þere men scholde dwelle
Wiþ-oute diuerce dedus · of' many done þingus.
But' al þat' badde is for a burn · here abouen erþe, 1000 — He who avoids evil
Huo so haþ chaunce to echue · & chese þe betture—
As men han wit' for to wite · þe wikke & þe gode— [Fol. 215]
He may nouht' claime to be cleped · clene god of' mihte,

---

habitamus in hoc seculo perpetuo moraturi, sed sicut perigrinantes, quia morte super-veniente pergimus ad alias regiones vel mansiones, nec manemus in perpetuis tabernaculis in hoc mundo. Nullum furtum facimus et pro nostra conscientia in publicum eximus. Non reputamus nos esse deos nec contra deum inuidia concitamur. Deus qui omnia creauit in mundo multas rerum varietates constituit, qui dedit homini liberum arbitrium vt de omnibus que sunt in mundo discernat et prouideat. Qui ergo omnia dimiserit et secutus fuerit

is God's friend.	Butᵗ godus frend may þe freke · frely be called ;	1004
	For we leden wel our lifᵗ · & louen to be simple.	
Ye say we are as gods.	In ȝoure sonde, sire kingᵗ · ȝe saide þis wordus ;—	
	þatᵗ we alle godus arn · as ȝe deme nouþe,	
	Or euere elles til hem · enuye we haue.	1008
	Butᵗ þe same þatᵗ ȝe so · by vs silfᵗ trowe	
	Longeþ, ludus, to ȝou · þat liuen so in ese.	
But ye are so rather,	For ȝe leden ȝoure lifᵗ · in lordschipe & in myrthe,	
	Ofᵗ noble kinde for ȝe come · & kid ben ofᵗ grete.	1012
being rich, and gaily clad.	In clene cloþus ȝe gon · & claimen to be riche ;	
	Al ȝoure minde is on mirþe · & mostᵗ vp-on goodus.	
	ȝoure fingrus ofᵗ fin gold · ȝe fullen wiþ ryngus,	
	As is wommenus wone · for wordliche glose.	1016
Your boastful deeds will make you proud.	Butᵗ, burnus, be ȝe ful sur · þo bostful dedeus,	
	Wher-fore ȝe holde ȝou her · hiestᵗ on erþe,	
	Schal ȝou procre to pryde · & to no profitᵗ ellus,	1019
	Butᵗ skaþe for ȝoure vn-skile · whan ȝe skapen hennus.	
Gold feeds no one.	Gold fedeþ no gome · ne no good soule ;	
	Butᵗ we þat selkouþus sen · & soþus mow knowe,	
	And kenne þe kinde ofᵗ þe gold · þatᵗ corsed is founde,	
	We faren alle to þe flod · þere we finde mowe	1024
	Gretᵗ plente ofᵗ gold · on þe ground ligge.	
We spurn it.	þanne we wollen ofᵗ þe watur · wilfully drinke,	
	& de-foule wiþ our fetᵗ · þe fine gold schene.	
	For gold, þouh itᵗ gay be · hitᵗ gaynus ful lite	1028
	Ofᵗ hard hongur and þirstᵗ · to helpe any peple.	

---

meliora non deus sed dei amicus appellatur. De nominibus igitur et continentur (*sic*) viuimus cur dicis aut dii sumus aut contra ipsos concitamur inuidia ? Hec siquidem suspitio quam de nobis habetis vos tangit. Nam ex multis prosperitatibus quas habetis multa superbia turgitati estis. Corpora vestra gloriosus (*sic*) vestibus ornatis et immittitis in digitis vestris aurea instrumenta. Sed quid vobis hoc prodest ? Ex auro enim anime vestre nullatenus salue fiunt nec humana corpora satiantur. Nos vero qui vtilitatem nouimus et ipsius auri naturam discernimus ; quando sitimus, pergimus ad fluuium vt bibamus. Ipsum etiam aurum si reperimus pedibus conculcamus. Aurum enim famem [*ed.* famen] non tollit nec sitim reprimit ; nec potest egritudines ab humanis corporibus variare. Si sitiret homo et aurum bi-

Haue a man neuere so miche · mischef of¹ houngur,   *A hungry man eats meat, not gold.*
He may hit¹ staunche wiþ mete · & menden his paine.
þouh þirst dreche him wiþ drouhþe · drink may him helpe,   *A thirsty man drinks water.*
A litil wetinge of¹ watur · his wo wol amende.   1033
ȝif¹ gold were to a gome · so good of¹ his kinde,
Whan men hit¹ helde in here hand · or hadde in here warde,
So scholde hit be to a burn · bote of his nede,   1036
His corsede couaytise · cofly to sese.
But¹ now, þe more þat¹ a man · may þer-of¹ winne,   *The more gold a man has, the more he wants.* [¹ MS. 'be']
þe more ȝernus he¹ ȝit¹ · to ȝeme at¹ his wille;
& he is mensked þe mor · amongus ȝou alle,   1040
For wel louus euery lud · þat¹ liche is him tille.
We sain þat¹ ȝour sory godes · of¹ wham ȝe so helpe,   *Your gods cannot heal the dead.*
Mow no manyr ded þing¹ · þorou hure miht¹ hele.
ȝe tenden michil in ȝour time · templus to bulde,   1044
& riche auterus riue · rere þere-inne;
þanne founde ȝe ȝour falce godus · with sorw for to here,
& quellen for to quemen hem · of¹ ȝour quike bestus;
& in þat¹ same sacrifice · ȝe seggen þe name   1048   *Yet ye sacrifice to them.*
Of¹ what¹ burn þat¹ hit¹ be · þat¹ wolde bone haue.
þin aldur-fadur, alixandre · al þis haþ vsed,
& alle kydde of¹ ȝour kin · kenden þis dedus;
þis is amongus ȝou men · in þis manere knowe;   1052
For þus ȝe erren echon · in erþliche werkus.   *Ye err, ye know not how much.*
Where-fore, seggus, we sain · for sake of¹ ȝour dedus,
How luþurly ȝe liuen her · litil ȝe knowen.
þow ȝe wiþ sinne be of-set¹ · suffre ȝe² nolle,   1056   [² MS. 'ne']
þat¹ we by-wepe in þis word · ȝour wikkede dedus!
& miche, þinkeþ vs, a man · menskeþ anoþur,   *To reprove you is a kindness.*

biberet, sitis non reprimeretur. Si esuriit et cibo refecto ex auro refectus fuerit, fames non repellitur. Si autem aurum esset bone [ed. hmōi (sic)] nature et acciperet illud homo, cupiditatis puniretur vicium. Quid ergo proficit aurum ? non purgat, non reprimit, non satiat, non sustentat; nullam cordi humano confert sanitatem nec vtilitatem. Quid inde vasa aurea componitis ? Nonne vasa lutea tantundem proficiunt, nisi quod mentes vestre magis propter splendorem auri in superbiam eleuantur ? Malum siquidem aurum est, quia

| | þat' a gome for his gilt' · goodly by-wepeþ. | 1059 |

For ho so woneþ in þis word · & wol nouh[t] y-knowe

He who ignores death should be struck down by lightning,
þat him is demed to deie · & doom schal abide,
Hit' is riht þat' þe rink · be reufully ended,
& smite to þe smeþe grownd · wiþ a smart' poudur;

as Salmoneus was."
As on sinful was seie · þat' salonien*us* hi3te, 1064
& euyl endid on erþe · and wrout' ful foule.

For þe lud on his lif' · a-losed him so noble,
þat he heuene hadde miht' · wi*th* hand*us* to reche;

[¹ MS. 'For þei']
For-þi¹ boþe for hur bost' · ben y-brend nouþe, 1068
Wiþ fir in þe fir-hil · to fend*us* by-tauhte.

þus mowe 3e finden in fabl*us* · of' philozofrus olde,
þat' spoken how þo spild men · spende*n* hur time."

This was Dindimus' last letter.
þus was þe lettere of' þe lud · þat' he last' sente, 1072
& mascedoni*us* mihty king' · menskliche hit' radde.

Whan he þe sonde hadde seye · he sente forþ newe,
þat' was to bragmanye brouht · & p*r*est' for to rede.

Alexander thus replies.
þanne radde cofly þe king' · þis kariede sonde, 1076
þat' þus tiþinge tolde · & tauhte þis wordus :—

How alixandre sente dindimus anoþ*ur* letter.

[*A picture.* VIII.]

"Alexander,
"Þe empe*r*our alixandre · of' armus a-losed,
þat' noble is & name-kouþ · & neuere man dradde,

[Fol. 215, back]
By godus chaunce þat' ys chose · chef' ou*ur* king*us*, 1080
& of' burn*us* y-bore · baldest of' mihte,

son of Ammon, to Dindimus.
þat amon þe grete god · in grac*i*ose tim*us*
By-gat' on olimpas · þe on*ur*able quene,
By-kenneþ king' dindim*us* · in kiþ þere he dwell*us*, 1084

[² MS. 'a fledde' (!). *See* l. 286.]
His a-seled² sonde · & saiþ in þis wise.—
3e sain, burn*us*, þat' 3e ben · best' echone,

---

quanto maiori quantitate habetur, tanto magis illud habendi cupiditate augmentatur.

Responsiua alexandri didimo regi bragmanorum.

[R]Ex regum et dominus dominantium Alexander filius dei Hamonis et regine Olimpie Didimo dicendo mandamus. Quoniam in

þatᵗ in ȝoure loþ-liche land · libben by kynde.
For so, seggus, ȝe ben · by-setᵗ in an yle, 1088   *Ye are so set in an island,*
þat þer may comen in ȝour kiþ · non vnkouþe peple;   *that no strangers come to you.*
Ne ȝe ne mowe ofᵗ þatᵗ march · in no manere wende,
Butᵗ, be you loþ oþur lefᵗ · lenge þer-inne.
& for ȝe, weihuus, ofᵗ þatᵗ won · wende ne mowe, 1092
Wel a-lowe ȝe ȝour lifᵗ · and ȝour land alse!
Al þe nede & þe noy · þatᵗ ȝe now suffren   *Ye say ye suffer by choice.*
By a-sentᵗ ofᵗ ȝour-silf · ȝe sain þatᵗ ȝe dryen;
& by þe sawe þat ȝe sente · to segge ofᵗ ȝoure fare, 1096
Ȝe arn liche ofᵗ ȝour lif · to swiche loþe burnus,   *Ye are like wretched prisoners.*
þatᵗ ben in dep presoun don · al hure daies time,
& han mirþus on molde · missed ful clene!
Butᵗ lawe lereþ vs & skile · þat ȝe ben leþur alle, 1100
& mow for ȝoure mischefᵗ · no mede haue;
For itᵗ comeþ ȝou ofᵗ kinde · in care to libbe.   *It is natural to you to live in sorrow.*
Sin ȝe wonen in þatᵗ won · þere wante is ofᵗ goodus,
þanne, seggus, semeþ hitᵗ nouhtᵗ · þat ȝe so wirchen 1104
For sake ofᵗ þe same god · þatᵗ sittus in blisse.
þere-for to wo þatᵗ is wers · wenden ȝe schulle,
Whanne ȝe parten fro þis paine · þat pinncheþ ȝou here.   *Ye shall suffer pain hereafter.*
þanne be ȝe men vp-on molde · mostᵗ to be-wepe, 1108
þatᵗ here to schame ben schape · & ay schulle aftur.
Ȝitᵗ wolen wikkede men · in þis word glade,
þouȝ þei ben damned to dul · whan hure day endus!
Ðo þatᵗ ludus in oure land · a-losed arn wise 1112
Ȝe holde folus in faiþ · & falce ofᵗ by-leue;
Hit longeþ, ludus, til us · ȝour lifᵗ to by-wepe,

---

talia mundi pericula vestra sedes est ab initio constituta, quod extra-
nei intrare non possunt nec vos ad eos vllatenus potestis pervenire,
Idcirco vestram obseruationem laudatis, et dicitis vos esse beatos quia
taliter estis inclusi vt si exire velletis et aliorum consuetudinibus vti
minime liceret; et ita volentes aut nolentes vestram consuetudinem
approbatis. Itaque secundum doctrinam vestram vita illorum qui
in carceribus includuntur debet non modicum laudari, qui quandoque
vitam penalem vsque ad exitum patiuntur. Et bona que habere dicitis cruciatibus illorum qui recluduntur in carceribus assimilantur. Et
quicquid de malis hominibus lex nostra iudicat, vos ipsi naturaliter

It is for us to mourn for you.	& make for ȝoure mischef{t} · mour[n]inge sich*us*.
	For wers faren no folk · founde vp-on erþe, 1116
	þan frek*us* þat{t} no frut{t} han · frely to libbe.
God has decreed you pain hereafter,	God þat iuge is of{t} ioie · haþ iugged ȝou alle
	To lenge aftur ȝour lif{t} · in lastinge paine ;
and misery in the present life.	& he haþ marked ȝou men · mischef on erþe, 1120
	þouh ȝe wene ȝou wise · & wittie of lor*us* !
	þere-fore, segg*us*, as y saide · for sake of{t} ȝour dedus
	Mede mowe ȝe of{t} god · in no man*ere* fonge ;
	ȝe ben vn-blessed of{t} lif{t} · for, burn*us*, y warne 1124
Your deeds are but misery to you."	þat{t} ȝe holden so her · holsome dedes
	Gret{t} wante is of{t} wo · & wikkede paine,
	þe whiche þe heie god*us* haten · & hure hole peple."
	Now tende we to touche more · of þis tale aftur ; 1128
Thus ends the letter.	For of{t} þis egre emp*er*our · þus endeþ þe lettere.
	Whan þis makelese man · þat most{t} was adouted,
	þe romme riden alixandre · richest{t} of{t} kingus,
	Hadde le[n]gged þere longe · & lettr*us* þe while 1132
	Endited to dindim*us* · as him dere þoute,
Alexander bids his men build a pillar of marble;	þere his burn*us* he bad · bulden of marbre
	A piler sadliche i-picht{t} · or he passe wolde ; 1135
	& þat{t} þei wrouhten a wrytte · & writ*en* þer-aboute :—
	" Hidur haue ic*h*, alixandre · wiþ myn help fare."
	Whan graue was þe gr*a*ie ston · þe grime king rydus,
and departs thence.	& alle meven his men · fro þe marke euene. 1139

How alixandre picht{t} a pelyr of{t} marbyl þere.

[*A picture.* IX.]

---

sustinetis. Unde fit vt qui a vobis sapiens dicitur apud nos iudicio reus appellatur. Uere itaque non beatitudine sed miseria potest vita vestra decorari. Sed per deos immortales iuro quod si ad vos ingredi possemus, vestra miseria derelicta faceremus vos armis et equis militaribus decorari.

Qualiter alexander fecit erigi columnam marmoream in signum victorie.

[I]Nterea precepit alexander vt in eodem loco columna marmorea mire magnitudinis figeretur, et iussit in eam hunc titulum literis grecis latinis et indicis conscribi : 'Ego alexander philippi Macedonis post obitum darii vsque ad hunc locum expugnando viriliter militaui.'

[*The following are all the rubrics from this point of the story to the end.*]

Quomodo alexander inuenit homines magnos et gigantes.

Quomodo alexander inuenit hominem agrestem pilosum et vocem habentem vt porcus.

Quomodo alexander inuenit arbores que nascebantur cum sole.[1]

Qualiter alexander peruenit ad vallem obscuram et ibi inuenit basiliscum.

Quomodo alexander non potuit ultra ire.

Quomodo alexander ascendit in montem.

Qualiter alexander peruenit ad arbores solis et lune.

Epistola missa ab Alexandro filius [*sic*] dei Hamonis regine Candacis.[2]

Quomodo regina Candacis introduxit Alexandrum in triclinium et eius figuram sibi ostendit depictam in membrana.

Qualiter alexander venit ad speluncam in qua erant dii qui sibi locuti fuerunt.

Quomodo Alexander deuicit duodecim reges.

Qualiter alexander fecit se per griffones in aere leuari.

Quomodo alexander petiit profunda maris.

Quomodo alexander pugnauit cum Rinocephalis.

Quomodo equus alexandri bucifallus fuit mortuus.

Quomodo Alexander venit ad fluuium tyrum.

Quomodo Antipater emit venenum et misit illud filio suo.[3]

Testamentum alexandri.

De vita alexandri et eius statura.

Nomina ciuitatum quas construxit Alexander.

De sepultura Alexandri.

The colophon is—Historia Alexandri magni finit felicitur Anno salutis. M.cccc.lxxxx. Finita vero die .xvi. mensis Nouembris. Laus deo.

· This and the paragraph to which it is a title have been already cited above. See p. 5.

[2] A name evidently borrowed from Acts.

[3] The story says that Alexander was poisoned by Cassander and Roboas, sons of Antipater.

NOTES.

[In these Notes, attention is drawn chiefly to a few of the more difficult *phrases* and *constructions*. For explanation of difficult *words*, see the Glossarial Index.]

1. 'When this wight found the weather to be such as he desired.' Cf. l. 922.

3. *Oridrace.* So in the MS.; it should rather have been *Oxidrace.* But the spelling of proper names is very corrupt in nearly all writings of the 14th century, and it is quite unnecessary to suppose that such a misspelling is to be laid upon the scribe. Even in the best MSS. of Chaucer, such names assume very singular forms, and we have no ground for supposing that the case would have been any different if Chaucer had written out his poems himself. Hence all such forms are best left as they stand, though it often happens that we can interpret them correctly by seeing through the disguise. Even in the Latin texts the spellings differ. We have *Exidraces* in the text of 1490 at the bottom of p. 1. In Julius Valerius (quoted in the Preface) we have " ad *Oxydracontas* iter suum dirigit."

4. *There*, i. e. where. Perhaps there are few things which cause more difficulty to a learner than his own inattention to the force of short words and particles of this kind. The whole force of a sentence frequently depends upon them, and the right perception of their value is often the clue to an *apparently* difficult sentence. This hint is applicable to the whole poem, and to all other poems. Cf. ll. 8, 495, 525, &c.

5. By some mistake, the translator gives the converse sense to that implied by the Lat. '*nulla* superbia.'

9. *Syte*, i. e. city, not site; Lat. '*ciuitates* non habent.' Cf. *selle*, i. e. cell; Piers Plowman, C. i. 5, *footnote*.

13. *Cuuus*, caves; here put for 'the men of the caves.'

18. 'He commanded to be sent to the man with his letter.' *Let sende*, commanded (men) to send, i. e. to be sent; a common idiom in this and contemporary poems; cf. l. 21, 43. See note to l. 245.

20. *Schamlese*, shameless; because he was not ashamed to go naked.

22. *Tid*, quickly; inserted to make the line run better. All words and letters between square brackets are insertions.

25. *Word*, world; a common spelling in this poem; spelt *ward* in Lancelot of the Laik, 3184. The G. *welt* preserves the *l*, but it drops the *r*.

27. *Seg*, O man. The number of words for man in this poem is considerable; and many of them are in the vocative case. Cf. *gome*, l. 30; *rink*, l. 31; *weiȝ*, l. 69; &c.

28. *Fare*, to journey, to go about among us. *To* is not used before infinitives, but only before gerunds, implying purpose. See l. 45.

35. *Happili*, by any hap or chance, haply. *Of kynde*, naturally.

50. *Wende gref þolie*, expected to suffer harm.

54. *That hem bi ferde*, that walked beside them.

62. 'Of other houses than are here we have no need.'

65. *For*, because; cf. note to l. 4.

71. 'That no death may harm us, we now ask.'

80. 'And, in order to win the world, goest so far (from home);' cf. Lat. 'discurris.'

81. 'How can you keep yourself from harm by your discernment and truth, (whilst endeavouring) wrongfully to bereave kingdoms of their kings?'

85. *Thei*, they, i. e. the gods; a sudden change of number. So in l. 100, *hur* means *their*; whilst in l. 101, *god* is again in the singular.

87. 'Since I have favour, by virtue of that grant, to become the most dreaded, I should now act like a wretch and enrage the Lord, if, for pain of any death, I were to flee from my destiny, that is marked out for me (alone), and for no other king.' *Wrouthe* and *wraþede* are past tenses subjunctive. So in l. 101 we have *sente*, i. e. were to send.

93. *Ride ferþe*, ride forth, ride away, go home.

110. 'Therefore I hasten to achieve (my lot), as my destiny is doomed for me.'

124. 'And fruit grew abundantly.' *Grow* is properly a strong verb; but *growed* is common in provincial English. "'Spec's I *growed*;" Uncle Tom's Cabin. Yet in l. 133 we have *growe* for *growen*, i. e. grown, the strong past participle.

132. 'That none should touch the trees, lest they should be delayed (in their way),' viz. by disease or death. On the verb *trinen*, to touch, see note to Piers Plowman, C. xxi. 27.

138. *Phison*, Pison; Gen. ii. 11. In l. 141 it is called *Gena* (Lat. text *gagei*, a misprint for acc. *gangen*). "Fluvius vero Ganges iste est qui nobis vocatur Phison;" Palladius de Bragmanibus, ed. Bisse, p. 2.

"There biside, withouten lees,
Hy founden a water y-hoten Ganges.
There ben Inne eles strong[e],
That beth thre hundreth fet longe;"
King Alisaunder; ed. Weber, 5790.

"With regard to the Pison, the most ancient and most universally received opinion identifies it with the Ganges. Josephus, Eusebius, and many others held this;" Dict. of the Bible, ed. by Dr. Smith; art.

Eden. The Skt. form of Ganges is *gañgá*, i. e. the 'goer,' the flowing; from *gam*, to go.

146. 'Saw men wander about on the other side of the river.'

151. *Stronde,* i. e. river; not 'strand' in the modern sense; cf. l. 165.

"Forgane thir stannyris schane the beriall *strandis;*"

i. e. over those pebbles shone the beryl streams; Gawin Douglas, Æn. b. xii. prol. l. 60.

155. *Heruest,* harvest; here the month of August; see the Latin text. In Palladius de Bragmanibus, ed. Bisse, p. 9, it is explained that the months of July and August were colder than the rest, and therefore healthier. So also St. Ambrose; p. 62 of the same volume.

156. As to these dragons, cf. Palladius de Bragmanibus, ed. Bisse, p. 10; and p. 63 of the same volume.

158. 'And grievous crocodiles, that hindered the king.' *Cocodrill* is the usual old spelling; cf. *cokedrill,* King Alisaunder, ed. Weber, 5720. This spelling was almost universal, and not confined to English; cf. Low Lat. *cocodrillus* (see the Latin text), whence Span. *cocodrillo,* and Ital. *coccodrillo.* By a still further corruption the Low. Lat. *cocodrillus* became *cocatrix,* whence our *cockatrice;* so that the common notion of the production of a cockatrice from an egg was no fable, but a fact.

171. 'The king soon commanded a good linguist to enquire quickly, in the speech of the country;' &c.

195. *Doþ for to grete,* i. e. causes Dindimus to be greeted; viz. by means of the letter.

197. *Sendeþ him-gon,* sends (a man) to go to him.

198. *Aftur him,* i. e. below him, under him, his followers.

205. 'But we little believe that.'

214. Obviously corrupt. The correction is easy; an old *w* looks extremely like *lk* or *ik,* and the word *sewe* might easily have been read as *seike,* and then turned into *sinke.* Read—'and fonde, for mi miʒht, ʒour fare to sewe,' i. e. and endeavour, as far as I can, to follow your habit of life. The phrase *for my might* is the right idiom.

221. *For,* because. 'Because I heard such a praise of your life.' The anonymous Latin text edited by Bisse (p. 85) begins at this point with the words "Sæpius ad aures meas fando pervenit," &c.

222. *In many done þinguns,* in things of many kinds; as in l. 999. *Done* is the pp. of *do;* lit. 'made,' and hence, make, fashion, kind; the pp. passing into a sb. by use. As to the phrase, it is an imitation of the common M.E. *many kinnes thinges,* i. e. things of many a kind; a phrase which has been twisted into the modern form 'many a kind of thing' by a complete inversion of the form of construction. So also, we have *alles kinnes thinges,* things of every kind, corrupted to 'every kind of thing;' and again, *nones kinnes thinges,* things of no kind, corrupted to 'no kind of thing;' and again, *what kinnes thinges,* things of what kind, or 'what kind of thing.' See further in the note to

Piers Plowman, C. xi. 128. See also note to the same, B. xviii. 298, for another example of *don* in the sense of 'make;' where, moreover, the gen. form *dones* is used.

235. 'It would not lose its light, nor burn the less,' lit. the later, i. e. less readily.

236. *Vn-wasteþ*; so in the MS., probably due to the final sound of the word *lasteþ*, which the scribe had in his mind as the next word to be written. Read *vn-wasted*, unwasted. But cf. l. 988.

238—242. This is from the other Latin text, which has—"Quapropter obsecro ut præbeas responsa quæsitis;" ed. Bisse, p. 86.

240. *Sende*, to send; infinitive. Omit the full stop at the end of the line, accidentally inserted. The sense is—'to send us tidings concerning that which we desire very readily to know from you, in order to ascertain the wisdom which ye exhibit,' lit. go with. Properly, the verb *kennen* means 'to make to know, to teach,' but it is also used, like G. *kennen*, Icel. *kenna*, in the simple sense of 'to know;' see ll. 308, 515. In l. 910 the causal sense clearly appears.

245. 'He bade (men) write a second letter concerning their life.' Observe *oþir*, i. e. second; and *lettrus*, i. e. a letter, like Lat. *literæ*.

263. *Wantede*, lacked; as in Shakespeare.

265, 266. 'But the humblest that lived might become his lord, and deal with him as with a fool that wants (lit. should want) his wits.'

275. 'With regard to the message thou sentest, (which was) to tell the truth about all the teaching of our life without delay.'

281. 'Ye have no leisure nor time to attend to my sayings.'

302. Alliteration imperfect. *Refe* is obviously a substitution for something else. The right word is *bruten*, to destroy, which see in the Glossary to Will. of Palerne, and cf. Alexander, fragment A., l. 888.

310. *We;* probably an error for *ye;* see note to l. 635.

313. 'Therefore we are seen to be sound,' i. e. hale.

314. *Hir*, here. *Henne passe*, depart hence, die.

325. 'But, by the arrival of natural decay, as the king of heaven decrees, we must fear death when the day (for it) comes.' *Cominnge*, i. e. coming, may stand as the reading; the sense is the same as in *bi ordre of oure kinde*, l. 327; and cf. *comeþ vs*, i. e. comes upon us, l. 331. These expressions answer to " secundum ordinem natiuitatis cuiuslibet" in the Latin text.

327. *Holde*, old. So also *hauter* = *auter*, altar, 728; *haþel* = *aþel*, noble, l. 856.

328. 'When our limbs lack might, and (when) we lose our (natural) heat.'

347. 'Nor do we desire to procure any man to go against them.' *Procre* was misprinted *prince* in Stevenson's edition, thus destroying the sense. *Nol*, i. e. *ne wol*, was misprinted *ne of.* In l. 366, *procred* was misprinted *proceed.* In l. 1019, it was printed correctly.

349. 'We fear no doughty one, nor any stern (cruel) deed,' i. e. attack. Or the reading may be—*ne no dede sterue*, i. e. nor to die any

death. Either sense will serve, and either may be read. As to *sterne*, cf. l. 429.

351. *Keuered*, covered. Hence, in the Latin text, *operata* is an obvious error for *operta*.

353. *Whon = won*, i. e. quantity; see l. 499. This curious word was once in common use; see Havelok, 1791, Piers Plowman, B. xx. 170. It occurs as late as in the old version of Chevy Chase, where it is spelt *wane*. The superfluous *h* in *whon* belongs to the word *wite*, i. e. *whit*, in the next line.

356. 'We turn quickly to a flood (that) is called Thabeus;' the relative being omitted. The river is called *Taberuncus* in Bisse's volume, p. 65.

359. *What so*, whatsoever, whatever. Evidently copied from 1 Cor. x. 31.

366. *Procred to goode*, procured for good, well intended.

368. 'We speak only the truth, and cease (keep silence) in good time,' i. e. before saying too much. *By time*, betimes.

371. Here *hauntep* appears to be in the singular, like *bringeth* in the next line. *That seggus hauntep*, that haunts people. More commonly, *haunten* = to practise; and we should rather read—*þat seggus haunten*, which men practise.

375. 'For we count it (poverty) as being rich, and easily find that it follows (*or* accompanies) our people till they depart hence,' i. e. die.

380. 'Because we do no misdeed, so as to suffer judgments,' i. e. to be condemned for it; cf. Latin text.

381, 382. 'We consider it as a virtue, in our land at home, that mercy is unknown amongst the men of our country; because we are never moved to shew mercy to any.' This is a singular statement, but answers to the Latin text, and is explained in the next sentence. 'We never offend God, nor any man here, whereby we should have to think about craving mercy, that God might forgive us.' We never think about mercy, because we never commit faults worthy of punishment.

389. *Galfule*. The MS. has *galsule*, but there is no such word, and the MS. rightly has *galful* in l. 668. The prefix *gal-* is clearly the A.S. *gál*, merriness, joy, generally used as an adj. and in a bad sense, viz. luxurious, lascivious. Cf. Germ. *geil*, rank, luxurious, lascivious; but occasionally in a good sense, bold, merry, spirited (Flügel). So also Du. *geil;* and cf. Icel. *gáli*, *gála*, *gáll*. In both the passages in the present poem, we must give it a good sense, viz. joyous, full of bliss, blessed; or else joy-giving, bliss-imparting.

391. *Glose you here*, to gloss over your sins here, to speak to you smooth things.

392. 'We loathe to essay all the lust of lechery.'

393. *Brigge*, probably a bad spelling of *brike*, *briche* or *bruche*, A.S. *bryce*, a breach, rupture, violation. 'Or to bring us to a violation (of chastity), so as to commit adultery.' Mr. Stevenson explains the word by 'strife;' obviously with reference to F. *brigue*, which Cotgrave

explains by. 'a canvas, private suite, underhand labouring for an office, &c.; hence, also, debate, contention, altercation, litigious wrangling about a matter.' But this is hardly the sense; rather compare *brike* in the sense of 'perilous state;' Chaucer, Cant. Tales, Group B, l. 3580. *Breke spouce*, to break espousal, is due to the (commoner) sb. *spusbreche*, i. e. spouse-breach, adultery; see ll. 787, 885; and cf. Ancren Riwle, p. 56; Ayenbite of Inwyt, p. 37.

400, 401. 'For we lighten (i. e. recreate, amuse) not our life by any wicked deed, on account of which we ought to be shamefully cut short of our days.' But this is not satisfactory. It is obvious that *liȝten* is an error for *liten*, i. e. stain; a close translation of *sordidamus* in the Latin. The Latin text also has a strange error; for *aerem* read *uitam*.

402. *Don deie*, cause to be dyed.

405. The MS. *tolk* is clearly miswritten for *to folk*.

406. *Hihten*, explained by Stevenson to mean ' honour, adorn;' a rare word. So *hiht* = improved, l. 408. And see l. 418. It is difficult to find authority for the word; but it is probably a peculiar use of A.S. *hyhtan* or *hihtan*, a derivative from *hyht*, hope. Grein gives the senses of *hyhtan* as (1) to hope; (2) to exult. To these Bosworth adds ' to increase,' with a reference which clearly shews that it was considered as equivalent to Lat. *augere*. In Spelman's edition of the A.S. Psalter, Ps. civ. 22, we find ' he *gehihte* folc his' as a gloss upon ' *auxit* populum suum.'

407. *Corn* is for *coren*, i. e. chosen, as in l. 415. *Comelokur corn*, chosen as being comelier. Similarly in l. 415, *kindeli coren* is literally ' naturally chosen,' i. e. chosen to be by nature, shaped by nature. *Than hur kynde askyþ*, than their nature requires; see note to Piers Plowman, C. i. 21.

415. ' As pleases the king of heaven.'

416. *Schine*, shun. So in l. 449, *schineþ* = shunneth.

417. 'To choose them for His children, who have changed the shapes He gave them.'

421. ' And shew themselves otherwise,' i. e. in another form.

426, 427. ' Nor make any man work our will, or serve us in worldly matters.'

437. The alliteration and l. 848 make the reading *boldus* (habitations) certain.

439. *Lome*, tool; cf. mod. E. *loom*. At least, such is the sense most readily suggested. But if it be intended as a translation of *Uascula de terra non facimus*, then *lome* may be loam, i. e. potter's clay. In l. 854, the word for 'tool' is *tol*.

440. *Owen aboute*, employ all round us.

442. The alliteration (a poor one) is on the vowels: *Al, any, erthliche*.

470. *Good of to lauȝe*, good to laugh at.

475. *Ta sain*, to say. The MS. really has *ta*.

477. *Seue sterres*, seven stars, i. e. the seven planets. We find, at different periods, three uses of this phrase. It means (1) the seven

planets, as here and in Richard de Redeles, iii. 352; with which cf. Additional Note to Piers the Plowman, p. 460 (C. xviii. 98); (2) the Pleiades, as in Cotgrave's "*Pleiade,* one of the seven stars," and in Puttenham, Arte of Poesie, lib. ii. c. 11, ed. Arber, p. 122; and (3) the seven stars in the Greater Bear, of which I cannot adduce any decisive instance, though the phrase most readily suggests this sense. The Lat. word *septentriones* refers to the Lesser Bear.

481. *Side,* wide, ample; a word retained till the 15th century. See Prompt. Parv. p. 455, note 2.

485. The translation is at fault. The sense is that the waves, however boisterous, do not eat away the sea-coast.

489. The Lat. text is clearly corrupt; and the translator is also at fault, and has given us nonsense. For in the English text, *he* can only be the wind (cf. *his* in l. 488); which gives—'the wind embraces and encloses the clear water.' He seems to have taken the reading *amplectitur,* and to have connected this sentence with the preceding one, with which it has no obvious connection beyond the reference of *illud* to *mare.* Instead of its being the *wind* which embraces the *sea,* the true reference is to the *sea* which embraces the *land.* This comes out more clearly in the other Latin text (see Preface) in Bisse's Palladius, p. 92. "Certamus etiam pelagus colore purpureo venustare, quod placidis et amicis excitatur semper fluctibus; non ferire germanam terram creditur sed amplecti, cujus multiformes pisces vagique delphini aequoris madidas undas atque saltus innocenter exercerent." It is clear that it was *this* text which suggested the mention of dolphins in l. 492.

492. 'There dolphins make a din.' Mr. Stevenson prints *diue,* against which there are two reasons:—(1) the MS. has *dine;* and (2) *maken diue* is not a correct expression. It is explained by the next line, 'that there they swim very quickly, and lash about with their tails.' The expressive word *swangen* is not mentioned in Stratmann; but Halliwell duly records the provincial "*swang,* to swing with violence," as an East of England word. Cf. G. *schwang,* a swinging motion; *schwanz,* a tail.

500. 'We much desire to go about in the dense woods.'

507. *That we the rede holde,* which we advise thee to observe.

509. *Thi pres,* thy press, i. e. throng of men, host.

510. 'Though it seem disagreeable (to you), it is not owing to us.' *Long in* must be an error either for *long on* or *long of,* i. e. along of, owing to.

512. *Balful no tened,* injurious nor vexed.

524—527. *Strondus,* streams; cf. l. 151. By the river *Erenus* is meant the Hermus (Gk. ἕρμος), a considerable river of Asia Minor, of which the still more celebrated Pactolus is a tributary.

529. *Drinkinke drawht* = drinking-draught, i. e. the draught of their drinking; not a very happily-formed compound.

533. *Oxian,* the ocean; a singular corruption. But the Latin has *horribile mare,* which can mean nothing else. Still clearer is the

sentence "Tu vero dixisti te ad Oceanum venturum et postea ad alium orbem;" Palladius, p. 27.

535. In the Latin text, for *supra* (so printed in the old edition) read *sopiri*. "Vos tartareum custodem sopiri posse pretio suggessistis;" De Bragmanis, ed. Bisse, p. 91.

540. 'Ye shew yourselves (to be) unnatural by killing your children.'

549. But ȝif, unless, except. *Alse*, also, as well.

550. *Gilte*, ye sin; see *gulten* in Stratmann. Instead of *Per dies tuos*, the translator has evidently had a text with the reading *Per deos tuos*, which is probably right; see *deos tuos* four lines lower down. Hence the sense is—'You greatly sin, O man, by example of (*or* by means of) your false gods, just as they were wont, when in this world, to act during their lives.' *Bi* here answers to the Latin *per*, instead of taking its commoner M.E. sense of 'with respect to,' as in l. 552.

552. 'For example, you may receive the truth as regards my saying, from (the instance of) Jupiter.'

555. *As a lie*, like a flame. See Piers Plowman, B. xvii. 207.

562. 'To her was lechery pleasing.'

570. 'Ye make boast of more than ye can perform.'

575. *Gol*, gold; the same spelling occurs in Havelok; see remarks in the Preface to my edition of that poem, p. xxxvii.

577. *You-silue to abowe*, to bow down to yourselves; cf. l. 675.

579. The first *liue*, meaning 'believe,' is better spelt *leue;* cf. *leuen* in l. 597.

591. Parenthetical. 'And, except each grave be fair and fine, ye think it a folly.'

592. *Lodlich* = *lothlich*, loathsome; the MS. reading *bodilech* is clearly miswritten for this word.

596. 'People know who (are they that) love them.' This is here supposed to be a Greek opinion.

601. 'On account of which the great God of heaven would be expected to hear us, (so as) to grant a man's petition when any one prayed to him.'

605. *For*, with the expectation that. *You help kiþe*, and vouchsafe help to you.

618. 'And all that men in this world should use,' lit. go with.

635, 636. The correction of *we* to *ye* is obvious; see the Latin text.

637. 'There may no boast or pride release you from suffering.' *Borewen*, be surety for, be bail for, release on pledge.

645. *A litil wordle*, a little world; in allusion to the Gk. term μικρόκοσμος, a microcosm or 'little world,' a term by which the old astrologers denoted man, under the impression that the parts of his body corresponded to parts of the universe or *macrocosm*. Hence it followed, according to the present argument, that each part of the human body was especially under the protection of its appropriate deity. For a particular application of the same principle, compare the influence of the zodiacal signs upon parts of the human body, as alluded to by Chaucer. "Euerich of thise 12 signes hath respecte to a certein parcelle of the body of a man and hath it in gouernance; as aries hath thin heued, & taurus thy nekke and thy throte, gemyni thyn armholes & thin armes, & so forth;" On the Astrolabie, ed. Skeat, pt. i. sect. 21, l. 48. And see Additional Notes to the same, p. 79; and Plate VII, fig. 19. The following passage from Gower's Confessio Amantis, bk. v, is so precisely to the point here that I quote it entire, for the reader's convenience.

> "The king of Bragmans, Dindimus,
> Wroot vnto Alisaunder thus,
> In blaming of the grekes faith;
> And of the misbeleue he saith,
> How thei for euery membre hadden
> A sondry god, to whom thei spradden
> Her armes, and of help besoughten.
>   Minerue for the heed thei soughten,
> For she was wys, and of a man
> The wit and reson which he can
> Is in the celles of the brayn
> Wherof thei made hir souerayn.
>   Mercurie, which was in his dawes
> A gret speker of false lawes,
> On him the keping of the tonge
> Thei laiden, whan thei speke or songe.
>   For Bacchus was a glotoun eke,
> Him for the throte thei biseke,
> That he it wolde wasshen ofte
> With sote drinkes and with softe.
>   The god of shulders and of armes
> Was Hercules, for he in armes
> The myghtieste was to fyghte;
> To him the limmes thei bihyghte.
>   The god, whom [that] thei clepen Mart,
> The brest to kepe hath for his part;
> For with the herte in his image
> That he addresse to his corage.
>   And of the galle the goddesse,
> For she was ful of hastinesse
> Of wrath, and lyght to greue also,
> Thei made, and seide it was Iuno.
>   Cupyde, which the brond of fyre
> Bar in his honde, he was the sire
> Of the stomak, which boileth euer,
> Wherof the lustes ben the leuer.
>   To the goddesse Ceres
> Which of the corn yaf hir encrees,
> Upon the feith that tho was take,
> The wombes cure was betake.
>   And Venus, through the lecherye
> For whiche thei hir deifye,
> She kepte al doun the remenant
> To thilke office apperteinant."

659. *Iubiter*, Jupiter. But the Lat. text has *Juno*, and it is remarkable that Gower follows it.[1] Either the Lat. text must be wrong, or else *deum* must be changed to *deam*. Cf. l. 697.

670. 'A dozen of wonders,' i. e. his twelve labours.

675. *Bollere*, hard drinker. On this word, see Notes to Piers Plowman, C. x. 194.

679. *Cupidus* is here in the dative case; 'to Cupid ye do all worship.'

682. 'And essayed (*or* followed after), whilst upon earth, that foolish fire.' Here *folie*, lit. folly, is used as an adjective. Cf. l. 688.

684. 'And kindles with the gleam all the lust of lechers;' Lat. libidinem accendit.

692. *Or any seggus ellus*, before any other persons besides. Ll. 691, 692 are due to the other Latin text—"Cererum frumenti datricem horrea ventris incolere;" ed. Bisse, p. 95.

696. The correction is obvious.

698. *He;* Juno is here supposed to be masculine, as in l. 717. 'And men say that he keeps a condemned spirit of the air, to speak wonders and foretell what is to happen, of wo or weal.' The sense of *in his worde one* is by no means clear; it may be 'by his word alone,' in which case *in* should rather have been *bi*. Or else it may mean 'in his world (sphere) alone;' only Juno was not reckoned as a planet or possessor of a sphere. *Spild* = condemned, ruined, fallen. Concerning spirits of the air, see Notes to Piers Plowman, C. ii. 127. The corresponding passage occurs in the text in Anonymus de Bragmanis, ed. Bisse, p. 95; which, however, gives quite a different turn to the passage, and makes Jupiter the god of the nose! "Jovem quasi aereum spiritum in naribus habere prætorium, Apollinem medicinæ et musicæ præceptorem palmarum habitacula possidere."

703. *Hin;* perhaps a mere error for *him;* yet it is the right form of the accusative. Cf. A.S. *hine*, G. *ihn*, the accusative, as distinct from A.S. *him*, G. *ihm*, the dative.

704. *Leueþ*, remains. Distinct from *leuen*, to believe; cf. l. 706.

708. Insert a comma after *godus; folk* is in the vocative case.

710. *That traie is to paie*, which it is a vexation (to you) to pay.

717. *Vn;* so in MS. Put for *on*, on.

719. *A swan;* evidently a translation of *cignum*, which would closely resemble *agnum* in a MS. And the text in Bisse's Palladius, p. 95, actually has the reading *cygnus*.

720. The corrections are easy; the MS. has *on vs*, where *on* is plainly not wanted, and *vs* = *vse* = use. And of course *vectus* is for *venus;* see Lat. text and cf. l. 693.

721. *On his den take*, taken in its den, i. e. nest.

732. *Mo*, more in number. *Telle*, count.

735. *Solepne;* so in MS. Read 'solēpne' = 'solempne.'

---

[1] So also in Bisse's Palladius, p. 95 :—"*Junonem* iracundiæ presidentem præcordia tenere."

736. Ill spelt. For *wile*, read *wol*. The sense is—' for every (one of them) expects to have from a man (i. e. worshipper) his own customary offering.' The passage in ll. 734—747 is not in the Latin text at the foot of the page, but it answers to the following passage in Bisse's edition of Palladius, p. 95 : " Nec patiuntur idem, si necessitas exigat, commune sibi pulvinar offerri, sed unusquisque Deus proprios flamines et sorte sibi datum munus assequitur, si tamen Dii appellandi sunt, quibus potestas non nisi in certis sibimet offerendis animalibus est data."

738. So in the MS., but it is nonsense. The right reading has since occurred to me, and is *obvious enough* when once guessed, though not easy to guess. For *y of reed* read *y-offred;* cf. ll. 711, 712, 718, 743. The sense is, of course—' Over such animals as are offered to them by men they have power, and over no other things.' The same thing is repeated below, in ll. 742, 743.

746. ' When the world fails,' i. e. comes to an end.

751. ' And every one (of them) is to pinch (*or* torment) that part of the body over which he presides, (in the place) where pain is unending,' i. e. in hell.

753. ' So many pains in the fire it will fall to your lot to endure.'

754. ' For your idle idols make you act ill.'

769. *Anȝ*, annoy, annoyance, harm ; cf. l. 816. ' It nourishes harm for you, because they hear you not.'

772. *To do wreche,* to wreak vengeance, to torment. Cf. l. 777.

773. *Aftur;* either ' after ' or ' according to '; here it is merely the former; cf. ll. 778, 781.

774. A corrupt line ; alliteration and sense are at fault. The right reading is easily seen. We have merely to insert the missing word *wreche* (cf. ll. 772, 777) after *schulle*. We thus get :—" For þei schulle wreche in þis word wirche for sinne," i. e. for they will have to work vengeance for sin in this world. Even thus, the words *in þis word* are not in a very good position ; but the same objection applies to l. 779 below, which see.

786. *Waken*, watch ; cf. *vigilans* in the Lat. text.

788. ' To you is lechery dear, and (you like) to live by stealing.'

791—801. There is no mention of Cerberus nor Hydra in the Latin text at the foot of the page ; but we find in Bisse's edition of Palladius, at pp. 96, 97, the following passage : " Tantalus est inexplebilis semperque sitiens cupiditatis aviditas; Cerberus mala ventris edacitas, cui quia non sufficit unum, terna ora collata sunt. Hydræ sunt vitiorum post satietatem renascentium fœditates; viperina corona est actuum sordidorum squalor horribilis."

794. *Foure hedus,* four heads (!). Read ' *thre* hedus.'

796. *Godus,* goods, property, wealth ; not ' gods.' So also in l. 963.

800. ' (Who) is greedy to catch condemned souls.'

801. ' And, whether he gets few or many.'

803, 804. ' For ye are famed (for being) covetous, and can never cease (from being greedy), but ever go about to acquire worldly wealth,'

805. An obscure line. Insert a comma after *is*, and another after *burnus*, thus isolating *burnus* as being a vocative case. Then take *al is* = it is all; and we get—'and it is all about (i. e. it is all done with the object), O ye men, in order to feed your body;' i. e. ye do it all to pamper the body.

834. *Ne;* so in the MS. Better *no*. On the other hand, we have *no* for *ne* very often; cf. l. 841.

842. *Enuye;* the correction is certain; see *inuidiam* in the Lat. text.

844. *Wisli*, certainly; not 'wisely,' as in l. 913.

851. *You wantus*, fails you. *You* cannot be a nominative. So in l. 891.

868. 'Wherefore let no man be pleased (satisfied) with his poor fare (in this life), nor expect to have any reward for his hard living.'

872. *Lengede*, were to remain (*or* dwell).

891. 'The custom of the world fails you;' cf. l. 851.

893. *For mischef*, on account of your hard lot.

907. *Reward*, regard; the original spelling.

916. *But*, except, unless, if it were not. The line is parenthetical.

918. *As*, according as; or, seeing that.

920. The MS. has 'tenē,' i. e. 'tenen.' But it should have been simply 'tene;' see l. 950. *Tid* is short for *tideþ*, i. e. betides, happens. 'For sometimes sorrow happens, and sometimes mirth.'

930. Read "*oþur* wise;" the hyphen was inserted accidentally. The sense is—'in yet another way.'

941—952. This passage is from the other Latin text, in Bisse's edition of Palladius, p. 102: "Quis enim aut audaciam requirit in puero, aut in adolescente constantiam, aut mobilitatem poscit in vetulo ? Multa sunt quæ visui nostro, alia quæ auditui, nonnulla quæ odoratui, vel tactui, vel sapori voluptuosa succurrunt, quibus ærumnarum quas ex labore contrahimus mulceatur asperitas; et ita modo saltationibus, modo cantibus oblectamur, nonnunquam [etiam]¹ suavitate odoris vel gustu dulcedinis aut contactus [blanda mollitie refovemur. Quorum omnium suggerunt nobis elementa materiarum, quæ etiam vite nostre creduntur esse principia. Quorum permixtione]¹ contraria humani generis structura conditur," &c.

941. *Cherched*, brought to church, "received into the church" after baptism; cf. Piers Plowman, B. i. 178, and the Notes upon it.

957. *Wonde*, fear; hence, refuse. *Won*, quantity, abundance.

969. *Wiþ oþur*, with another (seal ?). It seems to refer to *sel* in the preceding line.

971. *He dide*, he caused (men) soon to read it, i. e. he caused it to be read. *Not* 'he did read it.'

979. Insert a comma after "thee;" i. e. 'we cause thee to know and hear, O celebrated king.'

---

¹ The word 'etiam' and the passage 'blanda—permixtione' are denoted in Bisse only by dots; no doubt his MS. was imperfect. They are supplied from MS. C. C. C. Camb. no. 370, fol. 37, b.

988. *Yhanteþ*, written for *yhanted*, practised; cf. note to l. 236.

992. 'That we are (as) bold gods, to guide men.'

999. 'Of things of many a fashion,' i. e. of various kinds of things; see note to l. 222.

1002. Parenthetical. 'According as men have wisdom to know the evil and the good'

1007. The Latin text seems corrupt. The other text has—"Cur autem, quæso, visum est tibi nos continenter et pie viventes dicere Diis [Deos?], vel certe invidere Deo, siquidem justius in vos cadit ista suspicio?" ed. Bisse, p. 98.

1020. 'But (will bring upon you) harm for your want of discernment, when ye depart hence,' i. e. die.

1029. 'To relieve any one of severe hunger or thirst.'

1041. 'For every one well loves that which is like himself.' An allusion to the old proverb—"like to like," quoted by Gascoigne; or, "like will to like," quoted by Heywood. See Hazlitt's Eng. Proverbs, p. 265; and, in particular, Ray's remarks on "Birds of a feather flock together;" id. p. 90.

1042—1071. There is nothing answering to this in the Latin text at the foot of the page. It corresponds in some extent to the following: "Nam cum superbiam vestram nimiæ felicitatis tumor inflaverit, oblitique quod ex hominibus estis, firmatis Deum non curare[1] de mortalibus. Vobismetipsis templa fundatis atque aras erigitis, et immolationibus pecudum lætamini vos [in]vocari; hoc patri videlicet, hoc avo, cunctisque parentibus certum est fieri; hoc etiam tibi pyramidum forsitan promittit instructio. Quapropter furiosos vos esse dixerim, qui quod agitis ignoratis; . . . non sinitis ut miseriis vestris lachrymas saltem, quod est extremum munus pereuntium, dependamus (*sic*). Valde enim lamentandi estis, quibus inexpiabiles pro divinitatis injuria pœnæ præparantur: quarum certissimum documentum est Salmonei justa damnatio, qui fulgorem superni luminis æmulatus, quod imitabatur, expertus est; vel Enceladi sepultura, qui dum violentis ausibus aggredi cœlum manibus voluit, premitur tumulo montis igniti. Talibus remunerantur honoribus, qui se non cognoscunt esse mortales."— Anonymus de Bragmanis, ed. Bisse, pp. 98, 99.

1042. The reading *helpe* is absurd, and obviously corrupt; the word meant is plainly ȝelpe, i. e. boast. And the mis-writing of the word is easily accounted for, as the scribe's eye must have caught the last word of the next line, viz. *hele*.

1046. Perhaps corrupt. The stress of the alliteration falls upon *for*, which is not good; and the word *sorw* is suspicious. As it stands, it means—'And ye endeavour, with sorrow, to (make) your false gods hear;' and, even so, the construction is strained.

1058, 1059. 'And, it seems to us, one man much respects another, who righteously mourns for that other man on account of his sin.'

---

[1] The translator seems to have taken *curare* very literally, in the sense of to cure (*hele*), l. 1043.

1064. *Salonienus,* Salmoneus. See note to ll. 1042—1071, where the Latin original is given. Of Salmoneus we know that "his presumption and arrogance were so great that he deemed himself equal to Zeus, and ordered sacrifices to be offered to himself; nay, he even imitated the thunder and lightning of Zeus, but the father of the gods killed him with his thunderbolt, destroyed his town, and punished him in the lower world;" Smith's Classical Dictionary.

1068. *For-þi boþe,* wherefore both of them, i.e. Salmoneus and Enceladus. But the scribe has omitted the mention of Enceladus by name; see note above.

1084. *By-kenneþ,* makes known to.

1085. The MS. has "His a fledde sonde;" but the correction is easy, by help of the alliteration and l. 286.

1088. *By-set in an yle;* one here thinks of England! One reason why Englishmen "allow their lives and land" is, apparently, because they cannot easily get away! The Latin text has an especially satirical look about it; as if we are all said to be undergoing penal servitude in a prison.

1108. *Most to be-wepe,* most to be mourned for. Cf. l. 1059.

1124—1126. 'Ye are cursed in your life; for, men, I warn you that that which ye so esteem here to be a wholesome course of action is really great and woful penury and wretched pain.' Note *þat* = that which, in l. 1125.

1131. *Romme riden,* (who had) extensively travelled. *Romme* is here an adverb, and *riden* a past participle; the whole phrase forming an epithet.

1136. *Wrouhten,* should make. *Writen,* should write.

1137. According to Palladius de Bragmanibus (ed. Bisse, p. 2), the inscription was as follows:

ΑΑΕΞΑΝΔΡΟΣ. Ο. ΤΩΝ. ΜΑΚΕΔΟΝΩΝ. ΕΦΘΑΣΑ. ΜΕΧΡΙ. ΤΟΥ. ΤΟΠΟΥ. ΤΟΥΤΟΥ.

INDEX OF WORDS AND SUBJECTS

DISCUSSED IN THE NOTES.

[*Words* discussed are denoted by beginning with a small letter; *Subjects*, by beginning with a capital.]

abowe, 577.
aftur, 198, 773.
Alliteration, 302, 437, 442, 774, 1046.
alse, 549.
any = annoyance, 769.
askyþ, 407.
bewepe, 1108.
Body, parts of the, 645.
bollere, 675.
borewen, 637.
breke spouce, 393.
brigge, 393.
but, 916; but ȝif, 549.
bykenneþ, 1084.
by time, 368.
cauus, 13.
Cerberus, 791.
cherched, 941.
cocodrill, 158.
comelokur, 407.
corn, coren, 407.
dide, 971.
dine, 492.
don deie, 402.
done, 222, 999.
doþ for to grete, 195.
Dragons, 156.

Enceladus, 1068.
fare, 28.
ferþe, 93.
folie, *adj.*, 682.
for, 65, 214, 221, 605.
galfulc, 389.
Ganges, 138.
gilte, *verb*, 550.
glose, 391.
godus = goods, 796.
gol = gold, 575.
Gower quoted, 645.
grow, grow'd, 124.
happili, 35.
haunten, 371.
henne passe, 314.
heruest, 155.
hihten, 406.
hin, 703.
hir = here, 314.
holde = old, 327.
Hydra, 791.
Inscription on Alexander's pillar, 1137.
Juno, 698.
kennen, 240.
keuered, 351.

kiþe, 605.
lengede, 872.
let sende, 18.
lettrus, 245.
leueþ = remains, 704.
lie = flame, 555.
'Like to like,' 1041.
liten, 400.
liue = leue, 579.
lodlich, 592.
lome, 439.
Microcosm, 645.
mischef, 893.
ne = no, 834.
of kynde, 35.
Oridrace, 3.
oþir, 245.
oxian, 533.
Oxydracontæ, 3.
Pison, 138.
pres, 509.
procre, 347, 366.
Proper names, spelling of the, 3.
reward, 907.
romme riden, 1131.
Salmoneus, 1064, 1068.
schamlese, 20.

schine = shun, 416.
seg, 27, 371.
sende, 240.
Seven Stars, 477.
side, *adj.*, 481.
spild, 698.
Spirits of the air, 698.
spusbreche, 393.
stronde, 151, 524.
swangen, 492.
syte = city, 9.
there = where, 4.
tid, 22.
tid = tideþ, 920.
to, 28.
trinen, 132.
vnwasteþ, 236.
wantede, 263; wantus, 851.
what so, 359.
wisli = certainly, 844.
won, whon, 353, 957.
wonde, 957.
word, wordle, 25, 645, 698.
wraþede, 87.
writen, 1136.
wrouthe, 87; wrouhten, 1136.
yhanteþ, 988.

GLOSSARIAL INDEX.

[The following Index, though not quite a full concordance, is very nearly so. Though I may not have cited *every word*, I have not wittingly omitted *any*. For very common words, such as *in*, *is*, I have only supplied about a couple of references. In the case of more unusual words, I have inserted *many* references, but by no means *all*.
The following symbols are used in a special sense; viz. *v.* = infin. mood of a verb; *pr. s.* = *third* person sing. of present tense; *pr. pl.* = *third* person plu. of present tense; *pt. s.* = *third* person sing. of past tense; *pt. pl.* = *third* person plu. of past tense. In the case of other persons, the number 1 or 2 is added. Other symbols are the usual ones.
References to "Alex. A." are to the Alexander, fragment A, in my edition of William of Palerne.]

A, *emphatic*, one, 324, 706; *unemphatic*, a, 45, &c.
A, *art.* a, 45, 105, 127, 131, &c.
Abide, to abide, 982; to endure, 1061.
A-boue, *prep.* above, 116; Abouen, 1000.
Aboute, *adv.* around, 54, 122, 440; round about, 843.
Abowe, *ger.* to bow down to (yourselves), 577; 2 *p. pl. pr.* Abowen, ye bow down to, ye worship, 675. It is *not* followed by *to;* hence *to* may be omitted in Alex. A. 1167. Sometimes, however, *to* occurs after it; see *abuȝen* in Stratmann, p. 2. A.S. *ábúgan* (Grein).
Acorde, *ger.* to agree, 910; *acorde of*, to agree in, 875; Acordeþ, *pr. s.* is like, 482; Acordeþ to, agrees with, 903. O. F. *acorder*.
Aday, *adv.* by day, 425.
Addre, *s.* adder, 799; *pl.* Addrus, adders, 157.
Adoutede, redoubted, dreaded, 970; Adouted, 1130.
Afore, before, 405.
Aftur, after, 778, 781; afterwards, 167, 170, 1109; according to, 652, 773; Aftyr, after, 155.

Again, *adv.* in return, 817; again, 77; Agayn, *prep.* against, 347. *See* Agyn.
Age, *s.* age, 331, 931, 936, 939.
Agrisen, *pp.* terrified, afraid, 50. Cf. A.S. *ágrisan*, to dread (Bosworth).
Agyn, again, 246. *See* Again.
Ai-lastinge, everlasting, 70.
Air, air, 699.
Al, all, 153; *pl.* Alle, 37, 701.
Alaid, laid down, put down, quenched, 888. A.S. *álecgan*, to lay down.
Aldur-fadur, ancestor, 1050.
Alegge, *v.* to allege, 220.
Aliue, alive, 557.
Almus-dede, alms-deed, 870.
Alofte, on the top of, high amongst, 134; aloft, 503.
Alone, alone, 169, 641.
A-lose, *v.* to praise, 814; *pt. s.* Alosed, boasted (himself), 1066; *pp.* Alosed, renowned, 250, 554, 822, 1078, 1112; praised (as), renowned (as), 665, 694. O. F. *aloser*, to praise; from *los*, praise, Lat. *laus*.
Alowe, *v.* to approve of, 508; *pres. s.* Aloweþ, approves of, 212; 1 *p. s.*

Alowe, I approve of, 259; 1 *p. pl.*
Alowen, we approve of, praise, 398;
2 *p.* Alowe, ye praise, 1093; *ger.*
Alowe, to praise = to be praised,
874. O. F. *allouer*, to praise.

Alse, also, 549, 562, 722, 930, 1093.
See Al-so.

Al-so, as, 42, 117; al-so = as, *and is found alternating with it.* See Alse.

Am, I am, 74, 75, 98, &c.

Amende, *v.* to amend, 1033.

Amongus, *prep.* amongst, 28, 353, 486, 845, 901, 1040.

And, *conj. generally* &, 4, 5, 7, &c.

Angur, anger, 660.

Anied, *pp.* annoyed, 816. *See* Any.

Anon, anon, 816.

Anoþur, another, 1058.

Answere, *s.* answer, 63, 822 (*rubric*); *pl.* Answerus, 24.

Any, *s.* annoy, annoyance, sorrow, grief, 769. *See* Anied.

Any, any, 6, 220, &c.

Apere, *v.* to appear, 104.

Ar, we are, 377; they are, 775. *See* Arn.

Aradde, *pt. s.* read, 821. *See* Arede.

Araie, 1 *p. pl. pr.* we array, 599.

Arede, *v.* to read, read out, 248; *pt. s.* Aradde, read, 821. See *arœden* in Stratmann, p. 7.

Arereþ, *pr. s.* rears, raises, excites, 92.

Ariseþ, *pr. pl.* arise, 662.

Armus, *pl.* (1) arms (of the body), 672, 674; (2) weapons, armour, 377, 521, 822.

Arn, *pres. pl.* are, 198, 338, 1112; Arne, 62; 1 *p.* we are, 1007; 2 *p.* ye are, 1097. *See* Ar, *and* Ben.

As, *conj.* as, 27, &c.; *cf.* al-so, 42.

Aschamed, *pp.* ashamed, 421.

A-seled, *pp.* sealed, 226, 1085; Aselede, 286. *See* Asele *in* Gl. to Alex. A.

Asent, assent, 1095.

Asingned, assigned, 321.

Askape, *v.* to escape, 159.

Askeþ, *pr. s.* asks, 170; Askyþ, requires, 407; *pt. s.* Askede, 55. *See* Axeþ.

Askinge, *s.* asking, question, 244.

Aspien, *v.* to espy, enquire, ask; *let aspien*, caused to make inquiries, 172; 1 *p. pr. pl.* Aspie, espy, see, 343.

Astored, *pp.* stored, 114.

At, to, 370; at, 1, 352.

Aþel, noble, 822. A.S. *æðele*, Grein, p. 50. *See* Hathel.

Atir, attire, 599.

Atiren, 1 *p. pl. pr.* we attire, 403.

Atlede, *pt. s.* essayed to go, 15. *See* Attele *in* Gloss. to Alex. A. Icel. *ætla*, to aim at.

Auaunt, boast, 570.

Auht, *adj.* good, excellent, i. e. full, complete (said of strength), 936. See *æhte, ohte* in Gloss. to Layamon, and *aht* in Stratmann; and cf. *áhtlíce* = manfully, in A.S. Chron. an. 1071. [Mr. Stevenson explains it by 'increased'; but it is not easy to get the form *auht* out of A.S. *eced* or *ge-eced.*]

Auowen, ye avow to be, ye declare to be, 671.

Auterus, *s. pl.* altars, 1045.

A-wecchen, *pr. pl.* awake, arouse, 96; *pr. s.* Awecheþ, awakes, 485.

Axeþ, *pr. s.* requires, 916. *See* Askeþ.

Ay, *adv.* ever, 334, 342, 377, 567, 1109.

A eins, *prep.* against, 82.

Bad, *pt. s. subj.* should pray, 602. A.S. *biddan*, to pray.

Bad, *pt. s.* bade, 147; 2 *p. s. pt.* Bade, didst bid, 511. A.S. *beódan*, to bid.

Badde, *adj.* bad, 1000.

Bakke, *s.* a bat, 723. Cf. Dan. *aftenbakke*, a bat, lit. evening-bat.

Bal, ball, 934.

Baldere, bolder, 582; Baldest, boldest, 1081. *See* Bold.

GLOSSARIAL INDEX. 63

Bale, harm, evil, 163, 637; misery, 333; misfortune, 808.
Balful, *adj.* full of evil, angry, 512; grievous, 714.
Balfulli, cruelly, 598; Balfully, evilly, 775.
Banke, bank, 144.
Bannede, *pl.* cursed, 808.
Bar, *adj.* bare, 6; Bare, 33.
Baren, *pt. pl.* bore, 116. *See* Bere.
Baþ, bath, 423.
Be, *v.* to be, 103; *pr. s. subj.* may be, 68; whether (he) be, 418; whether (it) be, 867. *See* Ben.
Ben, we be, are, 33; ye are, 1012; they are, 200, 794, 1098. *See* Be.
Bere, *v.* to bear, 619; 2 *p. pr. s.* Berest, bearest, 342; *pr. s.* Bereþ, he bears, 683; Bereþ him, conducts himself, 574; *pt. pl.* Baren, 116.
Best, best, 224, 831, 1086; *def.* Beste, 260, 515.
Best, beast, 300, 608; *pl.* Bestes, 105, 858; Bestus, beasts, cattle, 54, 163, 598, 619, 872; *gen. pl.* Bestene, of beasts, 611, 640.
Bettere; þe bettere, the better, 404.
Bettur, better, 315; Betture, 1001; Betur, 103, 934; Beture, 962.
Be-wepe, *ger.* to lament, i. e. to be lamented over, 1108. *See* By-wepe.
Bi, by, 325, 327; beside, 54, 144, 152; as regards, respecting, with regard to, 209, 550; By, 560.
Bi, *for* Be, ye are, 636.
Bi, *an error for* Mi, my, 214. *See* Miȝht.
Bicliptb, *pr. s.* beclips, embraces, 489.
Bidde, *pr. pl. subj.* may ask, 68; 1 *p. pr. pl.* we ask, 239; *pr. s.* Biddeþ, prays, 613.
Bigat, *pt. s.* begat, 194; By-gat, 825, 1083.
Biggede, *pt. s.* built, pitched, 144. Cf. Dan. *bygge*, to build.
Bi-holden, *ger.* to behold, 46.
Bi-hote, 1 *p. s. pr.* I promise, 227. A.S. *behátan.*
Bihouus, *pr. s.* it behoves, 856.

Bileue, belief, 272.
Bi-reue, *v.* to deprive, bereave, 31; *ger.* rob, 82.
Biseche, 1 *p. s. pr.* I beseech, 206.
Bi-sette, *pr. pl.* employ, keep busy, 758. *See* Bi-setten *in* Alex. A. 437.
Bi-side, *prep.* beside, 160, 341.
Bi-þenke, *v.* to think about, 285; 2 *p. pr. pl.* ye consider, 782.
Bitide, *v.* to happen, 700.
Bi-ȝonde, *prep.* beyond, 145.
Blasinge, blazing, 523.
Blastus, blasts, 488.
Ble, *s.* complexion, 411; appearance, brightness, 523. A.S. *bleó*, hue.
Bled, *pp.* bled, 543.
Blendeþ, *pr. s.* does away with, lit. blinds, 624; *pr. pl.* Blenden, blind, 523. A.S. *blendan*, to blind.
Blessed, blessed, 624.
Bliken, *v.* to shine, look bright, 411. A.S. *blican*, to shine, blink.
Blinne, *v.* to cease, 803. *See* Alex. A. 398.
Blisse, joy, 541; *dat.* 330, 395, 1105; Blysse, 985.
Bliþure, more blithe, 411. *See* Blyþe.
Blod, blood, 611.
Blysse, bliss, 985. *See* Blisse.
Blyþe, *adj.* glad, happy, 624.
Bochours, *pl.* butchers (Lat. text *carnifices*), 750.
Bodius, *pl.* bodies, 320; Bodies, 423. *See below.*
Body, 644, 892; Bodi, 6. *See above.*
Bold, bold, 127, 713; *pl.* Bolde, 992; *def.* Bolde, 147; *voc.* Bolde, 512. *See* Baldere.
Boldus, *pl.* buildings, habitations, 437, 848, 852. A.S. *bold*, a dwelling; Grein.
Bole, bull, 737.
Bollere, *s.* lit. bowler, i. e. fond of the bowl, tippler, hard drinker, 675. *See note.*
Bone, *s.* boon, petition, 602, 764, 1049; *pl.* Bonus, 68, 768.

7 ⋆

Bonus, *pl.* bones, 594.
Boot, boat, 168; Bot, 183.
Bor, *s.* boar, 713, 736.
Bore, *pp.* born, 808.
Borewen, *v.* to bail, give security for a person, release on security, 637.
Borou, borough, town, 934.
Bost, boast, pride, 637, 1068.
Bostful, boastful, 1017.
Bote, *s.* advantage, profit, 962; remedy, 1036. A.S. *bót.*
Bote, but, except, 434.
Bourde, *dat.* jest, 469.
Bow, *s.* bough, 127, 135; *pl.* Bowus, 116, 351.
Braunchus, branches, 124, 134, 503, 729.
Bredde, *pp.* bred, by birth, 287; Bred, 175, 586.
Breke, *ger.* to break; *breke spouce,* to break espousals, to commit adultery, 393. *See* Spousebreche.
Brem, *adj.* loud, 503; *pl.* Breme, furious, 923. A.S. *breme,* renowned.
Brem, *adv.* mightily, furiously, 521.
Bremliche, *adv.* briskly (*but merely an expletive*), 134, 586. *See above.*
Brenne, *v.* to burn, 235; *pt. s.* Brente, burnt, 555; *pres. pt.* Brenninge, 683. A.S. *brinnan.*
Breste, *dat.* breast, 665.
Breþeren, brethren, 430; Breþurne, 287.
Brid, *s.* a bird, 134; *pl.* Briddus, 302, 956; *gen. pl.* Briddene, of birds, 503.
Brigge, *dat.*; *must be an error for* briche, i. e. breach, violation of the marriage-vow, adultery, 393. *See bruche* in Stratmann, p. 78; and cf. A.S. *bryce,* a breach, violation. And see note to l. 393.
Briht, bright, 923; Bryht, 521, 683, 926.
Bringe, *v.* to bring, 393; *pl.* Bringen, bring, 714; 2 *p. s.* Bringest, 521; 3 *p.* Bringeþ, brings, 372; *v.* Bringe forþ, to produce, 307.

Brod, *s.* brood, 302; kindred, 430.
Brode, broad, 968.
Brond, brand, 683.
Brouht, *pp.* brought, 430, 1075.
Broun, brown, dusky, 923.
Bryht, bright, 521, 683, 926.
Bryngen, ye bring, 719; *pr. pl.* Brynge, 632. *See* Bringe.
Bulde, *ger.* to build, 437, 1044; *v.* Bulden, 1134; 2 *p. pl. pr.* Bulde, ye build, 848.
Burde, *s.* bride, woman, 418; *pl.* Burdus, 893.
Buren, 2 *p. pl. pr.* ye bury, 593; *pp.* Bured, 775.
Burn, *s.* man, 103, 135, 175, 426, 574, 582; burn oþur burde = man or woman, 418; *pl.* Burnus, 147, 713.
Busiliche, *adv.* busily, 239.
Buskede, *pt. s.* got ready, endeavoured, 135. Icel. *búa-sk,* to prepare oneself.
Busy, busy, 426.
But, unless, 366; except, 10, 456; Butȝif, unless, 549, 571.
By, as regards, 795; by means of, 56.
Bydewen, *pr. pl.* bedew, 425.
Bygan, began, 972.
Bygat, *pt. s.* begat, 825, 1083.
Byhouus, *pr. s.* it behoves, 866.
By-kenneþ, *pr. s.* commends to, makes known to, 1084.
By-lad, *pp.* led astray, 906.
By-leue, belief, 1113.
By-secheþ, *pr. s.* beseeches, 811.
Byset, *pp.* beset, encompassed, 1088.
Bytauhte, *pp.* made over to, given over to, 1069.
By-wepe, *ger.* to lament over, 1114; 1 *p. pr. pl.* that we may lament over, 1057; *pr. s.* Bywepeþ, laments for, 1059. *See* Be-wepe.

Cache, *ger.* to catch, 800.
Caire, care, *i. e.* anxiety, eagerness, 29. *See* Care.

GLOSSARIAL INDEX.

Caire, *pr. pl.* go, 59. *See* cairen *in* Stratmann, p. 85.
Calf, calf, 612.
Callede, *pt. s.* called, 141; *pt. pl.* called, 527; *pp.* Called, 11, 138, 173, 356, 526, 799, 1004; 1 *p. pl. pr.* Callen, we call, 308.
Can, *pr. s.* knows, 932.
Care, anxiety, trcsble, 1102; misery, 679; Caire, eagerness, 29.
Carefule, *pl.* full of care, *i. e.* miserable, wretched, vain, 651; Careful, causing care, terrible, 158.
Carien, *v.* to carry, 184; ye carry, 725.
Carpe, *ger.* to talk, 179, 230; Carpen, 166, 455. Cf. Gl. to Alex. A.
Cas, case; *in cas*, perhaps, 228.
Casteþ, *pr. s.* casts, 483; *pl.* Casten, 767; *pt. s.* Caste, 480.
Catelus, *gen. pl.* of chattels, of goods, 370.
Cauys, *s. pl.* caves, 7; Cauus, 38, 52, 59, 434; people of the caves, 13.
Chalis, chalice, cup, 727.
Chariteuus, charitable, *or rather* meritorious, 894.
Chase, 1 *p. s. pr.* endeavour, *lit.* chase, pursue, 110.
Chaste, *adj.* 892.
Chaste, *v.* to chasten, 379.
Chaunce, chance, opportunity, 1001; fortune, 110; destiny, 1080.
Chaungeþ, *pr. s.* changes, 922; Chaunge, ye change, 569; *pr. pl.* Chaungen, 96; *pt. pl. subj.* Chaungede, should change, were to change, 417.
Chef, *adj.* chief, 107, 1080.
Cherched, *pp.* churched, *i. e.* brought to church to be baptised, 941.
Chere, *s.* cheer, face, look, cheerfulness, 83, 411, 727.
Chese, *v.* to choose, 941, 1001; *pt. s.* Ches, chose, 107; *ger.* Chese, to choose, 417.
Cheue, *ger.* to achieve, to succeed, 110.
Children, 53, 417.

ALEXANDER.

Chois, choice, 894; *pl.* Choisus, 997.
Chois, *adj.* choice, precious, 727.
Chose, *pp.* chosen to be, 1080.
Claime, *v.* to claim, 1003; *ger.* Claimen, 899; ye claim, 1013. *See* Clameþ.
Clameþ, *pr. s.* claims, 625.
Clanly, *adv.* cleanly, 833; purely, 629; Clanliche, cleanly, 288.
Clene, *adj.* clean, pure, true, 1003; clean, 496; pure, 623, 899.
Clene, *adv.* clean, entirely, 1099.
Clene-mindede, *pl.* pure in mind, 626.
Clennesse, cleanness, 625.
Clepeþ, *pr. s.* calls, 625; *pp.* Cleped, 636, 1003.
Clere, clear, 489.
Clergie, learning, 899.
Cleuen, ye cleave; *cleuen in*, cleave to, 636.
Closeþ, *pr. s.* closes, encloses, 489.
Cloþ, cloth, 402.
Cloþus, *s. pl.* clothes, 1013.
Cloudus, clouds, 118.
Cocodrillus, crocodiles, 158. See the note.
Cof, *adv.* quickly, soon, 42, 247. A.S. *caf*, prompt; Grein.
Cofli, *adv.* quickly, 48, 125; Cofliche, 64; Cofly, 1037, 1076.
Cold, *s.* cold, 331.
Colour, colour, 482.
Comaundede, *pl. s.* commanded, 125.
Come, *v.* to come; *come schal*, is to come, 363; *ger.* Come, 166; Come, ye come, 1012; *pr. s.* Comeþ, comes, 331, 436, 1102; it befals, 833; *no comeþ*, comes not, 905; 2 *p. s. pr. subj.* Come, mayst come, 29; *pt. pl.* Come, came, 818; *pp.* Come, 247.
Comeliche, comely, 730.
Comelokur, comelier, 407, 414.
Comine, common, 715; *comine peple*, people in general, the world at large, 875.
Cominnge, *s.* coming, due course, 325. (*Reading uncertain.*)

GLOSSARIAL INDEX.

Conne, *pr. s. subj.* may know, 571.
Conquerour, conqueror, 26, 60.
Conscience, 903; Consience, 767, 987.
Contre, country, 4; *pl.* Contres, 26.
Coren, *pp.* chosen, 415. *See below.*
Corn, *pp.* chosen; *comelokur corn,* chosen as comelier, 407; *kindeli coren,* chosen by nature, 415. *Coren* is the *pp.* of Chese, q. v.
Corn, corn, 725.
Corone, crown, 978.
Corsed, *pp.* cursed, 730, 1023; Corsede, 679, 1037; *pl.* Corsede, 767, 800.
Cortais, *adj.* courteous, 64; cortais i-kid = known to be courteous, famous for courtesy.
Coruen, *pp.* carved, *i. e.* shaped, made, 431.
Cost, *s.* coast, country, 141.
Costom, custom, wont, 504, 875; Costum, 715, 725; *pl.* Costomus, 60, 213. *See* Custum.
Couaite, *v.* to covet, desire, 213; 1 *p. s. pt.* Couaitede, I wished, 179; *pr. s.* Couaiteþ, covets, 942.
Couaitise, covetousness, 257, 370; Couaytise, 1037.
Couaitous, covetous, greedy, 800; *pl.* Couaitouse, 803.
Couþ, *pp. as adj.* known, famous, 191. A.S. *cúð,* known.
Craft, skill, 410, 414; *pl.* Craftus, crafts, trades, 837; skilful works, 702.
Crauen, *pr. pl.* crave, endeavour, 414.
Crye, *ger.* to cry, 385.
Custum, custom, 833. *See* Costom.

Daies, *s. pl.* days, 76, 444, 876, 928; days (of life), 401; *gen. pl.* days', 1098; *daies time,* course of your days, 584. *See* Day.
Daintè, pleasure, 876.
Dainteys, *s. pl.* dainties, 306.
Damned, damned, 1111.
Day, day, 118; lifetime, 670, 1111; appointed time, 326.

Ded, *adj.* dead, 130, 446, 634; Dede, 595.
Dede, *pt. pl.* did, 652. *See* Do.
Dede, *s.* deed, act, 222, 380, 400, 505, 634; *and see note to* 349; *pl.* Dedes, 212; *pl.* Dedus, 584, 595, 630, 909, 999; Dedeus, 694, 1017.
Defoule, *v.* to defoul, tread upon, 1027. O. F. *defouler,* to tread under foot.
Degre, degree, advance, 931.
Deie, *v.* to die, 399, 589, 1061.
Deie, *v.* to dye; *don deie,* we cause to be dyed, 402.
Deliten, 1 *p. pl. pr.* we delight, 505.
Deme, I judge, suppose, 965; ye suppose, 834, 1007; Demen, ye suppose, 870; *pr. s.* Demus, dooms, adjudges, decides, 325; Demeþ, 589; *pp.* Demed, adjudged, doomed, 78, 85, 110, 1060; considered, 958; *demed for wise,* accounted as wise, 218.
Demere, *s.* judge, ruler, 176.
Den, den, 446; nest, 721.
Dep, deep, 1098.
Dere, dear, 176, 218, 810.
Dere, *adv.* dearly, chiefly; *dere þoute,* seemed good, 1133.
Derely, *adv.* dearly, 364, 826.
Dereworþe, *adj.* noble, excellent, 243; Derworþe, precious, 721.
Derye, *pr. s. subj.* may harm, 71; *v.* Derie, 94. A. S. *derian,* to harm.
Desire, 1 *p. pr. pl.* we desire, 71, 306.
Destenè, destiny, 89, 984.
Deþ, death, 71.
Deuelus, *s. pl.* devils, 390, 608.
Dewus, *s. pl.* dews, 425.
Dide, *aux.* did, 248; caused; *dide hit red,* caused (men) to read it, 971; *dide calle,* caused to be called, 166; Dide him, *pt. s. refl.* put himself; *dide him forþ,* put himself forward, *i.e.* advanced, 138.
Dimme, *pl.* dim, 928.
Dine, *s.* din, noise, 492.
Dintus, *s. pl.* dints, blows, 85.

Discorden, 1 *p. pl. pr.* we disagree, 222; *pr. pl.* disagree, 273.
Dismembre, *ger.* to dismember, take limb from limb, 750.
Dispit, despite, reproach, 958.
Distroie, *ger.* to destroy, 79.
Dite, *s.* ditty, story, 819; Chaucer has *ditè;* tr. of Boethius.
Diuerse, diverse, 402; Diuerce, 492; divers, 999.
Diuisede, *pt. s.* planned, 670.
Do, cause; *we do þe to kenne*, we make thee know, 979; to do, 672. *See* Dide, Dede, Don.
Doctour, doctor, 249; Docktour, teacher, 973; *pl.* Doctourus, 778; Doctoures, 217; Docturus, 798.
Dolfinus, dolphins, 492.
Doluen, *pp.* dug, 447.
Dome, doom, 984; *pl.* Domus, judgments, 380.
Don, *v.* to do, shew (mercy), 901; 2 *p. pl. pr.* ye do, 273, 649; *pr. pl.* cause, 223, 754; *don þe to knowe*, do thee to wit, 422; *pp.* Don, ended, 118; put, 1098; *we don deie*, we cause to be dyed, 402. *See* Do.
Done, *s.* kind of, 222, 999. *See* note to P. Plowman, B. 18. 298.
Doom, judgment, 1061. *See* Dome.
Dosain, dozen, 670.
Doþ, *pr. s.* causes, 505, 880, 928; *doþ for to grete*, greets, 195. *See* Don.
Douhtie, *adj. as sb.* doughty man, warrior, 349; Douhty, doughty, 422.
Doun, down, 130, 446.
Doute, *v.* to fear, 326; *pp.* Doutede, dreaded, dread, 422; 1 *p. pl. pr.* Doute, we fear, 349.
Douue, dove, 721.
Dradde, *pt. s.* dreaded, 192, 823, 1079.
Dragonus, dragons, 156.
Drawen hem, draw near, 156.
Drawht, *s.* draught, 529.
Dreche, *pr. s. subj.* may vex, may afflict, 1032. A.S. *dreccan*, to vex.

Dredful, dreadful, 156.
Drie, *adj. pl.* dry, 529.
Drie, *ger.* to suffer, 753, 857; 1 *p. pl. pr.* we endure, 291. A.S. *dreógan*, to endure.
Drihten, *s.* the Lord, 88. A.S. *drihten.*
Drinke, *ger.* to drink, 355, 757; *v.* 1026.
Drinke, *s.* drink, 1032; Drynke, 791.
Drinkinke-drawht, drinking-draught, quantity drunk, 529.
Drouhþe, drought, 1032.
Drounke, drunken, 676.
Dryen, ye endure, 1095. *See* Drie.
Drynke, *dat.* drink, 791.
Dryue, *v.* to drive, 853.
Duk, duke, 970.
Dul, *s.* dool, sorrow, grief, misfortune, mourning, 89, 130, 778, 875, 1111. F. *deuil.*
Dulfully, *adv.* sorrowfully, 390. *See* above.
Dure, *v.* to endure, 364; *ger.* to last, 78, 364; 2 *p. pl. pr.* Duren, ye remain, 634.
Dwelle, *v.* to dwell, 998; *pr. s.* Dwelleþ, dwells, 616; *pr. pl.* Dwellen, 339; *pt. s.* Dwelde, dwelt, 247.
Dwelle, *s.* delay, 276

Echon, each one, 760, 851, 1053; Echone, 626, 888.
Echue, *v.* to eschew, 1001.
Eggen, *pr. pl.* incite, egg on, 757.
Egre, eager, keen, 1129.
Egrest, most eager, most keen, 251, 975.
Elde, *dat.* old age, 943.
Eldren, *pl.* elders, ancestors, 776; Eldrene, 468.
Eldure, elder, older, 936.
Ellus, *adv.* else, besides, 409, 1019; otherwise, 421, 862, 1008.
Emperour, emperor, 24, 812.
Enchesoun, *s.* reason, 107. O.F. *enchesun*, occasion, reason.

Ende, end, 75.
Endelese, endless, immortal, 669.
Endite, v.; let endite, caused to be written, 181; pr. s. Enditeþ, endites, indites, 810, 826; pt. s. Endited, wrote, dictated, 1133.
Enditinge, enditing, 243.
Endure, v. 269.
Endus, pr. s. ends, 1111; Endeþ, 1129; pt. s. Endid, perished, 1065; pp. Ended, put an end to, 1062.
Enemis, enemies, 338, 343.
Enforceþ, pr. s. forces, 688.
Engendreþ, engenders, produces, 587; pp. Engendred, 656.
Englaymed, pp. glued fast, held as by birdlime or a viscous substance, stuck fast, 676. "Gleymyn or yngleymyn, *visco, invisco*. Gleymows, *viscosus, glutinosus;*" Prompt. Parv. p. 198, q. v.
Enoine, ger. to anoint, 410.
Enquere, v. to enquire, 148.
Ensample, example, 233, 552, 566.
Enuie, envy, 283, 373; Enuye, 842, 993, 1008.
Ere, s. ear, 948; pl. Erene, 812. A.S. eáre, pl. eáran.
Eren, 2 p. pl. pr. ye plough, 201. See Erie.
Erie, ye plough, 847; Erien, 850; 1 p. pl. pr. subj. Erie, we may plough, 293. A.S. *erian*, Goth. *arjan*, cognate with Lat. *arare*.
Eritage, heritage, 981.
Erne, v. to earn, 201.
Erren, ye err, 1053.
Errours, pl. errors, 744.
Erþe, dat. earth, 57, 70, 86, 106; nom. 981.
Erþliche, earthly, 440, 1053; Erþeliche, 360; Erthely, 849.
Ese, ease, 360, 539, 757.
Et, *for* Eteþ, pr. s. he eats, 862. See below.
Ete, ger. to eat, 757; 1 p. pl. pr. Eten, we eat, 360; 2 p. ye eat, 539. See above.
Eucne, adv. exactly, *or* wholly, 1139.

Euere, for ever, 364.
Eueri, each one (severally), 106, 736; Euerich, 751; Euerych a, every, 86; Euery, 101.
Euyl, adv. ill, evilly, 1065.
Euyre, ever, at any time, 387.
Exkused, pp. excused, 277, 851.

Fablus, fables, 1070.
Face, 408, 410.
Faileþ, fails, 509; Failus, ends, 746; pt. s. Failede, lacked, 266.
Fain, adj. fain, anxious, willing, 237.
Fain, adv. gladly, 806.
Fair, fair, 113, 716; Faire, 45; pl. Faire, 495.
Faire, adv. fairly, 572.
Fairere, fairer, 405.
Faiþ, faith, 966; belief, 1113.
Faiþful, true, 65; faithful, 908.
Falce, false, 396, 550, 638, 643, 1046, 1113; Fals, 397.
Fale, adj. many, 317, 528, 633; *al so fale*, just so many, 643, 648. A.S. *fela*, much.
Falleþ, pr. s. impers. it falls (to him), it is (his) duty, 648; Fallus, befals, 323, 326; it suits, 753.
Fare, v. to go, 330; to act, go on, 266; to travel, 28, 45, 162; to act, 397; 2 p. s. pr. Farest, goest, comest, 79; pr. s. Farus, goes, comes, 113; it fares, 237; Fareþ, fares, happens, 795; 1 p. pl. Faren, we go, 332, 1024; 2 p. ye fare, go; *ȝe wiþ faren* = ye fare with, i. e. possess, 242; pr. pl. Fare, go, 376; Faren, go, 341; Fare wiþ, go with, use, 618; Faren, fare, 1116; Fare, pp. travelled, 1137; gone, advanced, 939; *fare wiþ*, to live upon, 202. *And see* Ferde.
Fare, s. fare, food, 868, 878; condition, 48, 150, 214; welfare, 986; doings, 1096.
Fast, s. fast, fasting, 538.
Faste, adv. quickly, 51.
Faute, fault, 303.
Fauure, ye favour, 740.

Feche, *ger.* to fetch, 125.
Feden, *ger.* to feed, 861; Fede, 805; Fed, to eat, 303; *pr. s.* Fedeþ, feeds, 955, 1021; *pp.* Fed, 497.
Fel, *pt. s.* fell, 130.
Fel, cruel, 664.
Feld, field, 105, 113, 295; *pl.* Feldus, 494. A.S. *feld.*
Fele, 1 *p. pr. pl.* we feel, 333.
Fendus, *pp.* fiends, 649, 705, 1069.
Fenked, *pp.* vanquished, 339. See Alex. A. 111. From F. *vaincre,* to conquer.
Fer, *adj.* far, 939; *adv.* farther, 162.
Ferde, *pt. s. subj.* would fare, *i. e.* would seem, 105; *pt. pl.* went, 54, 163; *pt. s.* Ferde, 55; happened, 137. *See* Fare.
Fere, fear, 346.
Ferke, *pr. pl.* 1 *p.* we hasten, 300. See *ferkien* in Stratmann, and *ferke* in Gl. to Alex. A.
Ferþe, *adv.* forth, on, 93.
Fet, feet, 1027.
Figure, 600.
Fihche, *ger.* to fish, 204.
Fihs, fish, 491; Fihes, 298; Fihch, 955; Fihches, fishes, 492.
Fihtere, fighter, warrior, 664.
Fihtinge, *pres. pt.* fighting, 79; 2 *p. s. pr.* Fihtest, fightest, 341.
Fillen, *pr. pl.* fill, 317, 795; 2 *p.* ye fill, 538.
Fin, *adj.* fine, grand, 591, 600, 1015.
Finden, *v.* to find, 1070; *ger.* Finde, 204; *pr. s.* Findeþ, supplies, 352; 1 *p. pl.* Finde, we find, 303; Finden, 962; we procure (what we want), 375; 2 *p.* Finde, ye find, 865; *pr. s. subj.* may find, 232; 1 *p.* I may find, 211.
Fingrus, *s. pl.* fingers, 332, 1015.
Finnede, *pp.* finned, furnished with fins, 298.
Fir, *s.* fire, 136, 753, 1069; Fur, 682.
Fir-hil, fire-hill, hill of fire; *it should rather be* fir-helle, *i. e.* hell of fire, 1069.
Fiȝhte, *ger.* to fight, 29, 37.

Fle, *ger.* to flee, 334.
Flech, flesh, 339, 688, 861.
Flechliche, fleshly, 334.
Fledde, 1 *p. s. pt. subj.* were to flee from, 89.
Fletinge, *pr. part.* swimming, 491. A.S. *fleótan,* to float, swim; see *fleoten* in Stratmann, *p.* 173.
Flod, *s.* flood, 531, 1023; *and rubric to l.* 137; 138, 146.
Flourus, *pl.* flowers, 495, 730.
Fode, food, 202, 298, 352, 354, 450, 860.
Fol, *s.* fool, 266; *pl.* Folus, 627, 1113.
Folewe, *v.* to follow, 232, 874; *pr. s.* Foleweþ, follows, remains with, 376; Folweþ, follows, 155; *pl.* Folewen, follow, 528.
Folie, folly, 591, 686, 880, 966; *pl.* Folies, 633; Foliuus, 806.
Folie, *adj.* foolish, 682.
Folk, folk, people, 37, 111, 146.
Folliche, foolish, 603, 740.
Fom, foam, 204, 491.
Fon, *s. pl.* foes, 339, 342, 346, 397.
Fonde, *v.* to endeavour, 214, 301 401, 567; to endeavour to fulfil, 528; Fonden, to endeavour, 874; *pr. s.* Fondes, attempts, endeavours, 112; *ger.* Fonden, to endeavour to fulfil, 457; 2 *p. pl. pr.* Fonde, try, try to achieve, 538; Fonden, ye endeavour, 643; ye seek after, 787, 871; 2 *p. s. pr. subj.* Fonde, mayst attempt, 37; *pr. s. subj.* fonde he fewe othur fale, whether he may seek after (*i. e.* obtain) few or many, 801. A.S. *fandian,* to seek after, prove, try, enquire into. *See* Founde.
Fonge, *v.* to receive, 1123; to receive, take, learn; *soþ fonge,* learn the truth, 552. A.S. *fón,* for *fangan.*
For, *prep.* on account of, 159, 163; *for wise,* as wise, 218.
For, *conj.* because, inasmuch as, 65, 221, 380, 654, 660, 664, 667, 669, 1092; in order that, 605; for, 31, &c.
Fordon, *pp.* ended, put an end to, 118.

Forgiuen, *v.* to forgive, 386.
For-leten, *v.* to leave entirely, forsake, 329.
Forsaide, aforesaid, 19; Fore-saide, foresaid, 113.
Forsaken, 1 *p. pl. pr.* we forgo, 377.
Forþ, forth, 1074; forward, 138; on, 939; *forþ bringe*, bring forth, 307.
Forþen, *v.* to carry out, fulfil, 570. Cf. mod. E. *to further*.
For-þi, for that reason, therefore, 110, 147, 206, 313, 558, 1068; Forþy, 910. *Written* forþei, 313, 558.
Forwes, *s. pl.* furrows, 294.
Foule, *adv.* foully, ill, 1065.
Foulen, ye defile, 633.
Founde, *ger.* to attempt, 392, 913; *v.* to experience, follow after, 392; 1 *p. pl. pr.* Founden, we endeavour, 334; 2 *p.* Founde, ye endeavour, 901, 1046; Founden, ye endeavour, 708; 2 *p. s. pr. subj.* Founde, mayst endeavour, 337; *pl. s.* Foundede, followed after, sought after, 682. *See* Fonde.
Founde, *pp.* found, 32, 152, 315, 1116; found to be, 1023.
Foundur, founder, 664.
Foure, four, 794.
Four-fotede, fourfooted, 300.
Fourme, 1 *p. pl. pr.* we form, fashion, 600.
Fram, from, 215; *see* Fro.
Fre, liberal, 953.
Freke, man, 1004; *pl.* Frekus, men, 120, 126, 953, 1117. A.S. *frec*, bold; *freca*, a hero.
Freliche, *adj.* excellent (lit. free-like), 126. (*Perhaps an error for* ferliche, *i. e.* wonderful.)
Frely, *adv.* freely, indubitably, 1004, 1117.
Frend, friend, 1004.
Friþ, *s.* frith, wood, forest of trees, 120. *See* Gl. to Alex. A.
Fro, *prep.* from, 52, 113, 480; From, 53; Fram, 215.
Frut, fruit, 116, 120, 126, 352, 953, 1117; *pl.* Frutus, 114.

Ful, full, 105.
Ful, *adv.* very, 2, 5, 113, 721.
Fulfille, *ger.* to fulfil, 563.
Fullen, ye fill, 1015.
Fulsome, *adj.* filled with food, satisfied, 497.
Fundeþ, *pr. s.* finds, 861.
Fur, fire, 682; *see* Fir.

Galful, *adj.* eloquent, 668; blissful, 389. The context in l. 668 requires the sense 'eloquent'; in l. 389 it is a mere expletive. See the note to l. 668.
Game, game, amusement, 470; *pl.* Gamus, games, 935.
Gan, *aux.* did, 121, 129.
Gay, gay, 883, 1028.
Gaynsaie, 1 *p. pr. pl.* we gainsay, speak against, 396; 3 *p.* Gaynsain, 420.
Gaynus, *pr. s.* it profits, 1028. *See* Gayne *in* Gl. to Wm. of Palerne.
Geduren, ye gather, 575.
Gentil, gentle, 23.
Ger, *s.* gear, equipment, 522.
Gete, *ger.* to obtain, get, 305; 1 *p.* I get, acquire, 84; 2 *p.* Getist, gettest, 30; 2 *p. pl.* Geten, ye get, 796.
Gien, *ger.* to guide, govern, 561; Gie, 992; *pr. s.* Gieþ, controls, 661, 670.
Gile, *v.* to beguile, cheat, 464.
Gile, guile, 748, 758.
Gilt, *s.* guilt, 386, 994, 1059.
Gilte, 1 *p. pl. pr.* we offend, 384; 2 *p.* ye sin, 550.
Gin, *s.* contrivance, 656.
Giour, *s.* guider, ruler, 703. *See* Gien.
Gise, guise, 883.
Giue, we give, devote, 305, 994; 2 *p.* ye give, 638; Giuen no of, ye care not for, 841; *imp. pl.* Giuus, give ye, 972.
Glad, 391.
Glade, *v.* to be glad, to rejoice, 472, 1110.

GLOSSARIAL INDEX. 71

Gle, *s.* glee, mirth, 789.
Glose, *v.* to flatter, 391.
Glose, flattery, 1016.
Glotenye, gluttony, 676.
Glotounius, gluttonous, 790.
God, *adj.* good, 561, 668, 690; *pl.* Gode, 274. *See* Goode.
God, *s.* property, 638; *pl.* Godus, goods, 604, 804, 987. *See* Good.
God, God, 36, 107; *dat.* to Gode, with God, before God, 476; *pl.* Godus, gods, 396, 550, 638; Goodus, 95; Godous, 772; *gen. sing.* Godus, God's, 315, 1004.
Godesse, goddess, 561; Goodesse, 690, 695.
Gol, gold, 575; Gold, 389, 1015, 1021.
Gold, *adj.* golden, 525; *or read* gold-ore, *a compound sb.*
Gome, *s.* man, 30, 83, 94, 101, 246, 550; *pl.* Gomus, 11, 522, 661, 796, 996.
Gon, *v.* to go; *sendeþ him gon*, sends (a letter) to go to him, 197. [The reading *ioie*, i. e. joy, would be far better; cf. l. 254.] *See below.*
Gon, *pr. pl.* go, walk about, 772, 883; 2 *p.* ye go, 1013.
Good, *s.* good, 30, 229; *dat.* Goode, righteousness, 989. *See* God, *s.*
Goode, *adj. pl.* good, 23. *See* God.
Goodesse, goddess, 690, 695. *See* Godesse.
Goodis, goods, property, 305; Goodus, 1103; *see* God.
Goodly, righteously, in a right spirit, 1059; well, 972; Goodliche, excellently, 246.
Goodus, *for* Goddus, i. e. gods, 95; *see* God.
Gostliche, spiritual, 772.
Goþ, *pr. s.* goes, walks, 101.
Gouernance, conduct, 568 (*rubric*).
Grace, grace, 84, 254; divine assistance, 673; ȝour *grace*, favour shewn to you, 606.
Graciouce, gracious, favourable, propitious, 193; Graciose, 1082; Graciouse, 824; Graciouce, pleasing, 954.

Graie, gray, 1138.
Graiþus, *pr. s.* prepares, makes ready, sends, 977. *See* Grayþe.
Grante (*miswritten* grane), to grant, 383. *See* Graunte.
Graspen, *v.* to grasp, snatch at (used with *on*), 502.
Graue, *s.* grave, 447; *pl.* Grauus, 590.
Graue, *pp.* graven, 1138; dug, 7.
Grauel, gravel, 525.
Graunt, *s.* grant, 87.
Graunte, *v.* to grant, 602; *ger.* 764; 1 *p. pr. s.* Graunte, I grant, 68; *pr. pl.* 709; *pp.* Graunted, 73.
Grauntinge, *s.* a granting, 254.
Grauus, *pl.* graves, 590. *See* Graue.
Grayþe, 2 *p. pl. pr.* ye prepare, 590; *pp.* Grayþed, prepared, made ready, 447. Icel. *greiþa*, to prepare.
Greden, 2 *p. pl. pr.* ye cry aloud for, implore, 606; ye pray, 764. A.S. *grǽdan*, to exclaim.
Gref, grief, harm, 50.
Grene, *pl.* green, 124.
Grene, *s.* green, i. e. green things, 502.
Gret, great, 452, 713; *pl.* Grete, 7; great men, 1012; *sing.* 124 (*or perhaps adv.*, i. e. greatly).
Grete, *ger.* to greet, 195; 1 *p. pr. pl.* we greet, worship, 274.
Gretinge, greeting, 977; *and see below.*
Gretiþinge, greeting, 254. [*Perhaps miswritten for* Gretinge, q. v.]
Grettest, greatest, 252, 976.
Greue, *v.* to grieve, 228; Greuen, 229; *pr. pl.* Greuen, grieve, 709, 770.
Grime, grim, 1138.
Grimmest, most fierce, 87, 252.
Griþ, *s.* protection, safety; *of griþ*, for their protection, 764. *See* Alex. A., 151.
Ground, *dat.* ground, 7, 10; Gronde, 119; Grounde, 447.
Groweþ, *pr. s.* grows, 931; Growus, 954; *pt. s.* Grouuede, grew, 124

(see note); *pp.* Growe, grown, 133; 1growe, 252.

Gruche, *pr. pl.* grudge, refuse (a prayer), 770.

Grym, *s.* anger, 50.

Grymmest, grimmest, most cruel, most stern, 976.

Guldene, golden, 522.

Gyen, *v.* to guide, 815; *ger.* Gye, to govern, 263.

Hadde, *s.* had, 1, &c.; *pl.* 7, 9, 41, &c.

Haddest, 2 *p. pr. s. subj.* if thou hadst, 339. *See below.*

Han, *pl.* have, 713, 1117; 1 *p.* we have, 199.

Handlinge, *s.* handling, 948.

Handus, *pl.* hands, 703, 1067.

Hap, *s.* good fortune, 749.

Happili, *adv.* by chance, haply, 35; Happily, 863.

Harde, hard, penurious, 869.

Harde, *adv.* hardly, in a meagre way, 856.

Hardy, bold, 935.

Harm, harm, 40, 46, 164; *dat.* Harme, 366.

Hast, thou hast, 28, &c.

Haste, haste, 168.

Hastly, hastily, soon, 155; Hasteli, 605.

Hate, 961.

Haten, *pr. pl.* hate, 408, 1127; 2 *p.* Hatien, ye hate, 842.

Haþ, *pr. s.* possesses, 642; hath, 47, &c.; 2 *p. pl.* ye have, 630.

Haþel, *adj. as sb.* noble person, noble, 219, 277, 348; man, 613 ; *gen. pl.* Haþelene, of noble or skilful men, 320; *voc.* O noble one, 856. *The same word as* Aþel.

Haue, *ger.* to have, 25; cf. 65, 84, 189, 277, &c.

Hauen, we have, 35, 310.

Hauke, *ger.* to hawk, 299.

Haunte, *ger.* to practise, 790; to keep company with, 565; *pr. s.* Hauntus, practises, 935; Haunteþ,

haunts, clings to, 371; *pr. pl.* Haunten, practise, 884.

Hauter, *for* Auter, altar, 728.

He, he, 2, &c.

Hed, *s.* head, 408; *dat.* Hede, 656; Heed, 658; *pl.* Hedus, heads, 794.

Heie, *adj.* high, 358, 601, 641, 1127; *pl.* 95. *See* Hie.

Heiede, *pt. pl.* hied, hastened, 51.

Held, *pt. s.* held, 815; *pl.* Helde, 1035; thought, 5.

Helle, *dat.* hell, 558, 799.

Helle-hond, hell-hound, Cerberus, 792; Helle-hound, 536.

Help, *dat.* help, 320, 733 ; army, host, 1137.

Helpe, *ger.* to help, 1029; *v.* 761; *pr. s.* Helpeþ, helps, 588.

Helpe, *an error for* Gelpe *or* ȝelpe, i. e. boast, 1042. *See* ȝelpen *in* Stratmann, p. 235.

Helplich, helpful, 673.

Helþe, health, 314.

Helyn, *ger.* to heal, 320.

Hem, *pron.* them, 16 ; themselves, 5, 10.

Hem-self, themselves, 917.

Hende, *adj.* handy, dexterous, skilful, attentive, 100.

Hendschipe, *s.* courtesy, 277.

Henne, *adv.* hence, 314, 376, 807, 1020.

Her, here, 35, 1125, &c.

Her-aftur, hereafter, 363.

Here, *ger.* to hear, 466 ; *v.* 502, 605, 979; Heren, 601; *pr. s.* Hereþ, 610; *pl.* Heren, 765 ; 1 *p.* we hear, 27; *pp.* Herd, 630.

Here, their, 8, 46, 1035, &c.

Herie, *v.* to praise, 648; 1 *p. pl. pr.* we praise, 358 ; 2 *p.* Herien, ye praise, 641, 731, 733. A.S. *hérian :* Grein.

Heringe, *s.* hearing, 948.

Herte, *s.* heart, 816; *dat.* 272, 358.

Herteli, *adj.* hearty, encouraging, bold, 95, 961. Lit. *heart-like.*

Hertely, *adv.* heartily, 613, 641, 731,

GLOSSARIAL INDEX. 73

Heruest, harvest, autumn, August, 155.
Heste, *s.* hest, 528.
Hete, heat, 328, 424, 687.
Heuene, heaven, 219, 475; *gen.* of heaven, 95, 325; *dat.* 131.
Heuys, *s. pl.* hues, 402.
Hiden, *v.* to hide, 10; *pp.* Hid, 40; *pt. pl.* Hidden, hid, 51.
Hidur, hither, 1137.
Hie, *v.* to hasten, 985.
Hie, high, 114, 435, 437, 985; *superl.* Hiest, 1018; Hieȝest, 16. *See* Hih.
Hih, high; *an hih*, on high, 848. *See* Hie.
Hihten, *ger.* to embellish, adorn, 406; Hihte, 891; *pr. pl.* Hihten, 418; 2 *p.* ye adorn, 728, 731; *pp.* Hiht, 408. Cf. A.S. *hyhtan*, to extol.
Hillus, *s. pl.* hills, 435.
Hilþe, health, 658.
Him, *dat.* to him, 727; *for* Hem, them, 416; *acc.* Hin, him (see note), 703.
Him-self, *dat.* (to) himself, 362.
Hir, *adv.* here, 314. *See* Her.
Hirde, *pt. s.* heard, 812; 1 *p.* 209. *See* Here.
His, its, 235; his, 1, &c.
Hit, it, 141, 366, 484, 485, 486, 489, 812. A.S. *hit.*
Hiȝte, *pt. s.* was named, 1064.
Hiȝþe, *dat.* height, 123.
Ho (*sic*), he, 166. [Prob. miswritten for *he.*]
Ho, who, 174.
Ho so, whoso, 1060.
Holde, *v.* to hold, 507; to observe, 213; *ger.* Holden, to protect, 435; Holde out, to keep out, 443; 2 *p. s. pr.* Holdest, hast, 532; 3 *p.* Holdeþ, possesses, 642; 1 *p. pl.* Holden, we consider, 381; 2 *p.* ye deem, esteem (as), 274, 1125; Holde, ye consider, deem, esteem, 558, 653, 1113; *pp.* Holde, held to be, 13, 176, 974; Holden, 16; kept, 687.

Holde, *for* Olde, *adj. pl.* old, 327.
Holdeus, *s. pl.* dwellings (Lat. text *domos*), 576.
Hole, *adj. pl.* whole, hale, 333; *sing.* entire, 565, 642, 961, 1127.
Holi, holy, 139, 219.
Holliche, wholly, 657, 792; Holly, 630.
Holsome, excellent, 1125.
Holus, *s. pl.* holes, 10, 434; Holis, 40, 51, 57.
Holwe, hollow, 10; Holw, 57; Holou, 434.
Hom, home, 46; *at hom*, 381.
Hondis, *pl.* hands, 683.
Hongur, hunger, 1029.
Hope, 733.
Hope, let him hope, 869; 1 *p. pl. pr.* Hopen, we hope, 363.
Hordom, whoredom, 557, 565.
Houede, *pt. s.* hovered, abode, waited about, 164. See note to P. Plowman, C. xxi. 83.
Hound-fich, dog-fish, 164.
Houngur, hunger, 1030.
Houp, whoop, call, 167.
Hous, house, 62, 434, 985.
Housinge, dwelling, habitation, 443.
How, how, 56, 887.
Hue, *pron.* she, 562, 656. A.S. *heó.*
Huge, 530; Hugeste, 488.
Hundred, 234.
Hungur, hunger, 863, 866, 881.
Hunte, *ger.* to hunt, 299.
Huo, who, 596, 943; Huo so, whosoever, 1001.
Hur, their, 407, 563. *See* Hure.
Hurde, *pt. s.* heard, 243; burde telle, heard tell, 14; 1 *p. s. pt.* Hurde, I heard, 221.
Hure, *dat.* to her, 562, 723; *acc.* her, 657, 695.
Hure, *poss. pron.* their, 16, 48, 123, 410, 418; Hur, 407, 411, 414, 733.

I, I, 65, 68. *See* Ich.
Iangle, *s.* jangling, prattling, idle talk, slander, 456, 462, 667.

GLOSSARIAL INDEX.

Iargoun, jargon, idle talk, 462.
Iaudewin, *adj.* (as an epithet of Jupiter, 659). The first syllable is obviously the O.F. *joe, ju*, or *jeu* (see Roquefort) still retained in F. *jeudi*, and derived from Lat. acc. *Iouem*, Jove. The rest of the word appears to be a mere variant of O.F. *devin*, Lat. *diuinus*. Thus the sense is 'divine Jove.' Stevenson prints *jandewin*, which cannot be explained.
Iboren, *pp.* born, 598; Ibor, 982.
Ich, I, 180, 215, 1137. See I.
Idolus, *pl.* idols, 632, 754.
I-eged, *pp.* egged on, incited, 556.
Ifounde, *pp.* found (to be), 497.
Igrowe, *pp.* grown, 252. See Growe.
I-kid, *pp.* known (to be), famous; *cortais ikid*, famous as being courteous, 64. See Kid.
Iliche, *adv.* equally, alike, 102.
I-like, like, 792.
Ille, *adj. pl.* ill, mischievous, 157.
Ille, *adv.* ill, 786.
Ille, *s.* evil, 754, 932.
In, *prep.* in, 10, 22, &c.
Inne, *adv.* within, in, 10, 435, 489; upon, 597.
Innocent, 932.
I-now, enough, 309, 318, 548.
Inpossible, impossible, 268, 915.
Ioie, joy, 502, 726, 977, 1118.
Ioiful, blissful, 659.
Ioilese, joyless, wretched, 553; miserable, 697.
Iproued, proved to be, 685.
Iput, *pp.* put, 291, 452.
Iren, iron, 851.
Is, *for* His, his, 731, 805.
Is, *pr. s.* is, 12, 26, &c.
Isaid, *pp.* said (to be), called, 100.
Isene, seen, 666.
Iset, *pp.* set, 454.
Isustained, *pp.* sustained, 620.
It, *pron.* it, 22, 68, &c.
Iuge, judge, 1118.

Iuggementis, *s. pl.* judgments, 462.
Iuggen, ye judge, esteem, 697; *pp.* Iugged, judged, 1118; condemned, 553.
Iwrouht, *pp.* wrought, made, 660.
I-ȝoulde, *pp.* yielded, given, 63.
Kairus, *pr. s.* turns, goes, 48. See Cairen, Karre.
Kallen, ye call, 651.
Kariede, *pp.* carried, sent, 1076.
Karre, *v.* to return, 986. See Kairus.
Kene, keen, bold, 536.
Kenne, *v.* (1) to know, 210, 515, 979; to perceive, 120; *ger.* to know, 48, 241; 1 *p. pl. pr.* Kenne, we know, 308, 1023; 3 *p.* Keneþ, know, 596; *pt. s.* Kende, knew, 42; 1 *p. pl.* Kenden, we knew, perceived, 257; *also* (2) Kenne, *v.* to make known, teach, 230, 278, 455; tell, 986; *pr. s.* Kenneþ, instructs, teaches, 910, 989; *pl.* Kennen, shew, 60; *pt. pl.* Kenden, have known, *or* have shewn, made known, 1051.
Kepe, *ger.* to keep, take care of, 74, 658; preserve, 686; *v.* to guard, 38, 81; *pt. pl.* Kepte, guarded, 52.
Kepere, keeper, 677.
Keture, *adj. pl.* braver, stronger, more famous, 578. See *kete* in Stratmann, and in Gl. to Wm. of Palerne. The true sense is not quite certain, and it is used in a rather vague way.
Keucred, *pp.* covered, 351.
Kid, *pp.* made known, famous, renowned, 26, 431; manifested to be, 803; begotten, 1012; bred, 173; *badly spelt* Kidde, 191; *pl.* Kidde, 581. See Y-kid. Kid = cud, *pp.* of M.E. *cuðen*; Stratmann, p. 109.
Kiddeste, best known, most remarkable, most notable, 13; most renowned, 978. See Kid.
Kide, kid, 612, 715.
Kille, *ger.* to kill, 300, 540; 1 *p. pl. pr.* we kill, 598; *pp.* Kild, 612.
Kin, kindred, 1051; *kinus nie*, near of kin, 986.

GLOSSARIAL INDEX.

Kinde, *nom.* nature, 910; *acc.* 1023; *dat.* 456, 1012, 1034; *of kinde*, by nature, 554, 905; *for kinde*, as (being) nature, by the name of Nature, 308. *See* Kynde.

Kinde, *adj.* natural, 331, 482, 989.

Kindeli, *adv.* naturally, 415, 903.

Kindus, *s. pl.* kinds, sorts, 490, 958.

King, king, 13; *pl.* Kinguus, 82, 90, 107.

Kiþ, *s.* country, land, 179, 455, 1084, 1089. *See* Kyþ.

Kiþe, *v.* to make known, shew, grant, 605; *kiþe ȝe ȝou*, ye prove yourselves, 540. *See* kiþen *in* Gl. to Wm. of Palerne.

Knewe, 2 *p. pl. pt.* ye knew, 397.

Kniht, knight, 127.

Knowe, *ger.* to know, 149, 422; to know about, 189; *pr. s.* Knowiþ, knows, 229; 2 *p.* Knowist, knowest, 77; 1 *p. pl.* Knowen, we know, 451, 844; 2 *p.* Knowe, ye know, 718; *pp.* Knowe, known, 1052.

Konne, 1 *p. pl. pr.* we can, 278; i. e. can do, 456. *See* Kunne.

Konninge, cunning, skill, 230, 583; knowledge, 905.

Kouþ, *adj.* known, famous, 578. A.S. *cúð*, known.

Kunne, ye can, 803; 3 *p. pl.* Kun, can, 763. *See* Konne.

Kydde, *pp.* born, produced, 1051. *See* Kid.

Kynde, *dat.* nature, 325; Kinde, 327; *of kynde*, by nature, 35; *nom.* 407. *See* Kinde.

Kyþ, *s.* kith, country, 173.

Kyþen, 1 *p. pl. pr.* we exhibit, make known, manifest, 504; 2 *p.* ye exhibit, shew, 651. *See* Kiþe.

Lacchen, *ger.* to receive, 70; Lacche, to catch, 298; *v.* Lacche, to catch, 298; *v.* Lache, 264, 576; *pr. s.* Lacchus, receives, 188; 1 *p. pl.* Lacche, we receive, 40; Lachen, we catch, 956. A.S. *læccan*, to seize.

Laie, 1 *p. pl. pt.* we lay, 448.

Laik, *s.* play, game, 465. Swed. *lek*, O. Icel. *leikr*, a game.

Lak, *s.* blame, 220. *See* Lakke.

Lakke, *ger.* to blame, 838, 897. Du. *laken*, to blame.

Lakken, *pr. pl.* lack, are deficient in, 328.

Lande, *dat.* land, 172, 665; Land, 174, 843; *pl.* Landus, 369.

Langage, language, 56, 142.

Large, large, ample, 113; i. e. large river, 526.

Lasse, less, 579; *lasse no more*, smaller nor greater, 704.

Last, *adv.* last, 1072.

Last, *conj.* lest, 132.

Laste, *v.* to last, continue, endure, 270, 322, 981; *pr. s.* Lasteþ, 236.

Lastinge, everlasting, 781, 1119.

Latur, *adv.* later, more faintly, 235.

Lauȝe, *ger.* to laugh, 470.

Lawe, law, 260, 379, 508, 513, 515, 1100; *pl.* Lawus, 506, 911; Lawes, 506.

Laweles, lawless, 906.

Lay, *pt. s.* lay, 563.

Lechoures, *gen. pl.* of lechers, 631; Lecherus, 684.

Lechourus, lecherous, 554; Leccherouse, 694; Lechorus, 755.

Lechurie, lechery, 788, 884, 887; Lecherie, 562; Leccherie, 681; *gen.* Leccheries, of lechery, 392.

Lede, *v.* to lead, 445; Leden, 858; *pr. s.* Ledus, carries, takes, 186; 1 *p. pl. pr.* Leden, we lead, 444, 1005; 2 *p.* Lede, 629; Leden, 1011.

Ledere, leader, 174, 974.

Lef, *adj.* dear, lief, 259; pleasant, 498, 1091; fond, 838; *lef oþur loþ*, pleasing or unpleasing, 867.

Legge, *ger.* to lay, 438, 592.

Lelliche, truly, 622.

Lem, *s.* gleam, brightness, 122; light, 234, 476, 520; flame, 684. A.S. *leóma*, E. g-leam.

Lenge, *ger.* to dwell, 1119; *v.* 781;

pr. s. Lengus, 558, 706; Lengeþ, 628; 2 *p. pl.* Lenge, 1091; *pt. pl. subj.* 1 *p.* Lengede, we were to dwell, 872; *pp.* Lengged, 1132. *See* Gl. to Wm. of Palerne.

Lengþe, length, 444.

Lengþe, *ger.* to lengthen, 76.

Lengure, *adv.* longer, 324.

Lente, *pt. s.* lent, i. e. gave, 413.

Lepus, *pr. s.* leaps, 168; *pl.* Lepen, 491.

Lere, (1) *ger.* to teach, inform, 66, 238; *pr. s.* Lereþ, teaches, 1100; 2 *p. s. pt.* Leredest, didst instruct, 850; *pp.* Lered, taught, 453; (2) Lere, *ger.* to learn, 260, 461; *v.* 216. A.S. *léran*, G. *lehren*, to teach.

Les, *adj.* false, 66. A.S. *leás.*

Lesen, *v.* to lose, 235; Lese, 322; 1 *p. pl. pr.* Lesen, we lose, 328.

Lesinge, *dat.* leasing, lying, 458. A.S. *leásung.*

Let, *pt. s.* caused; let sende = caused to be sent, sent, 18; let reden = caused to be read, 21; let bitake = caused to take, 43; *and see* 171, 181, 968.

Lettere, letter, 1072. *See* Lettres.

Lettest, 2 *p. s. pr.* hinderest, 520; *pt. pl.* Lette, hindered, 158.

Lettres, *s. pl.* letters (used in the sing. sense, i. e. a letter), 18, 20, 43, 181, 226, 245; Lettrus, 817, 820.

Leþur, wicked, 1100. See *leþerly* in Gl. to Wm. of Palerne.

Leue, (1) *ger.* to leave, let alone, 227; 2 *p. pl. pr.* Leuen, ye let alone, 946; (2) *intrans. pr. s.* Leueþ, remains, 704.

Leue, *ger.* to believe, 829; 1 *p. pl. pr.* we believe, 205, 329; Leuen, 597; 2 *p.* Leuen, ye believe, 628, 701, 706. A.S. *lýfan.*

Leue, *v.* to live, 56.

Leue, *s.* leave, permission, 293, 299.

Leue, *adj.* dear; þat ȝou leue were, that which may be dear to you, i. e. that which you most wish for, 67.

Leuus, *s. pl.* leaves, 501.

Leuyng, *s.* living, 355 (*rubric*).

Libbe, *ger.* to live, 833, 843, 894, 1102, 1117; *v.* 374; 1 *p. pl. pr.* Libben, we live, 288, 373; 2 *p.* ye live, 539, 867; Liben, 788; 3 *p.* 1087.

Liben, *for* Libben, ye live, 788.

Licam, body, 592; *gen.* Licamus, body's, 555. A.S. *líc-hama.*

Liche, *adj.* like, 1041, 1097; *adv.* like; *liche wel*, equally well, 106.

Lie, *ger.* to tell lies, 460.

Lie, a flame, torch, 555. *See* Piers Plowman, B. xvii. 207. A.S. *líg*, flame; *lég*, flame.

Lif, life, 66, 70, 76, 180, 1119.

Liftime, lifetime, 565, 681.

Ligge, *v.* to lie, 1025; 1 *p. pl.* Liggen, we lie, 446. A.S. *licgan.*

Liht, *s.* light, 235, 480.

Lihtede, *pt. pl. subj.* should light, 234.

Lihtliche, easily, 515.

Like, *ger.* to like, to be pleased, be glad, 316; *v.* to like, 404; *wel to like*, very pleasant, 926; *pr. s.* Likeþ, likes, 212; pleases, 445; Likus, *impers.* it pleases, 362, 576; *pr. s. subj.* Like; *no like*, let him not be pleased, 868; *pt. s. subj.* Likede, would please, 934; *pp.* Liked, pleased, 178.

Likful, *adj.* pleasing, delightful, 498.

Likinge, *pl.* pleasing, 949.

Likinge, wish, will, desire, 755; pleasure, 785, 887. *See below.*

Likinge, a sufficient quantity, enough to satisfy, 956.

Liknen, ye liken, 645; *pp.* Likned, likened, 802.

Lime, *s.* limb, 650, 704; *pl.* Limus, 328, 413.

Lin, 1 *p. pl. pr.* we lie, 441, 448.

Lisse, *s.* bliss, happiness, 476. A.S. *lis, liss.*

List, *s.* pleasure, desire, 189.

List, *pr. s.* it pleases, 441; 1 *p. pl.* Liste, we desire, 355; 2 *p.* List, ye please, 539. A.S. *lystan.*

Listene, v. to listen, 820; ger. Listne, to listen to, 768; pp. Listned, heard, 180, 199.

Lite, adv. little, 886, 932, 1028. A.S. lyt.

Litil, little, 168, 645, 878.

Litil, adv. little, 205, 324.

Liþus, imp. pl. listen ye, 820.

Liue, ger. to live, 911; pr. s. Liueþ, he lives, 324; 1 p. pl. we live, 270; 2 p. Liuen, ye live, 785, 1055, 1110; pt. s. Liuede, lived, 265, 562.

Liue, I believe, 579.

Liue, dat. life, 551; pl. Liuus, lives, 885; gen. pl. Liuus, lives', 596.

Liȝht, s. light, 122.

Liȝthe, 1 p. pl. pr. lit. lighten; but obviously an error for Liten, i. e. stain, 400. See note.

Lodlich, loathly, 592.

Lof, air; lof briddus, birds of the air, 956. Written for loft. See below.

Loft, s. the sky, 480; air, 474; of loft, either (1) of the sky; or (2) put for on loft, aloft, 476; on þe loft, aloft, 122. And see above.

Loken, ger. to look, 474; pr. s. Lokus, looks, 188.

Lome, s. either (1) tool (lit. loom); or (2) loam, clay (which better suits the context and the Lat. text; see note), 439.

Lond, land, 142; dat. Londe, 350. See Land.

Long, adj. long, 276.

Long, in phr. long in = long of, i. e. along of, owing to, 510.

Longe, adv. for a long time, long since, 178; a long while, 1132.

Longeþ, pr. s. impers. it belongs; a lud longeþ, it belongs to a man, 650, 1114; belongs, 458, 1110; Longus, 258; pr. pl. Longen, belong, 946, 949.

Lord, lord, 174, 316, 628, 665.

Lordliche, adj. lordly, 181, 576.

Lordschipe, dominion, lordship, power over, 76, 264, 428, 1011.

Lore, s. lore, learning, 453, 458; pl.

Lorus, teachings, lessons, 217, 224, 226, 457, 828, 1121.

Los, s. praise, 221.

Loþ, adj. loath, displeasing, distasteful, 284, 438, 460, 768, 867, 872; Loþe, hated, wretched, 1097; be you loþ oþur lef, be it unpleasant or pleasant to you, 1091.

Loþeth, pr. s. impers. it makes (us) loath, 392; 1 p. pl. pr. Loþen, we loathe, 272, 373.

Loþliche, loathsome, hateful, 1087.

Loue, love, 373.

Louen, ger. to love, 316, 404; v. 887; pr. s. Louus, 1041; 1 p. pl. pr. we love, 1005; 3 p. 596; pt. s. Louede, loved, 681.

Low, low, subject, inferior, 264; pl. Lowe, 441.

Lowe, imp. s. lower, let down, lay aside, 517; pp. Lowed, subjected, 519.

Lowe, for Loue, love, 253.

Loweste, most inferior, humblest, 265.

Lud, s. man, person, wight, 18, 106, 168, 324, 510, 515, 519; pl. Ludus, men, 56, 142, 284, 311, 355, 838, 843, 858, 1110, 1112, 1114; gen. pl. Ludene, of men, 773. A.S. leód.

Luf, adj. lief, dear, pleasing, 562, 788.

Lust, lust, 392, 555, 684; pl. Lustus, 334.

Luþur, adj. bad, evil, 272, 400, 569, 773, 946; bad, meagre, 868, 878; as sb. evil, 629. See Leþur.

Luþurly, adv. wickedly, 460, 1055; evilly, 785. See above.

Lym, lime, 438.

Lyuede, pt. s. subj. were to live, should live, 106. See Liue.

Maad, pp. made, 108, 889, 998. See below.

Made, pt. s. made, caused, 143, 413; 2 p. Madest, 527.

Main, strength, 663.

Maistrie, dominion, 433; supreme power, 535, 742.

78 GLOSSARIAL INDEX.

Maistrus, *s. pl.* masters, 108.

Makelese, matchless, peerless, 1130. *See* Makus; *and* Alex. A., 799.

Maken, *v.* to make, 852; to cause, 36; *pr. s.* Makus, makes, 879; 1 *p. pl. pr.* we make, 319; 2 *p.* ye make, 530; *and see* Maad, Made.

Makus, *s. pl.* companions, husbands, mates, 58. *See* Make *in* Gl. to Wm. of Palerne.

Man, a man, 36, 192; Men, 28.

Manere, *s.* manner, 248, 1123; Maner, 722; kind of (*without* of *following*), 734; Manere, 997; Manir, 335; *pl.* Manerus, 200, 897.

Man-kinde, mankind, 839, 914.

Many, many, 7; Manie, 26, &c.

Marbre, marble, 1134.

Marbyl, marble, 1139 (*rubric*).

March, *s.* mark, i. e. marches, boundary, country, 382, 845, 1090. *See* Marke.

Marke, *s.* march, i. e. region, country, 1139.

Marke, mark (?), 696.

Marked, *pp.* appointed, 1120; Markid, destined, 90, 109.

Massage, message, 248.

Matere, matter, 573.

Maugre, *s.* ill will, 544; *cf.* Maugray, in spite of, 895. F. *malgrè*.

Maumentrie, idolatry, 681 (*rubric*). Lit. Mahomet-ry.

May, *pr. s.* 1 *p.* I can, 285; 3 *p.* he can, 36.

Me, *dat.* for me, 109, 178; *acc* me, 177, &c.

Mede, reward, 869, 1101, 1123.

Medisine, medicine, 319, 702.

Medle, *ger.* to meddle, lie with, 893.

Medus, *pl.* meads, meadows, 494.

Meek, *adj.* sober, staid, 942; *pl.* Mek, 546; Meke, 626.

Megre, meagre, thin, weak, 889.

Mekenesse, meekness, 614; Meekness, 334.

Mekliche, meekly, 269.

Mel, *s.* meal, 304.

Membrus, *pl.* members, 707; Membrys, 644, 647.

Men, *s. pl.* men, 143, 433; *indef. pron.* one, people, folks (in sing. with sing. verb), 91, 141, 209.

Men, *adj.* mean, intermediate, 145.

Mende, *imp. s.* amend, 517; *v.* Menden, to mend, 1031.

Mene, *adj.* mean, common, 108.

Mene, *ger.* to mean, 12.

Menske, *v.* to grace, confer credit upon, 228; *pr. s.* Menskeþ, pays respect to, 1058; *pp.* Mensked, respected, 1040; 2 *p. pl. pr.* Mensken, ye worship, honour, 726. *See* mensk *in* Gl. to Wm. of Palerne.

Menskinge, favour, graciousness, mannerliness, 951.

Menskliche, courteously, 1073.

Ment, *pp.* meant, 28.

Mentaine, *ger.* to maintain, 667.

Mercy, 382, 383, 385, 900.

Meruailouse, marvellous, 210.

Message, 255; Massage, 248.

Mesure, *s.* a moderate quantity, 312; moderation, 791.

Mete, meat, 307, 312, 1031; *dat.* 859, 791.

Meuen, 1 *p. pl. pr.* we move, turn, apply, 466; *pr. pl.* Meven, move, 1139; *pp.* Meved, moved, 383.

Mich, *adj.* much, 229, 353, 1030; Miche, many, 180.

Miche, *adv.* much, 150, 500, 532, 667, 897, 1058.

Michel, *adj.* much, great, 285, 653.

Michel, *adv.* much, 550; Michil, 200.

Miht, 2 *p.* mightest, 533; Mihtest, 534; 2 *p. pl.* Mihte, ye might, 852; Miht, could ye, 887; *pl.* Mihte, might, 336.

Mihte, *s.* might, power, 328, 1003; Miht, 653, 739.

Mihteles, mightless, powerless, 732.

Mihtful, mighty, 663.

Min, my, 75, &c.; My, 67.

Minde, mind, 1014; *dat.* 285, 612; *haue in minde*, have in our minds, have to remember, 385.

Minegeþ, *pr. s.* makes mention of, recounts, 573; states, 614. *See* munegen *in* Stratmann, p. 356.
Minnge, *v.* to make mention, recount, 514. *See above.*
Minstralus, *gen. pl.* of minstrels, 702.
Mirie, merry, 927.
Mirthe, mirth, 464, 465, 726; *pl.* Mirþus, games, pleasures, 945, 1099.
Mischef, misfortune, 372; hardship, affliction, 1030; want, lack, 859; hard fare, 889, 893; evil fate, 1101, 1115, 1120.
Misdeede, misdeed, 394.
Mis-do, *v.* to act amiss, do wrong, 464.
Missed, *pp.* missed, lost, 1099.
Mithtelese, *adj.* might-less, i. e. weak, 712.
Miȝht, *s.* might, 214; *for mi miȝht*, to the best of my power; Miȝhte, 85.
Miȝhte, *pt. s.* might, could, 104; *pl.* 56; 2 *p.* Miȝt, mightest, 31.
Miȝhteles, mightless, unable, 74.
Mo, more, other, 90; more in number, besides, 732, 897. A.S. *má.*
Mod, mood, 927.
Modur, mother, 307, 586.
Molde, mould, i. e. the earth, 101, 546, 791, 839, 900, 1099; the world, 617; mould, part, 739.
Mor, more (in quantity), 742; greater, 94, 704.
More, *adv.* more, 210; longer, 322; *the mor,* the more, 1040.
Most, *adj.* greatest, 109; *adv.* most, 666, 1108.
Mosten, 1 *p. pl. pt. subj.* should have to, 385. *See below.*
Mote, ye must, 859, 895. A.S. *mótan,* to be obliged; pt. t. *móste.*
Mourne, *ger.* to mourn, 928.
Mourninge, *pres. pt.* mourning, mournful, 1115.
Mourninge, *s.* mourning, 472.
Mouþ, mouth, 951; Mouþe, 977.
Mowe, *pr. pl.* 1 *p.* we may, 290, 1024; we must, 100, 323; 2 *p.* ye may, can, 1090, 1092; Mow, 854; Mow, ye must, 858, 864; 3 *p.* Mowe, can, 478, 619, 761.
My, my, 67, &c.
Mylk, milk, 353.
Myrthe, mirth, 1011.

Nacion, nation, 149.
Nai, nay, 73.
Nakid, naked, 12; Naked, 34.
Name, name, 12, 149, 1048; to name = for a name, 139; *pl.* Names, 652.
Name-kouþ, known by name, renowned, famous, 823, 1079; Namkouþe, 979.
Namned, *pp.* named, 531. A.S. *nemnan,* to name.
Ne, not, 9, 76, 201, 384.
Ne, *for* No, no, 834.
Nede, *s.* need, 62, 614; necessity, want, 318, 857, 1036; trouble, 1094; *at nede,* in our need, 309.
Nede, *adv.* of necessity, 859.
Nedeþ, *impers.* it is necessary, 357.
Nedful, needy, poor, 879, 964; necessary, 292.
Nedfully, of necessity, 849.
Nedli, *adv.* by force of necessity, compulsorily, 149.
Neþeles, nevertheless, 267.
Nettus, nets, 297.
Neuere, never, 39, 192.
Newe, new, 22; new (messages), 1074.
Nie, nigh, near; *kinus nie,* near of kin, 986.
Nien, we annoy, vex, 995. *See* Nye.
Niht-brid, night-bird, nocturnal bird, 723.
Nime, *v.* to take, 292; *pr. pl.* Nime, take, 318. A.S. *niman.*
Nis, it is not, 894; is not, 379.
Nisetè, folly, 879.
No, no, none, 9; Non, 46.
No, nor, 120, 235, 281, 403; not, 868; no no = nor no, i. e. not any, 94.

Noble, noble one, 73; noble, 531, 823, 1066.
Noblete, nobility, 192.
Noht, not, 384.
Nolle, 1 p. pl. pr. we will not, we desire not, 344; Nol, 347; 2 p. ye will not, 1056.
Non, s. no, 46; pl. None, none, 340.
Nor, nor, 9, &c.
Norscheþ, pr. s. nourishes, 309; Norcheþ, produces, 769.
Note, s. use, utility, usefulness, 849. See Stratmann, p. 368.
Noþir, neither, 612; Noþur, nor, 612.
Nouht, nothing, 34, 998.
Nouht, not, 78, 151, 803, 1060; Noukt, 991; Nouht but, only, 625.
Noupe, adv. now, 71, 239, 583, 1007, 1068; Nowþe, 651.
Nouþeles, nevertheless, 816.
Now, 12, 1094.
Noy, annoyance, grief, 1094. See below.
Nye, v. annoy, injure, 340. O.F. nuire, Lat. nocere.

O, one, 97.
Of, prep. of (on the), 5, &c.; by, 74, 118; from, 119; some of, 126; concerning, 66, 780, 1056; out of, beyond, 1090; acorde of = agree in, 875; lauȝe of = to laugh at, 470; like of = be pleased with, 868.
Offren, v. to offer, 720; pr. pl. Ofren, 712.
Offrin, offering, 718; pl. Offringus, 711.
Ofset, pp. beset, 987.
Ofte, adv. often, 199, 452, 709, 711.
Olde, pl. old, 798.
On, prep. on, 7, &c.; in, 57, 548, 683, 721, 749; in the case of, 1064.
On, one, 794; þat on, the one, 526. See One.
On-cauȝt, pp. uncaught, 38.
One, dat. adj. alone, by itself, 548; alone, only, 698.
Onliche, only, 745.

Onurable, honourable, 194, 1083; Onorable, 825.
Onus, once; at onus, at once, 735.
Ony, any, 296, 320.
Or, ere, before, 40, 85, 468, 692, 1135.
Or ... or, either .. or, whether .. or, 359.
Ordre, order, rule, 327, 720.
Ore, s. ore, 525.
Ost, host, army, 3, 15, 533.
Oþirwise, otherwise, 419.
Oþur, other, 54, 107; an oþur, another, 103; pl. Oþure, other, 157.
Oþur, or, 310, 360.
Oule, owl, 723.
Our, our, 176; Oure, 38, &c.
Out-taken, except, 153.
Ouur, prep. over, 108, 151, 533.
Ouyrcomen, ger. to overcome, 338; Ouurcomen, we overcome, 345; Ouurcomeþ, he overcomes, 583.
Owen, pr. pl. possess, 440.
Owne, own, 745, 880.
Oxe, ox, 612; pl. Oxen, 296.
Oxian, s. the ocean, 533. [Here is meant the great river Oceanus, running round the world.]

Pacen, pr. pl. pass, pace, walk, go about, 741.
Paie, (1) ger. to pay (tribute), 710; pr. pl. pay, 716; (2) pr. s. Paieþ, pleases, 374.
Paine, pain, punishment, torment, 390, 395, 537, 553; penalty, 809; pl. Painus, torments, 753.
Painede, pp. inured to hardships, 268.
Paradis, Paradise, 140.
Parte, ger. to share, 104; v. to part, 395; pt. s. Partyd, departed, rubric to l. 1; 2 p. pl. pr. ye depart, 807; Parten, 1107; pp. Parted, distributed, 705.
Passe, v. to pass, go away, depart, 1135; 1 p. pl. pr. subj. Passe, may pass, go, 314; pr. s. Passeth, passes, flows, 140.

GLOSSARIAL INDEX.   81

Pay, pleasure, 315.
Pelyr, pillar, 1139 (*rubric*).
Penance, punishment, 807; penance, 291.
Peple, people, 4, 108, 815; assembly, 1127.
Perichen, *pr. pl.* perish, 452.
Peril, 452.
Perles, peerless, 915; Perlese, 140.
Pes, peace, 377.
Philozofrus, *s. pl.* philosophers, 457, 1070.
Picht, *pt. s.* put, placed, 1139 (*rubric*).
Pilegrimus, pilgrims, 983.
Piler, pillar, 1135. *See* Pelyr.
Pinchen, *v.* to pinch, torment, 751; *pr. s.* Pinncheþ, torments, 1107.
Place, place, land, 97, 130, 296, 847, 853; *pl.* Placus, 495.
Plain, *adj.* plain, flat, open, 495.
Plaunten, *v.* to plant, 853; Plaunte, ye plant, 847.
Plentè, plenty, 495, 1025.
Plokke, *ger.* to pluck, draw; *to plokke,* to draw (the plough), 296.
Plow, plough, 296, 847, 853.
Point, *dat.* point, state, 315.
Pokok, peacock, 716.
Pore, poor, 104, 527, 890, 983.
Poudur, *s.* powder, 1063.
Pouert, poverty, 374; Pouerte, 291.
Power, 705.
Praie, s. prey, 204.
Praien, 1 *p. pl. pr.* we pray, beg, 225; Prayen, 319.
Praiere, prayer, 766.
Praisen, ye praise, 560.
Preche, *ger.* to preach, 280; *pp.* Preched, 366.
Prented, *pp.* impressed, 256.
Pres, press, host, army, 161, 509.
Presoun, prison, 1098.
Prest, *adj.* ready, 1075.
Prest, *adv.* readily, soon, 161, 766.
Prestly, quickly, 225.
Preuey, *adj.* privy, 696.
Pride, 637.

Prince, 225, 509, 968; Prinse, 811; *pl.* Princis, 251; Princes, 975.
Pris, value, 716.
Pris, *adj.* noble, 161.
Procre, *v.* to procure, cause, 347; to insure, 1019; *pp.* Procred, turned, 366.
Profit, 1019.
Profite, *v.* to profit, 509; *pr. s.* Profiteþ, 280.
Profre, ye proffer, offer, 766.
Proud, 937; *pl.* Proude, 5, 11, 547.
Prouede, *no doubt an error for* Proude, 547; *see the word repeated in the same line.* Or it may mean "approved." Cf. l. 5.
Prouen, *v.* to prove, 937; *pp.* Proued, proved, known to be, approved, 5. *See* Prove.
Prove, 1 *p. s. pr.* I prove, test, 560. *See* Prouen.
Prow, *s.* profit, 366. O.F. *prou,* profit; Cotgrave.
Pryde, pride, 1019.
Prynce, prince, 16, 19, 111. *See* Prince.
Prys, *s.* value, esteem, 590; *prys holde of,* esteem, 937; *prys of hem helde,* thought much of themselves, 5.
Pulle, *ger.* to pull, pluck, 128.
Punched, *pp.* punished, 679, 747.
Purchas, *s.* acquisition, 807.
Purpre, *s.* purple colour, 482.
Put, *pp.* put, placed, 705, 983.

Quainte, *adj. pl.* knowing, wise, 17.
Quaintise, *s.* daintiness, pleasurableness, 950. O.F. *coint,* quaint, dainty, trim.
Quedfulle, *adj.* full of evil, 541. Cf. Du. *kwaad,* evil.
Quelleþ, *pr. s.* kills, 611; 2 *p. pl.* Quellen, ye kill, 608, 1047. A.S. *cwellan.*
Queme, *ger.* to please, 541, 608, 643, 1047; *pr. s.* Quemus, pleases, 177. A.S. *cwéman.*

ALEXANDER.   6

Queminge, *s.* pleasing, satisfaction, 950. A.S. *cwéman*, to please.

Quencheþ, *pr. s.* quenches, does away with, 950; *pl.* Quenchen, destroy, 541.

Quene, queen, 194, 825.

Quik, *adj.* living, 608; Quike, 1047.

Radde, *pt. s.* read, 819, 1073, 1076; *pp.* Rad, 969.

Raiken, 1 *p. pl. pr.* we wander, go, betake ourselves, 467. Icel. *reika*, to wander.

Rainus, *s. pl.* rains, 436.

Raþe, *adv.* soon, 2, 21, 93, 136, 337, 969; *As raþe*, as soon as possible, 121; *al so raþe*, 129.

Recche, 1 *p. pl. pr.* we reck, 369. A.S. *récan, réccan*.

Reche, *ger.* to reach, 1067.

Red, *s.* counsel, 398. A.S. *réd*.

Rede, (1) *ger.* to read, i. e. to be read, 1075; *v.* Red, 971; Reden, 21; 1 *p. s. pr.* Reed, I read, speak, 738; *pl.* Reden, we read, 467; (2) to advise; 1 *p. s. pr.* Rede, I advise, 337; *pl.* we advise, 507. A.S. *rǽdan*, to read, to advise. *See* Radde.

Rede, *pl.* red, 479.

Redileche, readily, easily, 375; Redely, 821.

Redlese, *adj.* devoid of *rede*, i. e. of counsel, 907.

Redy, ready, 789, 969.

Reed, *adj.* red; *or rather adv.* redly, 121.

Refe, to seize, 302. See note.

Regne, kingdom, 642; *pl.* Rengnus, 82.

Reke, *pp.* raked, raked over, buried slightly, 594.

Rekenen, 1 *p. pl. pr.* we reckon, account, 375.

Remewid, *pt. s.* removed, *rubric to l.* 137.

Rengnus, *s. pl.* kingdoms, 82. *See* Regne.

Renoun, *s.* renown, 369, 581.

Reproue, *ger.* to reprove, 220.

Rereth, *pr. s.* rears, 485; Rere, ye rear, 1045.

Resoun, *s.* reason, 398.

Reste me, rest myself, 93.

Reufully, piteously, 1062.

Reule, *s.* rule, 507.

Reuled, *pp.* ruled, 904, 915.

Reward, regard, 907.

Riche, rich, 104, 261, 337, 967; Richest, richest, 1131.

Richesse, riches, 31, 581; Ricchesse, 369.

Ride, *ger.* to ride, 112; *v.* 93; *pp.* Riden, ridden, travelled, experienced in travel, 1131.

Rif, *adj.* rife, full, 501; *pl.* Riue, abundant, 160.

Riht, *adj.* right, true, 261.

Riht, *adv.* right, 816.

Rihte, *dat.* right, justice, 416.

Rihte-wisnesse, righteousness, 258.

Rihtful, *adj.* righteous, just, 398.

Rink, *s.* man, 21, 31, 129, 151, 662, 821. A.S. *rinc*.

Ris, *s.* bough, 129, 501. See *hris* in Stratmann, p. 278.

Riue, *adj. pl.* rife, abundant, numerous, 160, 914, 1045. *See* Rif.

Riuer, river, 160.

Robbe, *ger.* to rob, 789; *pp.* Robbed, 524.

Romauncus, *pl.* romances, 467.

Rome, *v.* to roam, range, 146; *ger.* 501; *pt. s.* Rommede, 2; *pl.* Romede, 160; *pr. s.* Romwus, roams, wanders, 169.

Romme, *adj.* wide, 151. A.S. *rúm*, roomy, wide.

Romme, *adv.* far and wide, 80, 581; *romme riden*, much travelled, 1131. See above.

Ros, *pt. s.* rose, 121.

Roten, *ger.* to rot, 594.

Rotus, *pl.* roots, 662.

Rouh, rough, 594.

Rout, *s.* company, host, 524.

Ryde, *v.* to ride, 49; *pr. s.* Rydus, 1138; *pres. pt.* Rydinge, 2. *See* Ride.

Ryht, *s.* right, justice, 82. *See* Rihte.

Ryngus, *s. pl.* rings, 1015.

Sacrifice, 388, 542, 1048.

Sad, *adj.* firm, heavy, thick, clayey (*said of* earth), 912.

Sadliche, *adv.* firmly, 1135.

Saf, safe, saved, 830.

Sai, *pt. s.* saw, 115, 137; *pl.* Saien, 146.

Saide, *pt. s.* said, 41; *pl.* 61; 2 *p.* ye said, 1006; *pp.* Said, 111. *See* Sain.

Saile, *ger.* to sail, 297, 449; *v.* 533; *pr. pl.* Sailen, sail, 451; 2 *p.* Saile, ye sail, 203.

Sain, *ger.* to say, 475; Saie, 154; 1 *p. pl. pr.* Sain, we say, 368, 991; ye say, 646, 685, 689, 1095; they say, 798. *See* Saide.

Sake, sake, 283, 361, 559, 784, 830, 1105; account, 1054, 1122.

Same, same, 197, 780, 896, 1009.

Saue, *ger.* to save, 811.

Sauiour, saviour, 420; Sauyour, 784.

Sauouron, *pr. pl.* savour, give forth a scent, 496.

Sauur, *s.* savour, taste, 947.

Sawe, *s.* saying, saw, 42, 111, 209, 552, 646, 1096; *pl.* Sawus, 44, 459, 798.

Say, *pt. s.* saw, 187. *See* Sai.

Say, *imp. s.* say, 283. *See* Sain.

Schadde, *pt. s.* shed, 640.

Schal, 1 *p. s. pr.* must, 326; *pr. s.* is to, 700; shall, 213.

Schalk, *s.* man, wight, 20, 432, 449, 463. A.S. *scealc.*

Schame, shame, 401, 1109.

Schamfull, shameful, 463.

Schamlese, shameless, 20.

Schamly, shamefully, 809.

Schap, shape; *to schap,* in our shapes, 330; shape, or creation, 960; *pl.* Schappus, created forms, 417.

Schape, *ger.* to shape, form, 294; *pp.* Schape, shaped, formed, created, 412, 419, 809, 1109; intended, 918.

Schappere, *s.* creator, 479, 959.

Schar, ploughshare, 294.

Scharpede, *pp.* sharpened, 294.

Schast, chaste, 894.

Sche, she, 309.

Schene, *ger.* to cause to shine; *hem to schene,* to cause themselves to shine, to seem to shine, 412.

Schene, *adj.* bright, 1027.

Schent, *pp.* shamed, 809. A.S. *scendan,* to put to shame.

Schenure, *adv.* more brightly, more beautifully, 412.

Schewe, *ger.* to shew, 59; *pr. s.* Schewiþ, 463; *pr. pl.* Schewen, shew, 421; Schewen hem, shew themselves, 479; 2 *p.* Schewe, ye shew, 959; *pt. pl.* Shewden, shewed, 20.

Schinden, ye shame, disgrace, 960. *See* Shent.

Schine, *v.* to shun, avoid, 416; *pr. s.* Schineþ, shuns, 449.

Schine, *ger.* to shine, 117, 520; *v.* 121.

Schining, shining, 479.

Schippus, *s. pl.* ships, 449.

Scholde, *pt. s.* ought, 416; *pt. pl.* might, 108; would have to, 781; 1 *p.* we ought, 874. *See* Schulle, Schal.

Schop, *pt. s.* shaped, created, 330, 416, 432, 996. *See* Schape.

Schorted, *pp.* shortened, 401.

Schulle, 1 *p. pl. pr.* shall, 38; we must, are to, 322, 329; 2 *p.* ye must, ought to, 1106; Schullen, 720.

Sckaþe, *dat.* scath, harm, 81. *See* Skaþe.

Sclain, *pp.* slain, 344.

Sclepe, *v.* to sleep, 344, 441; *ger.* 535.

Sclowþe, *dat.* sloth, 344.

Scole, school, 453, 899.

Scorpionus, scorpions, 159.

Se, 1 *p. pl. pr.* we see, 399.

Se, *s.* sea, 203, 297, 481, 955; See, 91, 451.

Seohe, 1 *p. pl. pr.* we seek, 348.

Seg, *s.* man, 27, 49, 61, 206, 971; *pl.* Seggus, men, 165, 371, 580, 689, 1054; Seggeus, 478. A.S. *secg*, a man.

Segge, *ger.* to tell, 1096; 2 *p. pl. pr.* ye say, 657, 740; Seggen, 1048.

Seie, *pp.* seen, 1064; seen (to be), 313, 890.

Sel, *s.* seal, 182, 256, 817, 968.

Selkouþe, *adj.* strange, various, 475, 649; Selcouþe, 490, 925; Selkowþe, 917. Cf. Alex. A. 130.

Selkouþus, wonders, 1022. See above.

Seme, *v.* to seem, 405, 414; 1 *p. pl. pr.* Semen, we seem, 33; *pr. s.* Semeþ, it seems, 840; Semus, 929; 2 *p. pl.* Semen, ye seem, 890; *pr. s. subj.* Seme, may seem (to be), 231.

Semliche, *adj.* seemly, 111, 115.

Sen, *v.* to see, 478, 481; 1 *p. pl. pr.* we see, 475, 947, 1022.

Sende, *v.* to send, 18, 225; *imp. s.* Send, 207; *pr. s.* Sendeþ, sends, 197, 253; *pt. s. subj.* Sente, were to send, sent, 101; *pt. s.* Sente, sent, 361, 817; Sendyd, 973 (*rubric*); 2 *p.* Sentest, didst send, 255, 828; Senteste, 275; *pp.* Sent, 131, 511; Sente, 41.

Sengle, single, i. e. simple, 33.

Sertaine, certain, 321.

Sertefied, certified, made known, 27.

Sertus, *adv.* certes, certainly, 73, 177.

Seruantis, *s. pl.* servants, 362, 577; Seruauntus, 100.

Serue, *ger.* to serve, 316, 708; *v.* 427; *pr. pl.* serve, 797; 2 *p.* ye serve, 632; *subj.* Serue, may serve, 735.

Sese, *v.* to cease, 336; *ger.* to make to cease, put a bound to, 1037; *pr. s.* Seseþ, ceaseth, leaves off, i. e. becomes quiet, 91; 1 *p. pl. pr.* Sesen, we cease, 368, 471; *pt. s.* Sesede, ceased, 117; *pl.* Seseden, 119.

Sesoun, season, 154, 929; *pl.* Sesounus, 925.

Sete, *s.* seat, place, 988.

Seþ, *pr. s.* see, 91. *See* Sen.

Sette, *v.* to set, put, 295; *ger.* Sette, to plant, 912; *pr. s.* Settus, sets, 182; *pp.* Set, set, placed, 477, 481.

Seue, seven, 477.

Sew, *pt. s.* sowed, 692.

Seye, *pp.* seen, 1074. *See* Seie.

Sichus, *s. pl.* sighs, 1115.

Side, side, part, 86, 297.

Side, *adj.* large, ample, wide, 165, 481.

Sien, *pt. pl.* saw, 49; Sie, 126; 1 *p.* Sihen, we saw, 256.

Sience, science, 454.

Sihen; *see* Sien.

Siht, sight, 929.

Sike, *adj. pl.* sick, 313.

Sikur, *adj.* sure, 75.

Sikurede, *pt. s.* secured, i. e. assured, made them assured, 44.

Silf, self, selves, 33, 61, 75, 873, 1009; Silue, 454. *See* Vs.

Siluer, silver, 389, 575.

Simple, simple, poor men, 288; simple, 580; foolish, 873, 890; innocent, 459; easily pleased, 933.

Simpleliche, simply, in a simple way, 290.

Sin, since, 87, 99, 895, 914, 953, 963, 1103. *See* Syn.

Sinful, a sinful man, sinner, 1064.

Sinke, *an error for* Siwe *or* Sewe, to follow, 214. [To mistake *w* for *nk* or *uk* was very easy.]

Sinne, sin, 336, 406, 987.

Sinne, *ger.* to sin, 505.

Sire, sir, 225.

Siþen, afterwards, next, 47, 131, 478, 480.

Sittus, *pr. s.* sits, 1105; 1 *p. pl.* Sitte, we sit, 988.

Siȝht, sight, 119.

Skapen, ye escape, 1020.

Skarsete, scarcity, 871.

Skaþe, harm, damage, 159, 871, 990, 1020.

Skile, discernment, reason, 904, 1100; skill, 81.
Skiuus, *s. pl.* skies, 478.
Slepe, 1 *p. pl. pr.* we sleep, 359.
Slithe, *dat.* sleight, 564.
Slyhþe, *dat.* sleight, 301.
Smart, *adj.* causing pain, painful; *or perhaps* swift, quick, 1063.
Smellus, *s. pl.* smells, 949.
Smeþe, smooth, 1063.
Smite, *pp.* smitten, 1063.
Snelle, *pl.* quick, 437.
So, so, 49, 420, &c.
Sodainly, suddenly, 399.
Soffre, *v.* to suffer, 635; 2 *p. pl. pr.* ye suffer, 784.
Sofisen, *pr. pl.* suffice, 61.
Soile, *v.* to soil, 336.
Solas, solace, amusements, 471, 933.
Solepne, *for* Solempne, solemn, 735.
Solow, *s.* plough, 295. A.S. *sulh*, a plough.
Somerus, summers, 8.
Somme, *s.* sum, amount, 321.
Sonde, sending, i. e. message, 21, 41, 184, 511, 810, 826, 882, 967, 1006; *pl.* Sondus, messages, commands, 842; gifts, 959.
Sone, son, 616.
Sone, soon, 19, 817; *al so sone*, as soon, 117.
Song, song, 503.
Sonken, *pt. pl.* sunk, 119.
Sonne, sun, 115, 424, 477.
Sorw, sorrow, 1046. [But apparently corrupt.]
Sorwe, sorrow, 624, 877.
Sorwen, 1 *p. pl. pr.* we sorrow, 471.
Sorwful, *adj.* miserable, disastrous, 763, 835; sorry, 724; bringing penalty, 559.
Sory, wretched, 632, 639; miserable, 1042.
Sostaine, *ger.* to sustain, 917; *v.* 290.
Sote, *adj. pl. or adv.* sweet, or sweetly, 496.

Sote-sauerede, *pp.* sweet-savoured, 128.
Soþ, *s.* truth, 27, 44, 368; the truth, 451, 459; Soþe, 207; *pl.* Soþus, truths, 1022.
Soþli, *adv.* verily, truly, 9, 41; Soþliche, 100, 616; Soþly, 882.
Soueraine, *adj.* sovereign, 811; Souorain, 542.
Soule, soul, 329, 1021; *pl.* Soulus, 800; Soulen, 633.
Sounde, *adj. pl.* in good health, 313.
Southte (*for* Souchte), *pt. pl.* sought, 19.
Sowe, *ger.* to sow, 912; *v.* 295.
Space, space, duration, 885.
Spak, spake, 667.
Sparclus, *s. pl.* sparkles, sparks, 136.
Sparen, *pr. pl.* spare, i. e. let alone, 885.
Spatten, *pt. pl.* spat, spat forth, emitted, 136.
Speche, speech, 65, 172, 367, 623.
Speden, ye haste, 787.
Spedful, *adj.* helpful, 623.
Spedliche, speedily, 172.
Speke, *v.* to speak, 699; 1 *p. pl. pr.* we speak, 367.
Spende, 1 *p. pl. pr.* we spend, 367; 2 *p.* ye spend, 631; 3 *p.* Spenden, 1071. *See below.*
Spene, *ger.* to spend, 876.
Spille, *ger.* to destroy, 787, 835; *pt. pl.* Spilden, destroyed, 136; *pp.* Spild, condemned, 699, 1071.
Spirit, 699.
Spoken, *pt. pl.* spake, 1071.
Spouce, *s.* espousal, wedlock, 393.
Spouce-breche, adultery, breaking of espousal, 787; Spouse-breche, 885.
Spradden, *pt. pl.* spread, 123.
Spraies, *s. pl.* sprays, sprigs, branches, 123; Spraiuus, 729.
Spreden, ye spread, 729.
Springinge, springing, sprouting, 729.
Spronge, *pt. s.* sprang, grew, 133; *pl.* Spronngen, 123.

Spryt, spirit, 623.
Stable, firm, 587.
Stalþe, s. stealth, i. e. stealing, robbery, 788.
Stat, state, condition, 429, 686, 890.
Staunche, ger. to quell, stay, withhold, check, 938; v. to quench, 1031.
Stede, stead, place, 9, 114.
Stedefast, stedfast, 940.
Sterne, stern, grim, 52; stern, 349; on which see the note.
Sternere, sterner, greater, 429.
Sterres, s. pl. stars, 477. [The *seven stars* are here the planets, then seven in number.]
Sterue, v. to die, starve, 863. A.S. *steorfan.*
Sterus, pr. s. steers, goes, 185.
Stidie, ye studie (*Lat.* studium non habetis), 898.
Stifly, firmly, well, 686.
Stille, quiet, 574, 940; adv. continually, 97.
Stinte, v. to cease, 97, 530; stop, 143, 161; *stinte of,* cease from, 530; pr. s. Stinteþ, is quiet, 91.
Stiren, pr. pl. stir, 487.
Stirte, pt. s. started, moved hastily, 127.
Stiue, pl. stiff, violent, 487.
Stod, pt. s. stood, 114.
Stomak, stomach, 686.
Ston, stone, 438, 1138; pl. Stonus, 587.
Stonde, ger. to stand, 587.
Storie, s. story, i. e. meaning, 609; pl. Storrius, stories, 467.
Stormus, storms, 487; Stormys, 923.
Stounde, time, space of time, 97; season, 898; þat stounde, at that time, 609.
Stoute, stout, 940; Stouter, 429.
Straiten, pr. pl. confine, make narrow, oppress, 756.
Strem, stream, 144, 530.
Strenke, strength, 532, 674, 936.
Strenkþen, pr. pl. strengthen, 756.

Striue, ger. to strive, fight, 756.
Stronde, s. stream, 140, 151, 165, 530; pl. Strondus, 524.
Suffre, v. to suffer, 779, 873; to permit, 1056; ger. 75; 1 p. pl. pr. ye suffer, 1094.
Summe, some, 755, 756, 947, 948, 949; Somme, 757.
Sur, sure, safe, 9, 991, 1017.
Sustaine, ger. to sustain, 362, 797.
Swaginge, assuaging, 921.
Swainus, pl. swains, men, 855.
Swan, 719.
Swangen, pr. pl. flap, 493.
Swet, sweat, 310.
Swete, sweetness, 952.
Swich, such, 221, 443, 719; Swiche, 855, 1097.
Swimmen, pr. pl. swim, 493.
Swink, toil, labour, 310, 426, 442; Swinc, 921.
Swinke, ger. to labour at, 855. A.S. *swincan.*
Swiþe, adv. quickly, 921; very, 719; *ful swiþe,* very much, 493.
Sykur, safe, sure, 830.
Syn, since, 77.
Syte (*dissyllabic*), a city, 9.

Ta, *for* To, to, 475.
Tach, s. habit, 566; pl. Tacchus, ill habits, 463.
Take, to take, 854; pr. s. Takus, delivers, 182; *imp.* Tak, take, 233; pr. pl. Taken, 710; 2 p. 566; pp. Take, taken, caught, 721.
Tale, tale, story, 190, 365, 469, 1128; account, 66.
Talken, v. to talk, 148.
Taried, pp. tarried, i. e. made to linger, hindered, harmed, 132.
Tariynge, s. tarrying, delay, 818; Tariginge, 240.
Tast, s. taste, 357.
Tastinge, taste, 952.
Tauhte, pt. s. taught, 1077; pp. Tauht, 217.
Teche, v. to teach, 237; ger. 284.

Tellen, *v.* to count, compute, be aware of, 323; Telle, tell, be told, 14; 1 *p. s. pr.* Telle, I recount, 732; 2 *p. pl.* ye tell, 846; Tellen, 680, 701; *imp. s.* Tel, tell, 207.

Tempest, 484.

Temple, 714, 725; *pl.* Templus, 599, 1044.

Tempren, *v.* temper, control, 572.

Temted, *pp.* tempted, 98.

Tende, *ger.* to attend to, heed, 281; 1 *p. pl. pr.* we attend to, heed, 365; Tenden, 469; 2 *p.* ye heed, 846, 1044; 1 *p. pl. pr.* Tendide, we attended to, 217; *imp. pl.* Tendeþ, attend, 190; 1 *p.* Tende, let us endeavour, 1128; *pt. s.* Tendede, attended to, 813.

Tendere, tender, 952.

Tendeþ, *pr. s.* kindles, 684; *pp.* Tend, kindled, 233. Cf. E. *tinder*.

Tene, sorrow, affliction, 873, 950; vexation, 771; injury, 700; *pl.* Tenen, vexations, 920 (yet used with a sing. verb). *See below*.

Tened, *pp.* vexed, 512. A.S. *týnan*, to afflict.

Tenful, harmful, 566, 793.

Tente, *s.* heed, endeavour, 305; attention, 972.

Tentus, tents, 144.

þan, than, 62.

þanne, then, 17, 19, 21, 53, 59, 69, 447, 1104.

þare, there, 250.

þat, so that, 861; *rel. pron.* that, 5, &c.; *dem. pron.* 12, &c.

þe, *art.* the, 7, 10, &c.

þe, *dat.* to thee, 259.

þe mor, the more, 1040. A.S. *þý*.

þedirre, thither, 2; þidire, 15.

þei, *conj.* though, 37, 510.

þei, they, 6, &c.

þei-self, *for* þiself, thyself, 511.

þennus, thence, 98; þennys, *rubric to l*. 1.

þer-aboute, about it, 1136.

þer-by, by it, 619.

þere, *adv.* where, 446, 476, 495, 751, 1103; there, 51, &c.

þere-on, thereon, 182.

þerfor, therefore, 345, 1106.

þer-inne, therein, 164, 444, 982.

þerwiþ, therewith, 717.

þi, thy, 28, &c.

þiddire, thither, 156; þedirre, 2.

Thikke, *pl.* thick, 500.

þikke, *adv.* thickly, close, 116.

þingus, *pl.* things, 739, 996, 999; þinguus, 222; *gen.* þingus, 335.

þinkeþ, it seems; þinkeþ *vs,* it seems to us, 1058.

þirst, thirst, 1029, 1032.

þirsten, *pr. pl.* thirst, 529.

þis, *s.* this, 1, 22; *pl.* these, 61, 609, 818.

þo, those, these, 772, 958, 1112.

þolie, *ger.* to endure, suffer, undergo, 50, 380, 866, 984. A.S. *þolian*.

þorou, *prep.* through, 84, 85, 547; by means of, upon, 579.

þou, thou, 28, &c.

þouh, though, 484. *See* þouȝ.

þouhtous, *pl.* thoughts, 767; þouhtus, 95.

þoute, *pt. s.* seemed, 1133.

þouȝ, though, 232, 234, 708, 1111.

þrote, *dat.* throat, 677.

þus, *adv.* thus, 41, 396.

Tid, *pr. s.* betides, happens, 920.

Tid, *adv.* soon, 98, 207, 818; quickly, 356. See *Tit* in Gl. to Wm. of Palerne.

Tidi, *adj.* tidy, i. e. excellent, gorgeous, 599.

Tidliche, *adv.* quickly, 148. *See* Tid.

Til, *prep.* to, 48, 63, 148, 1114; *badly spelt* Tille, 166, 802; *him tille,* to himself, 1041; ȝou *tille,* for yourselves, 590.

Til, *conj.* until, 314.

Tilien, *ger.* to till, 854; *pt. s.* Tilede, tilled, 691.

Time, time, season, 217, 813, 323; *in time,* in due season, 712; *by*

GLOSSARIAL INDEX.

time, in good time, soon enough, 368; *pl.* Timus, 193
Tine, *v.* to lose, 36; *daies to tine,* to lose your lives, 589. *See* Gl. to Wm. of Palerne.
Titelid, *pp.* lit. titled; contained, arranged in order, 190.
Tiþinge, tidings, 14, 22, 813, 818, 1077. *See* Gl. to Wm. of Palerne.
To, *prep.* to, 3, 10, &c.
Tokne, token, 776.
Toknynge, tokening, token, 14.
Tol, *s.* tool, 854.
Tolde, *pt. s.* told, 22, 1077; *pl.* 776; *pp.* 793.
Tome, *s.* leisure, 281. *See* Gl. to Wm. of Palerne, p. 312.
Torche, torch, 233.
Touche, *ger.* to touch, touch upon, 135, 1128; *v.* 129.
Touchinge, touch, 952.
Touh, tough, 691.
Tounge, *dat.* tongue, 358, 668; *nom.* 572; *acc.* 573.
Traie, *s.* vexation, anguish, 710. A.S. *trega.*
Tre, *s.* tree, 133; *pl.* Tres, 115, 119, 123, 132; Tren, 853.
Trene, *adj. pl.* treën, of trees, 351.
Trewe, *pl.* true, 829.
Treweste, truest, 513.
Tribit, tribute, 710.
Trinde, *pt. s. subj.* should touch, 132. See the note.
Trowen, we believe, 615; Trowe, ye believe, 841, 1009; *pp.* Trowen, believed, trusted; *trowen on,* trusted in, 829.
Trowþe, truth, 910; Trouþe, 81; Truthe, 275.
Trye, *v.* to try, make trial of, 513.
Trystli, *adv.* trustfully, securely, 513.
Trysty, trusty, credible, 829.
Tuelf monþe, twelvemonth, year, 153.
Tulye, *ger.* to till, 846. *See* Tilien.
Turment, torment, 776.
Turnen, 1 *p. pl. pr.* we turn, 356; 1 *p. s.* Turne me, I turn myself, 98;
pr. s. Turneþ, turns, 365, 469; Turnus, turns, 965; it turns, 765; *pr. pl.* Turneþ, turn, 755; *pr. s. subj.* Turne, may turn, 484.
Tyme, time, 145. *See* Time.
Tyr, attire, 883. A.S. *tír,* Icel. *tírr,* glory, ornament; whence O.F. *atir,* attire.
Tyþinge, tidings, 207; Tiþinge, 240. *See* Tiþinge.

Varied, *pp.* varied, different, 200.
Verrai, true, 693; Verraie, 671.
Vertue, divine power, 693; Vertu, virtue, 381; *pl.* Vertues, deeds of valour, 671.
Vn, *for* On, i. e. upon, 717.
Vn-blessed, unhappy, 1124.
Vnblisful, unhappy, sad, 543.
Vnbliþe, *adj.* sad, 929.
Unclene, unclean, 636.
Vndigne, unworthy, 745.
Vndur, under, 219, 435.
Vndurstonde, ye understand, 609.
Vnended, endless, 751.
Vnharmed, unharmed, 227.
Vnkinde, unnatural, 540.
Vnknowe, *pp.* unknown (an unknown thing), 382.
Vnkouþe, unknown, strange, foreign, 1089.
Vnlich, unlike, 271.
Vnmihtful, powerless, 762.
Vnmihty, feeble, 893.
Vnrith, wrong, injustice, 568.
Vnsely, *adj.* unhappy, wretched, miserable, despicable, 987; wretched, 797.
Vnskile, want of skill, i. e. want of reason, folly, 1020.
Vnskilfully, without discernment, foolishly, 871.
Vnstedefast, unstedfast, 944.
Vnwasteþ, *for* Vnwasted, unwasted, 236.
Vnwise, unwise, 760.
Vois, *s.* voice, 131.

GLOSSARIAL INDEX.

Vp, *adv.* up, 483, 487.
Vpon, upon, 739; Upon, 39, &c.
Vppe, upon, 861.
Vs, *dat.* to us, 27, 331; for us, 447; *acc.* us, 28; Vs silf, ourselves, *an error for* hem silf, themselves, 873.
Vse, *v.* to use, 439, 508; 2 *p. pl. pr.* Vsen, ye use, 559, 845; *pr. pl.* Vsen, are wont, 865; use, are used, are wont to do, 202; use, make use of, 522; *pp.* Vsed, 839, 1050; been wont (to do), 713.
Vse, *s.* use, 720.

Wachinge, *s.* washing, 469.
Wahche, *pp.* washed, 423.
Waken, 1 *p. pl. pr.* we wake, 359; 2 *p.* ye wake, 786.
Wakrong, *adj.* wakeful, 537. Cf. A.S. *wacol,* wakeful; the suffix seems to be A.S. *ranc,* abundant; E. *rank.*
Walke, *ger.* to walk, 498.
Walleþ, *pr. s.* boils up, wells up, 499. A.S. *weallan,* to boil.
Wan, *for* Whan, when, 13.
Wante, *dat.* want, 867; penury, 857; misery, 1126; lack, 1103.
Wanteþ, *pr. s.* lacks, 860; Wantus, fails, lacks, 891; ȝou *wantus,* fails you, 851; 1 *p. pl.* Wante, we lack, 354; *pr. s.* Wanteþ, lacks, 860; *pt. s.* Wantede, lacked, 263.
Wardain, warden, 537.
Warde, *s.* keeping, 1035.
Warme, *ger.* to warm, 332.
Warne, 1 *p. s. pr.* I warn, 205; I declare, 1124; *pl.* we warn, 31.
Was, *pt. s.* was, 4, 8, &c.
Waste, *ger.* to waste, destroy, 545; *pr. s.* Wasteþ, wastes, 238; *pres. pt.* Wastinge, decaying, 980; *pp.* Wastid, wasted, 292.
Watur, water, 92, 436, 485, 1026, 1033.
Wawe, *s.* wave, 436, 485; *pl.* Wawus, 92, 483, 487.
Waxe, wax, 236.

Waxeþ, *pr. s.* grows, 926; 1 *p. pr. pl.* Waxen, we grow, 327.
We, *pron.* we, 27, &c.
Wede, garment, 6, 403.
Wedur, weather, 926; *pl.* Wedures, storms, 443.
Weduringe, weather, state of the weather, 922; Weduring, 1.
Weele, *apparently an error for* Wel, well, 367.
Weith (= weiht), wight, man, 1; Weiht, 185; Weiȝht, 150. *See* Weiȝ, Wiȝth.
Weiȝ, wight, man, 69; Weih, 231, 258, 943; Wehy, 736; *pl.* Weihes, 238, 618; Weies, 17, 58, 585, 864; Weihuus, 698, 922, 1092; Weiȝes, 783. A.S. *wiga,* a warrior.
Weke, *s.* wick, 236.
Wel, well, 91, 106; *wel to like,* very pleasant, 926.
Welde, 1 *p. pl. pr.* we wield, i. e. possess, 34; *v.* to possess, 289; *pr. s.* Weldus, possesses, 978.
Wele, *s.* wealth, 32.
Wele, *for* Wole, ye will, 820.
Wel-langaged, *pp.* learned in languages, 171.
Welle-springus, *pl.* well-springs, 499.
Welþe, *s.* weal, prosperity, 700, 919.
Wende, *v.* to wend, go, 178, 500, 1090, 1092; Wenden, 1106; *pr. s.* Wendus, goes, 3; 1 *p. pl.* Wende, 34, 990; 2 *p.* Wenden, ye turn, try, 804; 2 *p. s. pr.* Wendest, 80; *pp.* (weren) Went, 53.
Wene, *v.* to ween, suppose, 943; 2 *p. s. pr.* Wenst, thou weenest, dost suppose, 534; *pl.* Wene, ye imagine, think, suppose, 548, 1121; *pt. pl.* Wende, weened, expected, 50.
Wente, *pt. pl.* went, 6; *pp.* Went, 53. *See* Wende.
Were, *pt. pl.* were, 11; Weren, 5; 1 *p. pl. pr.* Weren, we were, 217; *pt. s. subj.* might be, 67, 470; would be, 872; should chance to be, 105; *pt. pl. subj.* Were, might be, 132.

Werk, work, 208, 378, 886; *pl.* Werkus, 567.
Werre, *s.* war, 282, 545, 664.
Werrede, 1 *p. pl. pt.* warred we, 39.
Wers, worse, 231, 783, 1106.
Wetin, 1 *p. pl. pr.* we know, we wit, 99.
Wetinge, wetting, moisture, 1033.
Wexe, *v.* to wax, grow, become, 938.
Wham, *dat.* whom, 793; *pl.* 780, 1042.
Whan, when, 1, 106; Whanne, 466, 1107.
What, 31, 173; whatsoever, 68; What so, whatsoever, 359.
Wherefore, on which account, 385, 394, 401, 404, 601.
Wherewiþ, wherewith, 852.
Whete, wheat, 692.
Wheþur, whether, 765.
Whi, *s.* man, 571. *See* Weiȝ.
Whi, why, 79, 432, 834, 836.
Whiche; þe *whiche*, which, 1127.
While, a time, period, while, 336; whilst, 236; þe *while*, whilst, 562; in the mean while, 1132.
Whit, white, 719.
Whitli, *for* Wihtli, nimbly, quickly, 185.
Whon, *for* Won, abundance, 353.
Wide, wide, i. e. great, 216.
Wide, *adv.* far and wide, 531.
Wifis, wives, 53; Wiuus, 403. *See* Wiuus.
Wihes, *s. pl.* men, 263. *See* Weiȝ.
Wikke, *adj.* wicked, 537; difficult; *wikke to staunche*, hard to check, 938; *pl.* wicked (men), 1002.
Wikkede, *adj.* wicked, 378, 1057.
Wikkednesse, wickedness, 786.
Wil, will, pleasure, 1, 96, 99, 427; Wile, 736; Wille, 72, 170, 606, 707.
Wilde, *adj.* wild, 4, 938.
Wilfully, voluntarily, by choice, 604; intentionally, 1026.
Wilne, 1 *p. pl. pr.* we desire, 289, 304, 350, 500; Wilnen, 461; 2 *p.* 898, 900; 3 *p.* Wilnen, desire, 567; *imp. s.* Wilne, desire, 516; *pt. s.* Wilnede, desired, 150; 2 *p. s. pr.* Wilnest, desirest, 257. A.S. *wilnian*.
Win, *s.* winning (*see* Lat. text), 350.
Wind, wind, 92, 436, 487, 488; *pl.* Windus, 484.
Wine, wine, 678.
Winne, *ger.* to win, 80, 450, 804; conquer, 548; to get, acquire, 1038.
Winus, *pl.* vines (Lat. *vites*), 847.
Wirche, *ger.* to work, 688; Wirchen, 427; *v.* Wirche, to do, 754; Wirchen, 551; Wirke, 46; 2 *p. pl. pr.* Wirchen, ye act, 907, 1104; Wirche, ye do, 832; ye work, 629; *pl.* Wirchen, work, do, perform, 717.
Wis, wise, 231, 534; *pl.* Wise, wise men, 12, 224, 973, 1112.
Wische, 1 *p. pr. pl.* wish, 69.
Wisdam, wisdom, 102, 211.
Wise, *s.* way, manner, 22, 45, 197, 680, 1085.
Wisliche, wisely, 516; Wisli, 844; Wisly, 913.
Wisse, *ger.* to instruct, 454; to inform, 762. A.S. *wísian*.
Wiste, *pt. s.* knew, 14; *pp.* Wist, known, 4, 944.
Wit, *s.* wisdom, intelligence, 96, 211, 534, 924; Witte, 23, 905; wit; 966; *pl.* Wittus, wits, 102, 266.
Wite, *for* Whit, whit, 354 (*or else* knowledge, acquaintance with; *but less likely*).
Witen, *ger.* to wit, know, 150; Wite, 1002; *v.* Witen, 208; Wite, 258; 1 *p. pl. pr.* Witen, we know, 473, 585; 2 *p.* ye know, 860, 922. A.S. *witan*.
Witeþ, *pr. s.* keeps, 698. See note, and Gloss. to Will. of Palerne.
Wiþ, *prep.* with, 3; against, 37, 341; along with, 342.
Withdrawe, *v.* to refrain from, 895.
Wiþinne, *prep.* within, 38, 338.
Wiþoute, *prep.* without, 66, 240.

Wiþoute, *adv.* outwardly, 340; *prep.* without, 6, &c.
Witiere, discoverer, 678.
Wittie, *adj.* wise, learned, 17, 1121.
Wiuus, *pl.* wives, 882, 891. *See* Wifis.
Wiȝth, wight, man, 39. *See* Weith.
Wo, torment, 746; woe, pain, 857, 1033, 1106.
Wodus, *pl.* woods, 500.
Wokus, *s. pl.* weeks, 153.
Wolde, *pt. s.* would, 45.
Wole, 2 *p. s. pr. subj.* thou will, 508; *pr. pl.* Wolen, will, i. e. wish, 1110; Wollen, we will, 1026.
Wolf, 860, 864.
Wombe, belly, 317, 690, 794, 797; *pl.* Wombis, 538.
Wommen, women, 557; *gen.* Wommenus, women's, 1016.
Won, *s.* plenty, fulness, abundance, 72, 499, 557, 575, 678; joy (?), 678; riches, 891. See *wán* in Stratmann, p. 548.
Won, dwelling, 1103; custom, 957. The same word as *Wone*, q. v.
Wonde, we turn aside from, forsake, 990; 2 *p.* ye shun, fear, 957; ye forsake, 886. A.S. *wandian*, to shun.
Wondrus, *pr. s. impers.* it makes me wonder, 886.
Wondrus, *pl.* wonders, 473, 670, 699.
Wondurful, wonderful, 4, 844.
Wone, *s.* custom, usage, 567, 1016; an accustomed offering, 736; *pl.* Wonus, customs, usages, 208, 844. A.S. *ge-wuna*.
Woneþ, *pr. s.* dwells, 1060; 1 *p. pl.* Wone, we dwell, 980; 2 *p.* Wonen, ye dwell, 1103; *pp.* Woned, wont, 378, 551. A.S. *wunian*.
Wonnynge, *s.* dwelling, abode, 8. See above.
Wonye, *ger.* to live in, 848. *See* Woneþ.
Worchen, *v.* to work, do, 99; 1 *p. pl. pr.* we work, do, 359; Worchin, 361; 2 *p.* Worchen, ye work, 680.

Word, word, 615, 621; Worde, 698; *pl.* Wordus, 461, 609, 1077.
Word, the world, 25, 80, 419, 473, 551, 557, 746, 832, 857; Worde, 430, 548, 779, 877. *See* World.
Wordle, world, 645. *See* World.
Wordliche, worldly, 32, 58, 72, 102, 354, 604, 804, 837, 913, 934, 1016; human, 891. *See* Word.
Wordliche, *adv.* in a worldly manner, 427.
World, 261; Worlde, 105, 359; *also* Word, Wordle, q. v.
Wormus, *s. pl.* serpents, 152, 157.
Worschipe, worship, 17, 25, 680, 717.
Worschipen, *pr. pl.* worship, 722; 2 *p.* ye worship, 604.
Worschipful, honourable, fine, 403.
Worþ, worth, 261.
Worþe, *ger.* to become, 87, 933; *v.* become, 265; 1 *p. pl. pr.* Worþen, we become, 446; 2 *p.* Worþeþ, ye become, are, 634. A.S. *weorþan*.
Worþi, worthy, 25, 746.
Worþliche, worthy, 615, 621.
Wost, 2 *p. s. pr.* knowest, 516.
Woxe, *v.* to wax, grow, 115; *pp.* Woxe, grown, 547; Woxen, 943.
Wraþe, *v.* to make angry, 994; 1 *p. s. pt. subj.* Wraþede, I should make angry, 88.
Wraþful, wrathful, 660.
Wraþþe, wrath, 662.
Wreche, vengeance, 772, 777. A.S. *wracu*.
Wrecheli, *adv.* wretchedly, very ill, 88.
Wreten, *pr. pl.* write, 24.
Wried, *pp.* turned aside, perverted, given to evil, 660. A.S. *wrigan*, to turn awry. See *wrien* in Stratmann.
Wriht, *s.* writ, 139. *See* Writ.
Writ, writ, 814; Wrytte, an inscription, 1136; Wriht, 139.
Writen, *pt. pl.* wrote, 1136; *pp* Writen, 139; Write, 244.
Wrong, *s.* wrong, 814.

Wrongful, evil, wrong, 777.
Wroþ, *adj.* wrath, 814.
Wrout, *pt. s.* wrought, acted, 1065; *pt. pl.* Wrouhten, wrought, made, inscribed, 1136; Wrouthe, 775; Wroute, did, 468; 1 *p.* Wroute, we wrought, we did, 387; *pp.* Wrouht, wrought, 139; 1 *p. s. pt. subj.* Wrouthe, I should work, should act, 88. *See* Wirchen.
Wrytte, a writing, inscription, 1136. *See* Writ.
Wyntyrus, winters, 8.

Y, *pron.* I, 110, 560, 732.
Ybore, *pp.* born, 1081.
Ybrend, *pp.* burnt, 1068.
Ybrouht forth, brought forth, 586.
Ycore, chosen (to be), 978. *See* Corn.
Ydemed, *pp.* ordained, 909.
Ydil, idle, 754.
Ygrowe, *pp.* grown (to be), become, 976.
Y-hanteþ = yhanted, *pp.* practised, 988.
Yholde, *pp.* held, possessed by, 863.
Ykid, *pp.* known to be, renowned as, 578. *See* Kid.
Yknowe, *v.* to know, learn, perceive, 1060.
Ylikned, *pp.* likened, 864.
Y-maad, *pp.* made, 617, 914; Ymad, 762, 839.
Ynow, enough, 956.
Ypotamus, *s. pl.* hippopotamuses, 157.

Yprofred, *pp.* proffered, offered, 187.
Y-punched, *pp.* punished, 395. *See* Punched.
Ys, is, 719, 1080.
Yschape, *pp.* created, made, 647.
Ysustained, sustained, 877.
Ywist, *pp.* known to be, 582.

ȝaf, *pt. s.* gave, 122.
ȝare, *adv.* quickly, yare, 241. A.S. *gearu*, prepared, ready.
ȝe, ye, 68, 242.
ȝeme, *ger.* to guard, protect, 674; to control, 1039. A.S. *gýman*, to take care of.
ȝer, life, lit. year, 215; ȝere, year, 203, 711; *pl.* ȝerus, years, 321.
ȝernus, *pr. s.* yearns, 1039; 1 *p. pl.* ȝernen, we desire, 241; *imp. pl.* ȝernes, ask ye, desire ye, 67; *pp.* ȝerned, 215.
ȝif, if, 29, 508.
ȝift, *s.* gift, 67; ȝifte, 69.
ȝit, yet, nevertheless, 734; moreover, 930.
ȝiue, *v.* to give, 674.
ȝorne, *adv.* eagerly, 179. A.S. *georn*, eager.
ȝou, *acc.* you, 65; *dat.* to you, 67; ȝow, you, 209.
ȝoung, young, 942.
ȝour, your, 178.
ȝoure, yours, 271.
ȝoursilf, yourselves, 1095.
ȝou-siluen, yourselves, 795.
ȝouþe, *dat.* youth, 215.

INDEX OF NAMES.

Alixandre, Alexander, 3, 15, 24, 55, 63, 170, 177, 191, 244; &c.
Amon, Ammon, 193, 824, 1082.
Appolin, Apollo, 701, 718.
Asie, Asia, 518.
Aufrik, Africa, 518.
Bacus, Bacchus, 675, 714.
Bragmanie, Bragmanye, the land of the Brahmans, 175, 1075.
Bragmanus, *pl.* Brahmans, 287; B. lond, 196, 250; B. prince, 968, 974.
Ceres, 689, 724.
Cupidus, Cupid, 679; Cupies, 730.
Dindimus, 176, 195, 243, 249, 810, &c.
Erenus, 526; see the note.
Europ, Europe, 518.
Gena, the Ganges, 141.
Genosophistiens, Gymnosophists, 11, 25.
Hercules, 669, 728.
Inde, India, 142, 147.
Iubiter, Jupiter, 553, 659; *gen.* Iubiterus, 656.
Iuli, July, 154.
Iuno, Juno, 697, 716.
Martis, Mars, 663, 712.
Mascedonius, Macedonian, 143, 145, 1073.
Mercurie, Mercury, 667, 726.
Minerua, Minerva, 653, 722.
Nilus, the Nile, 531.
Olimpias, Olympias (Alexander's mother), 194, 825; Olimpas, 1083.
Oridrace, 3; see note.
Oxian, the great river Oceanus, 533.
Paccolus, Pactolus, 527.
Paradis, Paradise, 140.
Phison, the river Pison, 138; *gen.* Phisonus, 146.
Proserpine, 560.
Salonienus = Salmoneus, 1064; see the note.
Thabeus (river), 536.
Tricerberus, Cerberus with the triple head, 536, 793.
Venus, 693, 720.
Yydra, Hydra, 799.

The manufacturer's authorised representative in the EU for product safety is Oxford University Press España S.A. of El Parque Empresarial San Fernando de Henares, Avenida de Castilla, 2 - 28830 Madrid (www.oup.es/en or product.safety@oup.com). OUP España S.A. also acts as importer into Spain of products made by the manufacturer.
Printed and bound by CPI Group (UK) Ltd, Croydon, CR0 4YY

20/03/2026

02075337-0011